Critical Applied Linguis

D1612473

WITHDRAWN

Now in its second edition, this accessible guide and introduction to critical applied linguistics provides a clear overview of the problems, debates, and competing views in language education, literacy, discourse analysis, language in the workplace, translation, and other language-related domains. Covering both critical theory and domains of practice, the book is organized around five themes: the politics of knowledge, the politics of language, the politics of difference, the politics of texts, and the politics of pedagogy.

Recognizing that a changing world requires new ways of thinking, and that many approaches have watered down over time, the new edition applies a sharp, fresh look at established and new intellectual frameworks. The second edition is comprehensively updated with additional research throughout and features new discussions of colonialism, queer theory, race and gender, trans-languaging, and posthumanism. With a critical focus on the role of applied linguists, Pennycook emphasizes the importance of a *situated, collaborative* perspective that takes the discussion away from questions of implementation, and insists instead that critical applied linguistics has to be an emergent program from the contexts in which it works.

This landmark text is essential reading for students and researchers of applied linguistics, multilingualism, language and education, TESOL, and language and identity.

Alastair Pennycook is Professor Emeritus of Language, Society and Education in the Faculty of Arts and Social Sciences at the University of Technology Sydney, Australia.

critical applied linguistics
a critical ^re introduction

Second Edition

Alastair Pennycook

Routledge
Taylor & Francis Group

NEW YORK AND LONDON

Second edition published 2021
by Routledge
605 Third Avenue, New York, NY 10158

and by Routledge
2 Park Square, Milton Park, Abingdon, Oxon, OX14 4RN

*Routledge is an imprint of the Taylor & Francis Group, an informa
business*

First edition published by Lawrence Erlbaum Associates, Inc., 2001

Library of Congress Cataloging-in-Publication Data
Names: Pennycook, Alastair, 1957- author.
Title: Critical applied linguistics : a critical re-introduction /
Alastair Pennycook.
Description: 2nd edition. | New York, NY : Routledge, 2021. |
Includes bibliographical references and index.
Identifiers: LCCN 2020058076 (print) | LCCN 2020058077 (ebook) |
ISBN 9780367547769 (hardback) | ISBN 9780367547776 (paperback) |
ISBN 9781003090571 (ebook)
Subjects: LCSH: Applied linguistics.
Classification: LCC P129 .P46 2021 (print) | LCC P129 (ebook) |
DDC 418—dc23
LC record available at https://lccn.loc.gov/2020058076
LC ebook record available at https://lccn.loc.gov/2020058077

ISBN: 978-0-367-54776-9 (hbk)
ISBN: 978-0-367-54777-6 (pbk)
ISBN: 978-1-003-09057-1 (ebk)

Typeset in Goudy
by KnowledgeWorks Global Ltd.

For the many friends, colleagues, and students
who have been part of this journey

Contents

List of Illustrations

Figure

Tables

Foreword: Decolonizing Critical Applied Linguistics

"There is no region, no culture, no nation today that has not been affected by colonialism and its aftermath. Indeed, modernity can be considered a product of colonialism" (wa Thiong'o 2009, p. ix).

In this extensively revised volume, Pennycook produces an extremely well written second edition of his book *Critical Applied Linguistics*. He updates critical scholarship by highlighting how critical applied linguistics is currently being carried out across the globe in diverse areas of applied linguistics. My main objective here is not to review the scholarship in critical applied linguistics but to ask to what extent critical applied linguistics is compatible with decolonial orientations to applied linguistics.

If there is no region, no culture, no nation that has not been affected by colonialism, this makes decoloniality mandatory and not "an option among others" (Mignolo, 2020, p. 4). In Europe, racism, xenophobia, antisemitism, and Islamophobia are among some of the means through which colonialism operates (de Sousa Santos, 2016, p. 17). Decoloniality is difficult work, but this does not make it impossible, as is evident in numerous publications that are framed around notions of decoloniality. For example, Casmir (2020) has written an elegant account of Haitian history, and Macedo (2019) has edited a readable account of the misteaching of foreign languages.

Decoloniality is necessary if we are to challenge the Eurocentricity that underlies most applied linguistics in diverse areas, such as second language acquisition, language policy and planning, and critical discourse analysis, among others. Decolonization of applied linguistics is necessary because colonialism, in addition to being a violent project, was accentuated by epistemicide. Epistemicide should be construed as the destruction of knowledge and memories of formerly colonized peoples (de Sousa Santos, 2016). Decoloniality in applied linguistics should, therefore, include a revival, a renaissance of Indigenous Cosmologies.

Even when evoking Indigenous Ontologies, it is necessary that the metropole and the colony exist in an unequal, but still reciprocally transforming relationship. There is no untouched indigeneity waiting to redeem an overheated, hegemonic metropole. But there are many peripheral worlds that have distinct, critical ways of being and knowing informed by indigenous genealogies that can provide contrasting, transformative insight (Jean Commaroff, personal communication).

It will be difficult for applied linguistics to be open to learning from decolonization and the global South because after five centuries of "teaching" the world, the global North seems to have lost the capacity to learn from the experiences of the world. It looks as if colonialism has disabled the global North from learning in noncolonial terms, that is in terms that allow for the existence of histories other than "universal" history of the West (de Sousa Santos, 2016, p. 19).

Critical applied linguistics can be meaningful (i.e., decolonized) if it leads to a restoration and renaissance of scholarship across the globe. In Africa, "Renaissance as rebirth and flowering, can spring only from the wealth of imagination of the people—and, above all, from Africa's keepers of memory" (wa Thiong'o, 2009, p. 124). If critical applied linguistics is to contribute to a decolonisation and intellectual renaissance, it has to be translated into local languages. In Africa, this should entail translation of critical applied linguistics into African languages, thus rendering it much easier to use in research into languages other than English. Otherwise, there will be an "abyssal line" between scholarship in African languages and that in English.

A decolonization of applied linguistics and Critical Applied Linguistics should be consistent with some of the major principles of *Epistemologies of the South* (de Sousa Santos, 2014):

1 A Western/Eurocentric understanding of the world is not the only understanding of the world.
2 There are alternatives to challenging this worldview, and what we need is unconventional thinking about alternatives.
3 The epistemic multiplicity of knowledges in the world is infinite, and no general theory can explain it.
4 An ecology of knowledge combined with intercultural translation is one alternative to a general theory.

It is necessary to decolonize applied linguistics so that it does not become an imperial project. Methodologically, "the use of decontextualized utterances and the formalist theorizing in linguistics are part of a much wider pattern. It is easy to see how empire enables a desocializing of knowledge, a separation of theoretical science from social responsibility" (Connell 2020, p. 156). Further, the tendency to focus on abstract grammars diverts attention away from the idiosyncrasies and actual practices of users of language who typically have a repertoire of languages. The objective of a decolonized applied linguistics should concentrate on the communicational biographies of speakers more so than on language which is inextricably tied to European ethnocentrism. A decolonized Applied Linguistics has to address the challenges posed to applied linguistics by methodological whiteness. Methodological whiteness is a consequence of a failure in applied linguistics to fully acknowledge the role played by race in the structuring of the world, thereby treating white experiences as a universal norm in language learning and language teaching.

Sinfree Makoni, Pennsylvania State University

References

Casmir, J. (2020). *The Haitians: A decolonial history*. Duke University Press.

Connell, R. (2020). Linguistics and language in the global economy of knowledge: A commentary. In A. Deumert, A. Storch, & N. Shepherd (eds.), *Colonial and decolonial linguistics: knowledges and epistemes*. Oxford University Press, pp. 150–156.

De Sousa Santos, B. (2014). *Epistemologies of the South. Justice against epistemicide*. Paradigm.

De Sousa Santos, B. (2016). Epistemologies of the South and the future. *From the European South, 1*, 17–29.

Macedo, D. (Ed) (2019). *Decolonizing Foreign Language Education. The Misteaching of English and Other Colonial Languages*. Routledge.

Mignolo, W. (2020). Critical dialogues. On decoloniality: Second thoughts. *Postcolonial Studies (Published 27 April 2020)*.

Thiong'o wa, N. (2009). *Something Torn and New. An African Renaissance*. Basic Civatas Books.

Preface

While this book is a product of 30 years' engagement with Critical Applied Linguistics, this revised edition is also a product of 2020 and forest fires, COVID-19, and Black Lives Matter. The forest fires during the Australian summer (and California and elsewhere) made life difficult for many of us, killed many millions of animals, destroyed property and livelihoods and showed us that climate change was deeply real. It also put many of us into a condition close to lockdown before the global pandemic forced us into our homes. COVID-19 made life much more difficult for many of us – this book revision has suffered because of lack of access to resources, and difficult writing conditions (three periods of 14-day isolation/quarantine in addition to general lockdowns) – but COVID-19 also drew attention to many other concerns: It showed us the workings of globalization as the virus spread rapidly but unevenly across the world, as borders were closed, as some countries were affected much more quickly than others, as we moved into online communication, and so on. It cast a harsh light on multiple forms of inequality: Women's work was hardest hit, for example, because of casual employment, particularly in service industries; working class, migrant, and communities of color suffered much more than their wealthy White neighbors because of a range of factors: Closer living conditions, work in frontline industries with greater exposure to the virus, job losses, using public transport and reliance on other public facilities, limited access to digital resources, unequal access to health services, and more. Amid all the panic, the pandemic spotlighted continuing forms of inequality, as issues or race, gender, class, housing, unemployment, and health intersected.

"We are all in this together" became a catch-cry of the pandemic and the need for concerted social action. But we weren't. Many lost their jobs; many old people died; the wealthy self-isolated in their holiday homes; the poor were incarcerated in crowded apartment blocks. It also showed generally that people are not well served by mendacious right-wing political leaders, who resisted the socialist-sounding idea that to resist the pandemic we need to act together, in unison. Indeed 2020 was another ugly year for the violent, racial, heteronormative, nationalist, xenophobic, misogynist rantings of a group of right-wing leaders, from the Philippines and India to Brazil, Hungary, and the UK and

USA, among others. Communal action, social health care, wearing face masks (bizarrely politicized in some countries) and more were anathema to conservative leaders, and thousands paid for this with their lives. Nonetheless, from these difficult material circumstances, as critical applied linguists we could see opportunities to use our critical tools in discourse analysis, literacy, education, and more, to work with colleagues and students to turn a critical gaze on events around us.

Less widely noticed was the fact that 2020 marks the 100th anniversary of the founding of the League of Nations, following the Paris Peace Conference in 1919. As Lake and Reynolds (2008, p. 5) explain, it was the rejection of the proposal for racial equality in the founding of this body that drew the "global colour line" that has divided the world on racial lines for the last century. If this moment of historical commemoration – 100 years of the global colour line – passed with little notice (there are after all enough other dates that might be equally marked), the Black Lives Matter Movement brought racial inequalities to a new level of social consciousness and political activism. It was not of course new in 2020 (Black Lives Matter started in 2013) but it rose to wider attention on the back of more Black deaths at the hands of police. And it echoed worldwide, with a strong focus in Australia (at demonstrations declared illegal, as elsewhere, because of COVID-19) on Black (Indigenous) deaths in custody, none of which has resulted in legal sanctions against police or prison officials. 2020 was a year of blackened trees, black masks, and Black political action in resurgence.

It was therefore a strange and difficult and disruptive year to be trying to revise this book. As I explain in the new introduction, this turned into a major project as I sought to reflect political changes over the last twenty years, to incorporate new directions and work in the field, and to improve the book's readability and usability. I had not thought revising this book would be as difficult as it has proved: All I needed to do was update a few sections, rework a few others, remove a few injudicious claims, make some ideas clearer. Not so. I have come to appreciate in the rewriting how huge and complex this area is and how inadequate my own understanding was and still is. I have tried in this book to give an overview of critical work across many areas, as well as to present my own critical take on these positions (though I've tried to achieve better balance in this revised edition). I hope therefore that this book will be of interest to those who found the old book useful, to a new generation keen to engage with these matters, and to a wider circle of applied linguists who can see why this is important. 2020 also gave me a renewed sense that all this matters more now than ever before.

My goal in this book has never been to develop a model for critical applied linguistics, but rather to explore why it matters and how it can work. The motivation comes out of 30 years of trying to relate critical work in many domains to my own fields of practice in applied linguistics. It comes out of trying to teach a course on critical applied linguistics, of finding ways to introduce critical perspectives to other courses. This has not always been a debate that has been easy to sustain and participate in over the last 30 years. The critical stance I (and others) have taken has caused resentment and anger. There have been nasty backlashes, attempts to discredit this sort of work, unpleasant parodies, refusals to discuss. But there has also been a great deal of support. I have been extremely privileged over the last decades to be invited to many parts of the world (from China, the Philippines, Japan, Malaysia, and Vietnam to Columbia, Brazil, and South Africa, from Northern Europe to North America), and in all these places, I have had wonderful conversations with a vast array of different people, trying to work out how our different projects intersect.

So I owe a great debt of thanks to many, many people over the last 30 years, and I am not going to try to name them. While acknowledgements can give credit to all those who have sustained this project through conversations, messages, talks, papers, discussions, and so on, they run the danger in this context of being divisive: Those thanked are doing critical work; those overlooked are not. Instead I just want to acknowledge and thank all those who turn up in the pages of this book, all those who have been part of this journey in different ways, from the origins of these ideas among the "critical crowd" at Ontario Institute for Studies Education (OISE) in Toronto, through my many debates and discussions with colleagues and students around the world. Many thanks to all these people. Let's keep the discussion going. I do want to thank Naomi Silverman at Lawrence Erlbaum, who liked the sound of the first version of this book and made it possible, and Elsa Auerbach, who gave it its final critical reading before publication. My thanks also to Karen Adler at Routledge, who saw that a second edition would be worth doing, and to the anonymous reviewers who made many useful and critical suggestions for this revised edition.

Finally, amid all else that was going on, 2020 turned out to be a difficult year on a personal level. In late October and early November – in the space of two weeks – Dominique Estival and I attended the funerals of my mother (Joan Pennycook) in the UK and her mother (Pierrette Chalono) and aunt (Jeannine Chalono) in France. These three strong, intelligent, caring women in their nineties, who had been so much part of our lives, and had done so much to make it possible for us to live the lives we have led, who had been the cornerstones or our lives for so long, were suddenly no longer with us. These were deeply sad times that put all the rest of this work in some perspective. So this revised edition is also in their memory. And with a final thankyou to Dominique, who has done so much to support and encourage me through these difficult times.

In isolation, November 2020.

Introduction

"We must change the world while constantly reinterpreting it" (de Sousa Santos, 2018, p. viii)

"Pessimismo dell'intelligenza, ottimismo della volontà" (attributed to Gramsci, 1929)

Thirty years have passed since I first made a case for critical applied linguistics (CALx) (Pennycook, 1990). Twenty years have passed since I developed that initial work into a book-length introduction (Pennycook, 2001). There is therefore a basic argument that if the field is still relevant today – and I think the case for this being so is very strong – it needs updating. This new edition, however, is far more than just an update. There are three important reasons why this book has been rewritten in much more extensive ways. They correspond in some ways to three questions posed by Friedrich et al.'s (2013, p. 120) critical reading of *Critical Applied Linguistics*:

- "Do the issues that critical texts tackle stay the same over time?"
- "Do the critical reflections of years past represent the particular problems of a time or particular ways of seeing the problems at a time?"
- "Are critical approaches bound to become watered-down as time passes?"

The first has to do with the sociopolitical context. Critical work has to be responsive to a changing world, and a great deal has happened in the last twenty years, from a more urgent need to deal with climate change to the rise of neoliberal political and economic forms of governance. Profound changes to communication and how knowledge is regarded have occurred alongside (and connected to) the growth of xenophobic populism. New social, cultural, political, economic and environmental conditions pose new questions for applied linguists. So while many of the same issues are still with us – we may be finally becoming more aware of the depths of institutional racism, but it sure isn't new – the political landscape is also always shifting.

The second instigation to change is that the field has moved on, sometimes in relation to these wider changes, sometimes as a result of shifting ideas across the humanities and social sciences. From the resurgence of political economic analysis and the growth of antiracist work to the development of decolonial, posthumanist, new realist, and other intellectual renovations, there is a wide range of new ideas to take on board. That is not to suggest that critical applied linguistics should take up any new intellectual trend that comes along: They have to be evaluated for their potential contribution to any critical project. Any number of 'turns' have been announced over the last couple of decades: the social, spatial, sensory, affective, practice, performative, decolonial, material, and more. Critical applied linguistics needs to be attuned to these developments – it has to be more dynamic than just adding a fixed political analysis to a fixed applied linguistic concern – but it needs to approach new ideas and frameworks (from translingual practices to southern sociolinguistics) critically. It has to be open to shifting intellectual currents, to new questions for investigation, to new ways of thinking, but with an eye always on the larger politics at play.

Critical approaches do get watered down over time, and the field has to move on. This is why de Sousa Santos' (2018) remark above about changing the world while reinterpreting it matters: A changing world (which we are also trying to change) needs new ways of thinking. One concern that I flagged at the end of the first edition was whether a growth in critical studies would lead to an inevitable weakening of critical work. Can we all be critical? I made a related point about sociolinguistic orthodoxies (ortholinguistic tendencies) (Pennycook, 2016) with respect to ideas such as 'codes': originally conceived as a way to avoid the problems of the language/dialect distinction, code got rewritten into the sociolinguistic script as 'language'. Liberal-conservative academia will always reinscribe innovative ideas into less interesting norms. So what has happened to 'critical work'? On the one hand, this has of course happened: Critical thinking – that apolitical approach to thinking – has taken over much of the agenda of critical literacy; critical discourse analysis has become more of a methodology than a political engagement. On the other hand, new critical avenues have emerged, and there is now a proliferation of approaches and domains in which critical work operates.[1]

Finally, there were a number of weaknesses in the first edition of the book that I have tried to resolve. It has been a popular and influential book, and I have had a range of responses to the book – someone told me they stayed up all night reading it (really?) while another told me they kept it on their bedside table (to help them sleep?), and others even referred to it as their 'bible'. Very kind and flattering, but for others it has been a difficult and sometimes exasperating book. Friedrich et al. (2013) say it left them "paradoxically distraught, ambivalent, and fascinated, and we like to think Pennycook would actually like that" (p. 136). Well, yes and no. An introduction to a complex field will always run into various tensions: How to explain a range of ideas from different fields without becoming too long or too dense? The first version erred toward density, and I have tried to resolve this not with the other option (length) but rather greater clarity. A second difficulty surrounds the desire to cover different positions (both critical and noncritical ways of doing applied linguistics) while also arguing for a preferred vision. It is impossible in some ways to avoid this, but the earlier version seemed too ready to categorize, to fix and dismiss other ways of thinking. I have tried therefore to be a bit more even-handed. This does not mean less critical, or more open to any attempt at criticality, but it requires a better evaluation of all critical standpoints for what they offer and where their weaknesses lie. I can't promise an easy read (though I've tried to improve things considerably) but I hope I can offer a greatly refreshed text that will provide new impetus to engage in critical applied linguistic work.

Radical Hope in A Troubled World

I started my first foray into critical applied linguistics with a brief overview of contemporary political concerns:

> We live in a world marked by fundamental inequalities: a world in which 40,000 children die every day in Third World countries; a world in which, in almost every society and culture, differences constructed around gender, race, ethnicity, class, age, sexual preference and other distinctions lead to massive inequalities; a world increasingly threatened by pollution and ecological disaster (Pennycook, 1990, p. 8).

From there, I went on to explain why this all mattered for applied linguistics (a central issue to which I return below). So how have we done since then? On the matter of infant mortality, there are some grounds for optimism: According to the World Health Organization (WHO, 2019) the total number of under-5 deaths worldwide has declined by 59% since 1990: Only around 5.3 million children under 5, or 15,000 per day, died in 2018. In 1990, 1 in 11 children died before reaching age 5; today it is about 1 in 26. This is surely progress, a result of collaborative action from local and international organizations to improve the health of children and their mothers. Progress, yes, but to write that 'only' 15,000 children under the age of 5 die per day is a deeply uncomfortable statement. And deep inequalities lurk behind these global averages: Mortality among children under 5 in sub-Saharan Africa is 15 times higher than in high income countries, and half of all under-5 deaths occurred in just five countries: India, Nigeria, Pakistan, Ethiopia, and the Democratic Republic of the Congo. The developmental narratives behind such statistics are also evolving, with the *triple burden of malnutrition* now including not only undernutrition and hidden hunger (at least half of all children under five globally suffer a lack of essential nutrients that often goes unnoticed until it's too late) but also obesity. And this is not only poor versus wealthy countries but also within many nations.

The advances that have been made in health, therefore, are unevenly spread, both across and within countries. This takes us to the broader question of global inequality. We should be in no doubt that we are living in times of increased inequality (Piketty, 2014), the interventions on behalf of capital and the enlightenment by the 'new optimists' (e.g., Pinker, 2018) notwithstanding

(Hickel, 2018). As analysis of capital shows, the redistribution of income in wealthy nations that occurred in the middle of the 20th century has been reversed in the last 30 years, with increased capital in the hands of a tiny minority, increased inequality across many societies, and a return to the patrimonial capitalism of the 19th century. For Pinker (2018) this negativity should be challenged: He makes a case against what he sees as the pessimism of critical analysis, even suggesting that "Intellectuals hate progress" (Pinker, 2018, p. 39). Pinker believes we should be more optimistic, and in particular celebrate the enlightenment ideals of reason, science, humanism, and progress. We need to be very cautious with such arguments, however: As others have shown (Lent, 2018), the data to support broad optimism are deeply flawed and drawn from organizations that produce such information in order to support the global status quo. And while optimism may at times be preferable over pessimism, neither position presents a program for change (optimists don't need to; pessimists don't see the point). This is better reframed in terms of intellectual pessimism coupled with political optimism, or radical hope.

The global status of women presents a similar picture. In some areas – education and literacy for girls, for example – there has been very real and powerful progress, and yet violence against women and widespread discrimination against women and girls in health and education, at home and in the labor market continues (UNDP, 2020). No country in the world has achieved gender equality, and the world is not on track to achieve it: overall progress in gender inequality has been slowing. This is not pointless pessimism (Why can't you look on the bright side of things?), or a glass-half empty mentality (it all depends on how you look), or a hatred of progress (things are better than they were): This is to celebrate progress where it has occurred, to identify where it has not, and to continue to struggle for change. The other claims made by the new optimists – that enlightenment ideas of reason and humanism are being threatened – also need discussion. It is not in fact the case that critical theories are opposed to reason and humanism, but rather that they are skeptical about the universalizing claims made in their name. Those who stake out a claim to Enlightenment ideals do not have exclusive rights to rationalism or an understanding of humanity.

This is not so much a form of moral or epistemological relativism – another of those tired assertions that is both philosophically naïve (conflating pluralism and relativism; see Berlin, 2003) and politically suspect (aligning with an interest in moral absolutes) – but a form of intellectual activism that insists that ethnocentric declarations should be no more encouraged in philosophy than in other fields. While blinkered optimism obscures the inequalities we need to address, it nonetheless draws our attention to the need for some kind of hope. We need ways of doing critical work that offer more than dystopian narratives of the world. This raises questions of *radical hope* (Heller & McElhinny 2017, p. xv) and struggle for change rather than bland positivity and admiration for the way things are. A lot of commentary during the coronavirus pandemic – a period when it was admittedly hard to avoid a slide into dystopian thinking

– aimed to be critical, but seemed more pointlessly negative, arguing that this was all about an attempt by governments, international business interests, oligarchs, and so on to seize and maintain power over people. This, it seems to me, was not usefully critical, but rather unhelpfully negative.

There are indeed real concerns for the casually employed that have been exacerbated by the pandemic, and many forms of structural inequality have come to light as we see the disproportionate effects on different communities in terms of health, unemployment, schooling, hygiene, food security, and much more. This is a battle we need to continue to fight in solidarity with many people. It also matters both for the continued quality and freedom of thought in academic life, and for the possibilities of continuing critical work: For people on casual contracts – insecure, overworked, and open to institutional manipulation – taking an overt critical stance may become an option that is hard to maintain. The conditions under which I have been able to formulate critical applied linguistics are very different from those faced by many contemporary academics. In the current context of growing distrust between staff and management, increased governance in teaching, the undermining of the knowledge common through commodification of research findings, the massive casualization of the workforce, and the manipulation of staff, data, and marketing (Connell, 2019), the new enterprise university has become a very difficult place to work, and especially to do critical work.[2]

The distinction between critical work, which necessarily assesses inequality in many contemporary aspects of society, and dystopian visions that stoke pessimistic interpretations of the future, can be hard to separate but it is an important one. It is captured by the motto attributed to Antonio Gramsci: Pessimismo dell'intelligenza, ottimismo della volontà: Pessimism of the mind, optimism of the will.[3] This suggests we have to maintain a project of intellectual critique – pointing to injustices, calling out discriminations, illuminating inequalities – while also believing that things can be changed by concerted political action. The idea of "radical hope" derives from Lear's (2006) reading of Native American Crow leader, Plenty Coups' articulation of hope in the face of devastating cultural loss and with no clear pathway for change: "What makes this hope radical is that it is directed toward a future goodness that transcends the current ability to understand what it is. Radical hope anticipates a good for which those who have the hope as yet lack the appropriate concepts with which to understand it" (Lear, 2006, p. 103).

This in turn has inspired Australian Indigenous activist Noel Pearson (2011) to articulate a project of *radical hope* for Indigenous Australians in the face of racism and profound inequalities, a hope that rests on education: "Our hope depends on how serious we become about the education of our people" (Pearson, 2011, p. 16). Radical hope acknowledges the fundamental injustices that inform many aspects of daily life, yet it also insists that we have to find ways forward, even if the endpoints remain unclear. Neither utopian claims that everything is going well, nor dystopian visions that everything is getting worse can provide the core of a critical applied linguistic project (especially since the *applied* element needs to be able to articulate projects for change). Neither should a challenge that we don't have all the answers hold us back from articulating some form of radical hope for an alternative future.

A Changing World

Displaced People and Precarious Work

My 1990 paper also identified the problem of "pollution and ecological disaster." *Climate change* wasn't so much on our radar 30 years ago, but it was already clear we were not treating our planet well. If some still argue that inequality is not as bad as organizations such as Oxfam make out (it's worth reminding ourselves that it was Oxfam that named the "one percent" that claim a huge proportion of global wealth), those that argue against climate change now find themselves marginalized by a sizable majority. Indeed so far have we come that we now talk in terms of the Anthropocene, an acknowledgement of the destructive force that humans have become for the rest of the planet. The assumptions of modernity – that nature is external, a resource to be exploited, that humans are separate, self-governing, on an upward spiral of self-improvement to escape the limits of nature – have come under scrutiny as we have finally started to reject the "separation between Nature and Human that has paralyzed science and politics since the dawn of modernism" (Latour, 2015, p. 146). The world is scrambling to avoid further ecological devastation while access to water, food, and basic resources comes under even greater threat through climate change and inequitable distribution.

While much that is troubling many of us now was also therefore troubling enough of us 30 years ago – "the financial crisis is deepening, authoritarianism is thriving, and racism permeates society" (Gounari, 2020, p. 17) – there are also new trends that need critical analysis. It is common to think of the present as a time of crisis, but there do seem to be grounds for particular concern in the current moment. 2020 is arguably a time of historical disjuncture, with millions of refugees struggling to find alternative places to survive among increasingly reluctant and hostile hosts (and these needs often cast aside amid the pandemic panic). In 2020, there were over 70 million "displaced people": 41 million "internally displaced," 26 million classified as refugees and 3.5 million seeking asylum (UNHCR, 2020). Walls and fences have meanwhile become the new response to these mobile populations with the rise of trenchant forms of xenophobic and isolationist populism in many parts of the world. The rise of neoliberalism has also brought us new challenges (Harvey, 2005). We were already critiquing what was commonly called "economic rationalism" in the 1990s, and many of the sins now associated with neoliberalism were evident then: Trickle-down economics, tax cuts for the wealthy, excessive privatization, unrestricted deregulation, shrinking government, opposition to social welfare. The key elements of redistributive welfare – parties supporting social democracy, trade unions, fair tax systems – have been challenged by the austerity of neoliberalism, the growth of migration, and the re-emergence of nationalist and xenophobic politics, shifting political debate from a shared commons to an exclusionary discourse.

This redistribution of income away from labor and toward profit is bringing greater inequality as capital is concentrated in the hands of the very rich, while huge economic disparities are ideologically normalized. This has led to a new emergent class of mobile, impoverished, and insecure workers that is supporting growing extravagances by the wealthy while the very idea of welfare and the public good is increasingly on the retreat. These changing labor conditions have been described in terms of what Standing (2014) describes as the *precariat* – a precariously employed and mobile proletariat that lacks security in relation to the labor market, training, income, and representation. However we may want to get at questions of class analysis (Block, 2014), migrant workers, from cleaners and construction workers to aged care and domestic workers, present a class that poses problems for classic class analysis because of its mobility and dispersion and the very unlikelihood of its capacity to organize in opposition. The notion of the precariat has come in for considerable critique: It becomes problematic when it is applied both to mobile aged care workers and, for example, to casual academics (exploited though they are), and overlooks the point that in many parts of the world, precarious work has always been the norm (Munck, 2013). It nonetheless gives us a way of understanding the difficulties and insecurities of undertaking work under conditions of mobility and transience.

Hashtags and White Applied Linguistics

Back in 2000, we didn't have #MeToo or #BlackLivesMatter movements. We didn't even really have hashtags (they were an obscure option on your keyboard for things like #2). We did, however, have racism, misogyny, and sexual misconduct. Dell Hymes' widely-attested history of sexual harassment is a case in point (Educational Linguist, 2018; Elegant, 2018). There has been much discussion of whether his inexcusable – though it was excused and hidden at the time – behavior should lead to him being 'cancelled' (as some have put it), whether his work should be ignored, or whether his work and sexual misconduct can be separated (Ennser-Kananen, 2019). While we need to confront these concerns in applied linguistics, they may also obscure wider issues: The discussion about whether we should cite Hymes or not still fails to engage with the question as to why we're not citing women of color, Indigenous scholars, and many others. Hymes or not Hymes cannot be the endpoint of our discussion.

2020 was also the year when the Black Lives Matter movement finally (and for terrible reasons) got the notice it deserved. It shed light on many things, but above all the deep histories and structures of institutional racism. It made many people confront in deeper ways their complicity so that in applied linguistics we have started to ask not just why there are so few people of color but why White people feel so comfortable in this field: And this ties to the colonial roots of linguistics, and the separation of language from all that it is part of: Bodies, lives, stories, histories, articulations of the past, the present, and the future. It has been a White applied linguistics that makes it possible for people in the field to avoid their own complicity in maintaining White Power (Kubota, 2019; Motha, 2020). As the #TESOLsoWhite and #AAALsoWhite movements have made clear, the racial disparities within our field run deep (Bhattacharya, Jiang, & Canagarajah, 2019).

Epistemological racism – the dominance, normalizing, and continued reference to White Eurocentric forms of knowledge – is deeply entwined in our applied linguistic knowledge practices, favoring certain people and worldviews and forms of knowledge over others (Kubota, 2019). As Motha (2020, p. 129) puts it, we need to uncover "the multitude of ways in which applied linguistics has functioned as an important and effective vehicle for White supremacy and relatedly empire, with the very roots of the discipline dependent on racial inequalities and racial hierarchies." Applied linguistics, she continues, "lives in a complex and interdependent relationship with White supremacy, despite the assumption in wide circulation that an innocent and detached applied linguistics is attainable." Even for many of us who have long argued against the chimerical notion of an innocent and detached applied linguistics, there are profound complicities here that we have to address.

Truth, Conspiracies, and Matters of Concern

The world of hashtags also takes us to another set of concerns: The vast changes to modes of communication and the organization of knowledge that have occurred over the last twenty years. Of particular importance here are the transformations to the information commons or shared knowledge base (the commons or common, to which we return, refers to public ownership or use, and has become another gathering point for opposition to the increased privatization of everything). The privatization or individuation of knowledge and information – through targeted news and information feeds in social media – presents a difficult problem for critical work. We do not need particularly sophisticated discourse analytic tools to understand that Donald Trump's talks and tweets were racist, homophobic, misogynist, and more, though we can learn a great deal by looking at how this speech style operates: rather than merely deriding or objecting to his language, we need to understand how it appeals to audiences, how gestures, mockery and particular formulations have certain effects (McIntosh and Mendoza-Denton, 2020). From a more applied linguistic point of view, it is important to understand how a comment such as "He speaks perfect English" (Trump referring to a Latinx Border Patrol Agent) functions as a form of *raciolinguistic exceptionalism*, whereby White supremacist and colonial relations are formed, embedded, and maintained through ideologies of language and race (Alim & Smitherman 2020).

But 'post-truth politics' (Fish, 2016) present us with other difficult concerns, characterized by a willingness to issue warnings and make claims and promises for electoral advantage with no clear basis in real or future events (Block, 2019). We need to go further than merely suggesting these are questions of lying for electoral advantage – politicians have been doing this for a long time – and move instead toward an understanding that this is not so much a case of "lying," which still potentially relies on a related belief in truth, but of having no interest in either: "calling Trump a liar, besides being a truism, does nothing to advance our understanding of how he uses language, through bullshitting, to portray himself as a charismatic autocrat" (Jacquemet, 2020, p. 124). Jacquemet's focus on "bullshit" points to the ways that such figures are engaged in neither truth nor falsehood, but rather discourse that they hope will produce certain effects. At the same time, populist conservatives urge their followers to do the same, promoting anti-institutional thinking, and suggesting people should mistrust the news, universities, scientists, or just knowledge in general.

This poses a very obvious challenge for all of us working in institutions that purport to produce knowledge. This is complexified by contemporary discourses on 'conspiracy theories' – antimask, antivaccine, anti-5G discourses were given considerable air-time in 2020. Critical work itself is often seen to be peddling its own conspiracy theories: This is what Davies (1996) accuses Phillipson's (1992) *Linguistic Imperialism* of doing – suggesting that the Applied Linguistics Department of Edinburgh University was the control center of the capitalist English Language Teaching (ELT) conspiracy. Critical analysis will always be subject to this critique: The structural inequalities identified through critical work are seen by some as suggesting they are the intentional and hidden goals of a certain group. Perhaps some critical work lends itself to this critique (if critical analysis is not well grounded or well argued, it is easier for critics to suggest it is peddling conspiracies), but the growth of conspiracy discourses as they spiral through social media, and the need to oppose them, are another threat to critical social analysis.

All of this poses a major challenge to how we consider language and discourse. Critical work has sought in some ways to do something similar to these popular discourses by questioning claims to truth and pointing to covert agendas: What else was the take-home message of critical discourse analysis other than 'don't trust the news media'? So when, for example, so-called climate skeptics align themselves with critical analysts (whether critical philosophers of science or critical discourse analysts) on the basis that both are skeptical of claims to 'trust the science' or to 'believe what you read,' we have to start to rethink our relation to 'the truth' and *matters of concern* (Latour, 2004). All of this suggests that the issue is no longer one of showing that right wing populist racists are just that, or showing that they achieve their rhetorical goals in certain ways, but also of asking ourselves what is happening to language and discourse in a new era where 'bullshit' rules. Latour (2004) urges us to rethink our relation to truth, discourse, and matters of concern if critical work is to maintain its force and relevance.

Much more could be said about the state of the world in 2020. A key question that recurs, however, is why all this matters for applied linguistics. It is one thing to worry about climate change, gender inequality, and neoliberalism, some might argue, but there's no particular reason to let these concerns impinge on our work as applied linguists concerned with language education, language policy, language in the workplace, and so on. This has always seemed a very disingenuous argument. Some have suggested that we can't engage with these concerns because they are not part of our professional expertise. And we don't have the tools to make ethical choices between good and bad ways in which the world works. Seriously? The challenges posed by human destructiveness, environmental degradation, diminishing resources, our treatment of animals, or the Whiteness of our profession present a range of ethical and political concerns that are deeply interconnected with questions of language. While this does of course depend on your understanding of language – old and inadequate models derived from linguistics have been allowed to operate for too long with a vision of language separated from the world (Nakata, 2007) – it is evident that such matters of concern are bound up with questions of language and discourse, and applied linguists cannot ethically avoid them.

We cannot duck issues of class, race, gender, sexuality, or disability, as if they were of no consequence to our field. We cannot be effective applied linguists dealing with language and the law, second language education, or language revival, to name a few areas, without having some kind of activist agenda (see Chapter 7). We now have a better grasp, for example, of how race is intertwined with native speakerhood: we cannot treat the notion of the native speaker without understanding processes of *raciolinguistic enregisterment* (Rosa and Flores, 2017a). Nor, when we try to understand language in the context of domestic labor, can we disentangle class, gender, migration, and the global forces that lead women from poorer countries such as the Philippines into domestic work elsewhere (Lorente, 2017). We cannot engage with social questions or with the implementation of ideas and practices without confronting the world around us. If globalization and neoliberal economic ideologies and politics have fragmented older class structures and produced instead a mobile, insecure, workforce, then applied linguistics surely needs to engage with this. If there are deep seated inequalities in the ways knowledge is produced, affirmed and distributed, then surely we have to seek ways to change this. To do so, however, we need new ways of thinking and doing applied linguistics.

Guarding Against Change

We have made huge strides forward in applied linguistics and related fields in the past twenty to thirty years. There has been positive change in this respect, despite efforts to hold it back. The development of critical applied linguistics in the early 2000s was met with a number of rearguard actions by the disciplinary gatekeepers of applied linguistics. In a section of Kaplan's (2002) preface to *The Oxford handbook of applied linguistics*, he explains that:

> The editorial group spent quite a bit of time debating whether critical (applied) linguistics/critical pedagogy/critical discourse analysis should be included; on the grounds that critical applied linguistics rejects all theories of language, expresses "skepticism towards all metanarratives" (Lyotard, 1984) and rejects traditional applied linguistics as an enterprise because it has allegedly never been neutral and has, rather, been hegemonic (Rampton, 1997), the editorial group decided not to include the cluster of "critical" activities. (Kaplan, 2002: pp. v–vi)

A similarly-worded text (with the same references) also occurs in Davies' (1999, p. 126) introduction to the field. This is quite a remarkable statement of exclusion, especially for a handbook of applied linguistics. Work that aims to connect applied linguistics to broader social formations – critical discourse analysis, critical literacy, critical approaches to language policy, and so on – is excluded on three very doubtful criteria. First is the strange claim that critical applied linguistics rejects all theories of language. Critical approaches to applied linguistics of course operate with theories of language, though they have been appropriately skeptical particularly of normative theories derived from mainstream linguistics. A skepticism toward grand narratives, meanwhile, is surely a useful intellectual tool, particularly when trying to deal with minority concerns and questions around the politics of difference. It is also, it should be noted, only applicable to some critical approaches: more traditional Marxist-based work has been quite happy to maintain a grounding in grand narratives. Finally, the concern about neutrality misses the point that such a field of practice requires applied linguists to take a stance. There is no point in working on minority language education, for example, without an element of advocacy.

It has always been rather unclear, however, whether the issue is that these disciplinary guardians dislike the politics or object to the epistemological challenges. I used to think, given the strangeness of these claims, that they were a smoke screen for what really bothered the custodians of the field: There has always been a level of uneasiness in mainstream liberal applied linguistics with the political standpoint of various forms of critical work. The overt political stance on issues of inequality, racism, sexism, or homophobia, from some perspectives, unacceptably "prejudges outcomes" (Davies, 2005, p. 32). As Widdowson (2001) argues, by taking an *a priori* critical stance (rather than maintaining a critical distance – to use a different sense of the critical), critical applied linguistics may impose its own views on the objects of inquiry, taking inappropriate stances on the social world that may be hypocritical because of the impossibility of choosing between different ethical and political concerns. There are of course real issues here (to which I return in later chapters) since critical work does indeed need to be good academic work (critical ethnography needs to be good ethnography; critical discourse analysis needs to be good discourse analysis) but the stance that it is too hard to make ethical and political choices on matters of concern is surely inadequate.

The political stance taken by critical projects, however, is not itself the guardians' central concern. Critical approaches are not such a threat politically to a general liberal consensus. We like to think that they unsettle the status quo, but liberalism has always been able to accommodate critical stances within its own diversity. It is rather the epistemological task of making applied linguistics political that is a more important challenge to the field. While it is tempting to read the dismissal of critical applied linguistics as a rejection of critical politics, these arguments suggest a different level of disquiet, a worry about the threat to the security of the discipline if it is to accommodate forms of work that are overtly political. Liberal applied linguistics is better able to accommodate the political stance of critical applied linguistics (even if it finds it uncomfortable) than the epistemological challenges it perceives to its disciplinary security. This is evident in Davies' (1999: 145) *An introduction to applied linguistics* where he warns of the threat of critical applied linguistics as "a judgmental approach by some applied linguists to 'normal' applied linguistics on the grounds that it is not concerned with the transformation of society." A defense of 'normal' applied linguistics on the grounds that a lot of work was done to establish its disciplinary coherence overlooks the particular inclusionary and exclusionary interests of such disciplinarity (particularly as embedded in conservative institutions of the West/North). It is not the supposedly judgmental attitude or the will to change society that is at stake here but rather the threat to 'normal' applied linguistics and the ways in which critical applied linguistics is seen as "dismissive totally of the attempt since the 1950s to develop a coherent applied linguistics" (Davies, 1999, p. 141).

What is being defended here is not so much the discipline itself but rather the nature of that discipline; hence the strange comments about rejecting all theories of language and grand narratives, and threatening what is normal. This is an attempt to hide behind the narratives of liberalism to obscure the particular racial and classed and gendered positions from which this is being articulated (Mills, 2017). Our vision of the world is the normal one, it is argued, and we reject attempts to unsettle it. Critical applied linguistic work that aims not only to add a political dimension to standard applied linguistic work (discourse analysis with a critical edge, pedagogy with an agenda for social change) but also to challenge the epistemological assumptions behind ideas such as language has always been a more challenging proposition to the disciplinary custodians. Ultimately it is the epistemological challenge posed by the political stance that is the real focus. This rearguard action is particularly regrettable because rather than undermining applied linguistics, critical approaches have been at the forefront of pushing the field forward. Fortunately, we have moved on from such belief in the importance of coherence and normality. Now an Oxford handbook (García, Flores, & Spotti, 2017) on language and society can not only include chapters on language, power, and discrimination but can start from "critical poststructuralist positions" (p. 2) as a basic premise. It is now far less controversial to suggest that languages are social products rather than natural kinds, and thus that *language is politics* (van Splunder, 2020, p. 9), indeed that it is *political from top to bottom* (Joseph, 2006) (see Chapter 3).

Material, Racial, Queer, and Other Turns

A great deal of work over the past twenty to thirty years has built on and developed the earlier efforts at doing critical applied linguistics, and I have tried to weave as much of this as possible into this revised book. Whether this work derives from the broad changes outlined in the earlier section on social change, or whether these are more autonomous academic shifts, remains an open question, and one that raises larger issues of what determines or influences epistemological change. It seems fairly evident, for example, that the rise in studies of neoliberalism and political economy is a reflection of changes to political and economic relations (and also their direct effects on academic workplaces), but it is less clear whether the various 'turns' (social, affective, multilingual, and so on) are a result of social change or a greater academic awareness of matters of concern. There has been considerable discussion, for example, as to whether the multilingual turn (May, 2014) derives from an increase in evident multilingualism in places that had not noticed it so much before (particularly urban spaces in the Global North) or whether it derives from changes to language ideologies whose impetus comes from elsewhere (the voices of scholars from the Global South finally being heard, for example). In many ways, of course, these questions are deeply intertwined, but it is nevertheless useful to consider whether, from the first perspective, critical work should properly derive from and focus on real material change, or whether, from the second perspective, critical work may also derive from new ways of thinking about social and political relations.

Neoliberalism and the Material Turn

It is clear that the incursion of neoliberalism into so many areas of contemporary life has driven the expansion of critical applied linguistic analysis, from studies of the language of neoliberalism (Holborow, 2015) to research on neoliberalism and education (Flubacher & Del Percio, 2017) and the effects of neoliberalism on how we think and act (Martín Rojo & del Percio 2019). The case that neoliberalism now permeates everything – not just socioeconomic relations, but how we think, work and relate to others (Ratner, 2019) – has brought powerful new analyses to many contexts of importance to applied linguistics. This focus on neoliberalism has been accompanied by the return of class as a proper, analytic concept. Here Block (2014; 2018a) and his collaborators have been crucial in bringing social class, analyses of political economy and an emphasis on redistribution into the field. This has been a very welcome development in (critical) applied linguistics, bringing a much sharper edge to studies of social inequality, or of the political economy of global English (O'Regan, 2021). As with all such developments, however, we also need to consider a few potential pitfalls.

There is a danger of turning neoliberalism into the catch-all foe of all critical work, and also of overlooking the importance of *libertarian political economy* with its disdain not only for state-based provision of education, health or security but also for financial regulation or any other forms of limitation on freedom. (Benquet and Bourgeron, 2021). The argument that a focus on diversity makes us complicit with neoliberalism, which has co-opted difference for its own ends (Flores, 2013; Kubota, 2016), needs to be heard but also questioned. As Canagarajah (2017) explains, it is important to distinguish between the language ideologies that inform communicative practices that we might understand as conforming to neoliberal ideologies and practices, and those that have more often been the focus of critical applied linguistics. Put another way, just because some critical applied linguists focus on aspects of diversity (urban multilingualism or minority languages, for example) doesn't mean they are therefore complicit with neoliberal orientations to diversity.

To give a related example, if we point out that neoliberal agencies have an extractive and commodity-oriented approach to resources (the privatization and extraction of formerly public assets such as land, water, forests, minerals, and so on), this does not render all talk of linguistic resources complicit with neoliberal governance. Relatedly, the rise of critiques of "language commodification" (Duchêne & Heller, 2013, amongst many others) has usefully pointed to ways in which languages have been increasingly valued as commodities within the global economy, and thus to the ways that certain forms of multilingualism (in elite languages) accrue more value than others. A problem, however, is that this notion of commodification carries less critical weight than at first sight: It does not sit comfortably within a neo-Marxian framework of commodification (Block, 2018b; Simpson & O' Regan, 2018), reifies languages in unhelpful ways, suggests that profit should be secondary to expressions such as pride, and ends up critiquing language learning for material gain.

Class has arguably been missing from applied linguistics for at least two reasons: a lack of critical social analysis ('socioeconomic class' was assumed to be a transparent and uncontroversial category against which language variables could be mapped), and a poststructuralist focus on discourse at the possible expense of material relations. While the first point is a welcome corrective to the inadequate sociology that often underpins sociolinguistic analysis (a point made long ago by Williams, 1992), the critique of poststructuralist work has often been misguided, engaging in caricatures of an apolitical field of study concerned with identity, agency, and the individual. These arguments unfortunately echo reactionary critiques of "postmodernist neo-Marxists" – a catchphrase of the "intellectual we deserve" (Jordan Peterson) (Robinson, 2018) – while missing the point that poststructuralism has a strong political pedigree (if it has been watered down in the bourgeois academy, so too have other critical approaches), and has never promoted individualist accounts of people or agency (indeed quite the opposite). This is not what subjectivity is about (McNamara, 2019).

The problem ultimately is that while critical approaches based on political economy bring a much-needed dose of social reality to frameworks based on a consensual notion of society – where inequality is a systemic given rather than an incitement for change – the tendency toward totalizing analyses (there is no subject position outside neoliberalism) fall into their own trap of political determinism: These analyses themselves can only reflect neoliberal interests. For those of us still clinging on to full-time jobs in tertiary education in a time of mass casualization, furthermore, we need to be careful we do not overlook the roles we play – despite our critiques – in sustaining the daily practices of neoliberal regimes (performance reviews; accountability systems, and so on).

The insistence on material rather than discursive relations (sometimes dressed up as redistribution rather than recognition; Block 2018c) may also take us down an unhelpful path. It is of course equally unhelpful to insist that everything is discursively constructed, and the material is only a product of our social imagination. The problem is that the distinction itself is problematic, a product of neo-Marxian bifurcations of infrastructure (the material base) and superstructure (cultural and ideological reflections of that base). As Butler (1990) made clear long ago, the discursive-material dichotomy needs a serious re-evaluation. It is ultimately unproductive to insist on discursive analysis or socioeconomic analysis at the expense of each other, or to insist that one is primary, or causative of the other. They are intertwined and complimentary, and we would be better served if both worked together. A concern is that neo-Marxian views on the centrality of economic and material relations (which are indeed matters of concern) make particular claims to what materiality matters. Studies in "new materialism" have sought an alternative vision, not by denying the significance of political economy and economic deprivation but by suggesting that it should not constrain the meanings we can give to materiality (Bennett, 2010). These arguments take us toward studies that attempt to rethink the divisions between material and non-material worlds (Barad, 2007). These issues will be discussed in greater depth in Chapter 3, particularly in light of the posthumanist turn.

Finally, although it is now common to include discussions of *intersectionality* – an understanding that class, gender, and race, as well as other categorizations around which social differences are formed, are always intertwined – there remains a tendency to maintain that class and political economy nonetheless remain the bedrock of critical analysis because of its focus on the redistribution of material resources. And yet, as Flores and Chaparro (2018) note, race is equally bound up with the unequal distribution of resources: By putting gender, race, sexuality, and so on into their 'identity' box (or assigning them to matters of discourse or recognition), political economists run the danger of suggesting that the inequalities formed around race – both lived forms of daily discrimination and patterns of material deprivation – are secondary to class. It is instead more useful to develop "a materialist antiracist approach to language activism" that combines an analysis of race and class with "a critique of White supremacy and capitalism" (Flores & Chaparro, 2018, p. 380). Raciolinguistic analyses have brought a new and urgent focus to applied linguistics, but so have other turns toward sexuality, multilingualism, and the Global South.

Raciolinguistic and Queer Turns

Race as a focus of critical analysis has received a major emphasis in recent years, not least through the recent development of *raciolinguistics*. It was there in earlier versions of critical work: we spoke often of "class, race and gender," but without much more careful and particular analysis of all three terms, how they intersect and also how they differ. The invocation of these terms fails to address the deep-seated discriminations of White epistemologies. Kubota and Lin (2009) urge greater understanding of how race is intertwined with questions of native speakerhood: Because of the "tendency to equate the native speaker with white and the non-native speaker with non-white" (Kubota & Lin, 2009, p. 8) people of color face discrimination as non-native speakers, and non-native speakers are stigmatized within a racial order. Racial discrimination and White normativity are deeply embedded in practices and ideologies of English language teaching (Jenks, 2017) and to try to understand the global spread of English without taking into account race and Empire is simply to miss the key issues (Motha, 2014). An increased focus on race has brought an insistence that we need to reverse the white gaze, to see that our categories of analysis are the product of racialized positionalities.

While it is clear that applied linguistics can no longer continue to ignore race, neither can it afford to overlook questions of sexual identity and orientation. Twenty years ago, very little applied linguistic work had taken up the significance of Judith Butler's (1990) critical reworking of gender. Since then a range of work (see Chapter 4) has opened up our understanding of gender, sexuality, and sexual identity. Levon and Mendes (2016, p. 1) explain that a focus on "the linguistic behavior of specific groups of speakers (lesbians, gay men, etc.)" has been superseded by a focus on "how sexuality (in all its guises) emerges through linguistic practice." This as we shall see has been part of a wider sociolinguistic shift from macro-sociolinguistic studies of correlations between groups and linguistic features toward a more critical approach to language practices (Bell, 2014). This relates to the shifting landscape of sociolinguistics, which has now started to reconverge with its long-lost cousin linguistic anthropology. This newly invigorated focus – what Bucholtz and Hall (2008) call *sociocultural linguistics* – has brought a range of cultural and political concerns as well as ethnographic tools to the rather limited earlier approaches to language and society.

This has in turn reinvigorated applied linguistics, as new forms of analysis and action have come into play. From an applied linguistic perspective, Nelson (2009, p. 3) asks how language teaching practices were and should be changing in light of "the worldwide proliferation of increasingly visible lesbian, gay, bisexual, transgender, and queer identities and communities and the widespread circulation of circulation of discourses, images, and information pertaining to sexual diversity". While discrimination against – and criminalization of – sexual identities and activities continues across the world, applied linguistics has opened up (partially, and not without struggle) to LGBTIQA+ concerns and Queer Theory. Now it has become possible not just to do critical analysis of discourses about sexuality, but to ask more searching questions about what it would mean to Queer the field more generally, to unsettle normative assumptions about language, affect, and the body (Thurlow, 2016), or to ask how gender, discourse, and sexuality look different from a southern perspective (Milani & Lazar, 2017).

Translingual and Decolonial Turns

A range of so-called turns regularly sweep across the humanities and social sciences, from the linguistic, discursive and performative, to the ecological, spatial, somatic, sensory, affective, and material. Critical applied linguistics needs to be both attentive to such epistemological trends – many provide productive new ways for thinking about social concerns – and also cautious lest new fads are not addressed critically. Various turns of particular relevance to applied linguistics need careful consideration in this light. As May (2014) notes, a number of areas of applied linguistics have undergone a 'multilingual turn'; indeed multilingualism, he suggests, "is the topic du jour, at least in critical applied linguistics" (p. 1). Nonetheless, it is clear that a multilingual turn in itself does not constitute a critical orientation. The recognition of multilingualism as the norm from which we should observe language learning and use is important but without a broader social agenda around the political economy of multilingualism, a multilingual turn does not carry enough critical weight in itself. The "critical perspective" on multilingualism developed by Blackledge and Creese (2010) takes a stance against "powerful repeated discourses" that "minority languages, and multilingualism, are the cause of problems in society" (p. 6), arguing instead for an understanding of the complexity of multilingual practices. A broader, critical multilingual agenda does not just aim to make multilingualism visible within the blinkered field of second language acquisition but also to work with a goal of "equitable multilingualism" (Ortega, 2019), or a focus on how multilingualism may be understood very differently in the Global South (Pennycook & Makoni, 2020),

The related translinguistic turn also needs to be weighed up for its critical orientation. The explosion of work that has invoked a translingual position, a questioning of the separability of languages and the separation between languages and other communicative resources (Canagarajah, 2013) is clearly in need of some kind of explanation. There are several trends in translinguistic work (to which I return in Chapter 3 and elsewhere): On the one hand studies that focus on the mixing of supposedly separate languages (either sociolinguistic studies of language use or more applied work in pedagogical contexts), and on the other, studies that focus more on the expansion of semiotic domains: not just multimodality but semiotic assemblages. As Jaspers (2018, p. 2) has reminded us, however, some of the claims about the emancipatory potential of translanguaging may be misplaced: Translanguaging is "likely to be less transformative and critical than is often suggested." Jasper's point is that the idea that social change can be brought about by changing the ways languages are used and taught misses the point that social forces of inequality are far greater than this. García (2014) has often stressed, however, that her work should be understood as part of a broader decolonial project, challenging the identities and structures of the modern/colonial world system, which brings us finally to the last of the turns I shall consider here.

Recently the field had been challenged by decolonial and southern theory, by the insistence on rethinking the world through a different lens. There remains in mainstream applied linguistics a deplorable blindness toward contexts and ideas outside the Global North. In book after book, conference after conference, article after article, academics from a narrow range of contexts – mainly European and North American – discuss research on specific contexts and generalize these to the wider world. Under claims of commonality – humanity, language, and disciplinarity – classed, raced, and locality-based understandings of language use are assumed to be applicable to the majority world elsewhere (Grosfoguel, 2007). An inequitable knowledge hierarchy ensures that certain assumptions about language, diversity and education are given precedence over other possibilities. The "lingering inheritance of coloniality and its unequal distribution of knowledges, bodies, and languages" persists. Applied Linguistics needs to take this seriously in order to "avoid, albeit unwittingly, continuing the legacy of coloniality." (de Souza, 2017, p. 206). The various strands of southern theory – de Sousa Santos' *southern epistemologies* (2014) or Mignolo and Walsh's (2018) *decolonial insurgency* (p. 34) that aligns with other forms of praxis and pedagogy "*against* the colonial matrix of power in all of its dimensions, and *for* the possibilities of an otherwise" (p. 17) – are setting a new and crucial agenda for critical applied linguistics. This has opened the space for considering the implications of Indigenous ways of knowing and doing (Todd, 2016; Yunkaporta, 2019) for our field. And this means changing the ways we think about language, place, knowledge, and community; it means shifting the kinds of political activism and research we are engaged with.

Changing the Book

I have chosen not just to add this introduction to an unchanged book, but rather to make major revisions to the book throughout. There are some inevitable tensions in writing about critical work. One is that it may become exclusionary: Many people want to feel that their work is *critical* (a result in part of the various meanings of the term critical). To draw a line and say that one approach is critical and another is not will always be contentious. At the same time, however, critical work has to adopt some kind of normative version of what it is about: Not all work is critical in the sense that it is developed in this book. There was always a tension in the first edition between the acknowledgement of neo-Marxian critical work (linguistic imperialism, critical discourse studies) and my tendency to favor poststructuralist (postmodernist, postcolonial) work. Much of this work, I now feel, was framed too much from a poststructuralist/discursive framework. The problem was that my avowed stance on critical work spent too much time promoting various 'post' positions at the expense of more traditional approaches.

Here I have tried to bring more balance, to show what each brings to the table. I am not promising complete balance – there are good reasons for suggesting why some approaches are limited and others offer more scope – but I have tried to make this more nuanced. While I do not want to buy into simplistic critiques of poststructuralism, I want to make a better case in this revised edition for the mutual positions of what I termed "emancipatory modernism" and "problematizing practice" (I have also changed some of these terminologies). This is not to suggest that modernist and postmodernist positions are easily reconcilable – as Kramsch (2021) clarifies, the one operates from a reductionist position in which some 'have power' while others do not, while the other suggests a more complex diffusion of power – but rather that it is more useful to weigh up various positions carefully, rather than positioning one in favor of the other. Put another way, I was rather too keen in the first edition on all 'post' positions – just as in the present we are perhaps too invested in all 'trans' positions – at the expense of others.

I am less intent on staking out a poststructuralist rather than a neo-Marxist position, as was arguably the case in the first edition. Instead I hope to see when and how these can work together, and what other possibilities can take us beyond this distinction. While I still have limited patience for simplistic critiques of 'post' or deconstructionist positions (that label such work as politically correct, relativist, or other terms from the reactionary bag of tricks), I do see more clearly the weaknesses of various stances and the strengths of others. Instead I have sought to shed light on central concerns within critical work, issues to do with structure and agency, genre and voice, reproduction and resistance, and so on. While I want this updated version to be less exclusionary – or at least to avoid so much boxing with clumsy labels (such as 'emancipatory modernism') – it is also very important that it has clear criteria for what is and is not critical. Friedrich et al. (2013) take up the question (raised in the first edition) of whether a conservative politics could also be part of a critical project (can one do critical applied linguistics with a conservative agenda?). The point is worth discussion, but is ultimately contradictory. There is a normative politics embedded in the critical applied linguistics I am arguing for: It is about social change, discrimination, and inequality, ideas that are anathema to a conservative mindset (which, in case we need to remind ourselves, is at best about keeping things the same and more often about returning to an idealized past). It is important not to define critical applied linguistics narrowly and exclusively; but conservative values surely have no place here.

Another issue that constantly emerges around critical work is that it can be difficult to read. Hall, Wicaksono, Liu, Qian, and Xu (2013, p. 5), for example, suggest that critical applied linguistics may often be alienating for language teachers because of its "uncompromising ideological stance" and "the highly abstruse nature of much of its discourse." While I have certain reservations about the framing of such critiques – the juxtaposition of critical applied linguistics and "classroom realities," for example, sets up a problematic distinction (issues of racial discrimination *are* classroom realities) and may also underestimate the capacities and interests of teachers, busy though they often are – to ignore such comments would be to overlook some very real concerns. I certainly try to avoid suggesting ideological rigidity. There are aspects of doing critical work that mean there are areas on which many of us are not prepared to compromise (a focus on equality, for example, and a rejection of ways to address inequality that fail to grasp key economic and political processes at play), but at the same time, it is important that critical applied linguistics can be flexible in how it addresses such concerns. Second, in order to take up issues of disadvantage, critical applied linguistics has to grapple with difficult ideas – structure and agency, ideology and discourse, colonialism and decoloniality, sexuality and discrimination, amongst many others – and then to explore both how these areas intersect with each other and how they relate to language and applied linguistic concerns. Nonetheless, the onus is still on making this accessible to as wide a range of people as possible, so I have worked hard to make this text more accessible and less abstruse than the first edition.

I have sought to trim down unnecessary or outdated discussions while also keeping enough of the references and older debates.[4] A revised version of the book can help bridge recent critical work with the past and provide historical depth to a field that spans over 50 years of critical scholarship. I have added many new and pertinent references and discussions, but I have also retained many original references to show that these debates have been around a long time. There is plenty of contemporary critical applied linguistic work going on, from critical pedagogy to critical literacy, from antiracist pedagogy to decolonizing theory. While new work draws its inspiration from new contexts, new movements, and new ideas, it is also important that we are able to see the history of this work. While I have updated the book considerably, I have tried not to cull too much of the older work just because it's old. The challenge therefore has been to develop critical applied linguistics in a less dogmatic way and with fewer attempts to distance and critique other critical approaches, but to nonetheless show what things are necessary for critical applied linguistics. Friedrich et al. (2013, p. 131) "resent the view that looking critically means always looking skeptically" but I can't see how or why we would avoid a skeptical stance. Critical applied linguistics must have a standpoint that critiques inequality. It cannot just advocate for a better world (as do some approaches such as "peace linguistics"). It has to maintain a critique of contemporary modes of doing applied linguistics (without so much labeling, and without unnecessary critiques of work that really doesn't matter). It must have modes of grounded action that can address issues at a grassroots level. This brings me to my final point.

In the last chapter I have sought to better address the question as to what we can do as applied linguists. Makoni (2003) has suggested that without explicit means to engage with local communities, critical applied linguistics may end up being another hegemonic framework that fails to engage. Throughout this new edition, as well as in the final chapter, I have sought to emphasize the importance of a *situated, collaborative* perspective that takes the discussion away from questions of implementation, and insists instead that critical applied linguistics has to be an emergent program from the contexts in which it works. The first edition of this book focused more on the establishment of the field of critical applied linguistics. Here, by contrast, I have sought to make this less important than issues of advocacy and activism. The question remains, of course, as to what we can do as (critical) applied linguists. Block (2018c) urges us to make redistribution (fundamental changes in the economy toward more equitable distribution of wealth) central to our work and to recognize the limitations of recognition (focusing on discrimination along lines of race, gender, and sexuality). This raises a central question about our role as critical applied linguists: It is one thing to bring better analyses of material inequality into our work, but the question remains as to the relation between that work and social change. How do we work toward change in the contexts of our work, where issues of language sit at the heart of forms of inequality?

Notes

1. Journals such as *Critical Inquiry in Language Studies, Critical Multilingualism Studies, or Multilingual Margins: A journal of multilingualism from the periphery* (naming its critical stance through its southern eyes) have emerged over the last few years.
2. Indeed, the difficulties and complicities involved in working in contemporary universities have led me to make a decision to leave my current employment. By the time this book is published, I will no longer be working as an institutionalized academic.
3. Gramsci attributes this phrase to Romain Rolland. He explained his own position - "sono pessimista con l'intelligenza, ma ottimista per la volontà" (I'm a pessimist with my mind, but an optimist of the will) in a letter from prison in December 1929).
4. I have also taken seriously Kubota's (2019) injunction to revisit whom we cite. I have endeavored in the second edition to have a much better range of authors, positions, geopolitical concerns, languages, and so on. This has also entailed cutting out some of the tired old debates (and authors) in the field.

1 Introducing Critical Applied Linguistics

Critical applied linguistics is a critical approach to the theory and practice of applied linguistics. For such a statement to have much meaning, however, we need at the very least an understanding of the scope and meaning of the term *critical* and the ways it has been taken up in applied linguistics. In this first chapter, therefore, I shall focus on two main aspects of critical applied linguistics: An overview of what critical work in general entails, and a discussion of domains of critical applied linguistics. In the following discussion, I will distinguish between critical thinking and critical theory, and provide some initial background (developed in Chapter 2) to crucial components of critical work, including critical social theory, radical hope, and activism. In the second part of the chapter, I will discuss briefly how different domains of critical applied linguistic work operate, including critical sociolinguistics, critical discourse analysis (CDA), critical literacy, critical approaches to translation, critical second language pedagogies, and critical language testing (CLT). These will be discussed in more depth in subsequent chapters focusing on the politics of language, difference, text, and pedagogy. This first chapter therefore will make it possible to develop a better understanding of this "critical approach" to applied linguistics, linking it to questions of power, inequality, and social change.

We might also arguably need a clear understanding of the scope and meaning of applied linguistics, though I do not intend to get into an extended discussion of this topic. A lot of time has been spent – much of it fairly fruitless – trying to define applied linguistics. We have fortunately moved on from the days when it was indelibly tied to language education, and particularly to teaching English as a second or foreign language. We have also moved on from the interminable discussions about whether we are mediating between linguistics (as defined elsewhere) and language education (linguistics applied) or whether applied linguistics has some more autonomous status (Markee, 1990; Widdowson, 1980). I prefer to think of applied linguistics less in disciplinary or inter- or transdisciplinary terms and more as temporary assemblages of thought and action that come together at particular moments when language-related concerns need to be addressed (Pennycook, 2018b). What this means will become more evident as we look at various domains of critical applied linguistics throughout the book.

What Does It Mean To Do Critical Work?

Apart from some general uses of the term – such as "Don't be so critical," which suggest that to be critical is to be unhelpfully negative about things – two related and common uses of the term can be found in *literary criticism* and *critical thinking*. The first suggests an ability to evaluate and comment on literary texts (or other texts and aesthetic objects in the case of television, film, or food critics), to convey to others the reasons for certain aesthetic judgments. While there is great variety these days in the ways such critical work operates (blogs and social media have opened up such work to a much wider range of forms than in an earlier era of newspapers and television), the genre largely mixes aesthetic and evaluative discussion in order to explain and justify why the author likes this book, film, CD, poem, wine, meal, and so forth. *Critical thinking*, by contrast, puts greater emphasis on forms of rational thinking. Seen in the Western tradition as dating back to Socrates, this tradition seeks to evaluate factual evidence, emphasizing objectivity and unbiased thought. It is used to describe a way of bringing more rigorous analysis to problem-solving or textual understanding, a way of developing more *critical distance* as it is sometimes called. Its focus is on forms of reasoning (induction, deduction, and abduction, for example) and the ability to evaluate an argument. This form of "skilled critical questioning" (Brookfield, 1987, p. 92) can be broken down into a set of thinking skills, a set of rules for thinking that can be taught to students.

In an age when learning 'skills' has become a key goal for many educational institutions, and when self-directed learning guides have become big business (see, for example, Paul & Elder, 2001), the teaching and learning of these critical thinking skills have been linked to better decision-making, smarter thinking, and various improvements to one's life, and have come to dominate both popular and academic understanding of what it means to be critical. Critical thinking refers to "an educational goal, a skill that can be acquired, developed, and sharpened and is reached individually" (Gounari, 2020, p. 11). It is based around notions of logic and reasoning, and is tied to goal-directed learning, and a specific program of guided thinking. It is this sense of *critical* that has been given some space by various applied linguists (e.g., Atkinson, 1997; Widdowson, 2001) who argue that critical applied linguistics should operate with this form of critical distance and objective evaluation. Although there is much to be said for such an ability to analyze and critique – I am by no means *against* it – it is a different approach to critical work that is the focus of this book. The sense of the critical that is central to critical applied linguistics draws on an alternative lineage of work that makes social critique central. It is concerned with questions of injustice, inequality, and discrimination.

A Critical Understanding of Language and Society

From this perspective, critical applied linguistics is concerned with the interrelationships among (adapting Janks, 2000) *domination* (contingent and contextual effects of power), *disparity* (inequitable access to material and cultural goods), *discrimination* (ideological and discursive frames of exclusion), *difference* (constructions and realities of social and cultural distinction), and *desire* (operations of ideology, agency, identity, and transformation). Whether this *a priori* focus on power and inequality means that such forms of analysis are always biased, lacking the objectivity central to any forms of analysis (and therefore in opposition to critical distance), will be an important focus of further discussion. Two basic positions refute such a criticism: On the one hand, many working in a *modernist* tradition maintain that critical inquiry can remain objective and is no less so because of its engagement with social critique. On the other hand, those working from a more *postmodernist* position reject the claims to critical distance, insisting that the claim to objectivity – indeed the subjective-objective distinction itself – is an unhelpful construction that leads us nowhere. These three approaches – critical thinking, modernism, and postmodernism – are sketched out in Table 1.1. We should be cautious not to set them too strongly against each other – they are much more complexly interwoven than this suggests – or to suggest these are fixed and closed traditions of thought – there is far more cross-fertilization than this kind of schema suggests – but it is important to understand there may be very different approaches to power, knowledge, and change at stake.

Whatever position one takes on critical work, it is clear that rather than basing critical applied linguistics on a notion of teachable critical thinking skills, or critical distance from social and political relations, critical applied linguistics has to have ways of relating aspects of applied linguistics to broader social, cultural, and political domains. One of the shortcomings of work in applied linguistics generally has been a tendency to operate with what I elsewhere (Pennycook, 1994a) called *decontextualized contexts*. It is common to view applied linguistics as concerned with language in context, but the conceptualization of context is frequently one that is limited to an undertheorized view of social relations. One of the key challenges for critical applied linguistics, therefore, is to find ways of understanding relations between, on the one hand, concepts of society, ideology, global capitalism, colonialism, education, gender, racism, or sexuality and, on the other hand, classroom utterances,

Table 1.1 Three Approaches to Critical Work

	Critical Thinking	Modernist critical theory	Postmodern critical theory
Politics	Liberal individualism	Neo-Marxism	Feminist, anti-racist, queer, and southern theory
Theoretical base	Humanist rationalism	Critical Theory	Poststructuralism
Goals	Objective thinking skills	Redistribution and ideology critique	Recognition and transformation

translations, conversations, genres, second language acquisition, media texts, and so on. Whether it is critical text analysis, or an attempt to understand implications of the global spread of English, a central issue always concerns how the classroom, text, or conversation is related to broader social cultural and political relations.

It is not enough, however, merely to draw connections between microrelations of language in context and macrorelations of social inquiry. Rather, such connections need to do at least two things: First, they need to draw attention to the ways in which these small- and large-scale operations are always part of each other: A racist utterance is not best understood as an individual insult by one person to another but as part of wider social concerns: It simultaneously draws on broad racial ideologies and reinforces them. This is why Hacking (2004) insists on the need to find a space between discourse in the abstract, as described by Foucault, and face-to-face interaction, as discussed by Goffman: Foucault, as Hacking explains, "gave us ways in which to understand what is said, can be said, what is possible, what is meaningful" yet he did not give us ways of thinking about "how, in everyday life, one comes to incorporate these possibilities and impossibilities as part of oneself. We have to go to Goffman to begin to think about that." (Hacking 2004, p. 300). McNamara (2019) makes a similar point when he connects conversation analysis (CA) with Butler's (1997) idea of performativity: In order to understand the wider workings of the world, we have to look locally at the microactions of language use. Similarly, however, we should not get too caught up in the minutiae of language lest we lose sight of the bigger picture. We need a way of looking at language that not only looks at society or institutions, that not only includes an understanding of the interactions of the everyday, but that also seeks an understanding of how such interactions are institutionally framed and such institutions are interactionally realized.

Second, the focus has to be from a critical approach to social relations. That is to say, critical applied linguistics is concerned not merely with relating language contexts to social contexts but rather does so from a point of view that views social relations as problematic. A great deal of work in sociolinguistics has tended to map language onto a rather static and consensual view of society (Williams, 1992), though this has been changing considerably over the last decade as the 'new sociolinguistics' has brought more critical questions to the table. Critical sociolinguistics (discussed in more depth in Chapters 2 and 3) is concerned with a critique of ways in which language perpetuates inequitable social relations. From the point of view of studies of language and gender, the issue is not merely to describe how language is used differently along gendered lines but to use such an analysis as part of social critique and transformation. A central element of critical applied linguistics, therefore, is a way of exploring language in social contexts that goes beyond mere correlation between language and society, and instead raises more critical questions to do with domination, disparity, discrimination, difference, and desire (Table 1.2).

Table 1.2 Five Ds of Critical Work

Domination	Contingent and contextual effects of power
Disparity	Inequitable access to material and cultural goods
Discrimination	Ideological and discursive frames of exclusion
Difference	Social and cultural distinctions
Desire	Operations of ideology, agency, identity, and transformation

Critical Theory and Beyond

This focus on the inequitable operations of society has a long history. One strand that many have turned to is Critical Theory, a tradition of work linked to the Frankfurt School and such thinkers as Adorno, Horkheimer, Walter Benjamin, Erich Fromm, Herbert Marcuse, and more recently, Jürgen Habermas. A great deal of critical social theory, at least in the Western tradition, has drawn in various ways on this reworking of Marxist theory to include more complex understandings of the ways in which the Marxist concept of ideology relates to psychoanalytic understandings of the subconscious, how aspects of popular culture are related to forms of political control, and how particular forms of positivism and rationalism have come to dominate other possible ways of thinking. At the very least, this body of work reminds us that critical applied linguistics has to engage with the long legacy of Marxism, neo-Marxism, and its many counterarguments. Critical work has to involve analysis of inequitable work conditions, the functioning of capitalism, the role of ideology, and an understanding of society as conflictual rather than consensual.

Looking more broadly at the implications of this line of thinking, we might say that *critical* here means taking social inequality and social transformation as central to one's work. As Poster (1989, p. 3) puts it, "critical theory springs from an assumption that we live amid a world of pain, that much can be done to alleviate that pain, and that theory has a crucial role to play in that process." I am reminded here of a moment recounted by Habermas, the prolific heir to this critical tradition, when he went to visit Herbert Marcuse, his predecessor and author of such classic works as *One Dimensional Man* (1964). Just before Marcuse's 80th birthday, the two had had a "long discussion on how we could and should explain the normative base of Critical Theory." Two years later, Habermas visits Marcuse in the intensive care unit of a hospital. The dying Marcuse returns to the previous debate: "Look, I know wherein our most basic value judgments are rooted—in compassion, in our sense for the suffering of others" (Marcuse as cited in Habermas, 1985, p. 77).

This moment is worth recalling, for amid the fierce debates over different approaches to critical work – and considering too that the Frankfurt School has been demonized in conservative circles as the source of those familiar enemies of conservative (and often anti-Semitic) thought, 'cultural marxism' and 'political correctness' – it is worth reminding ourselves that it is perhaps compassion that connects our work. If compassion sounds perhaps a bit easy or religious or patronizing, this is not so much compassion based on soft sympathy for others so much as compassion grounded in a sharp critique of inequality. Following Poster (1989), we might add that critical applied linguistics is an approach to language-related questions that spring from an assumption that we live amid a world of pain, and that language plays a very significant role in both the production and the possible alleviation of some of that pain. Yet critical applied linguistics is not just about compassion or the alleviation of pain: It is also about the possibility of change.

There are a number of very important additions that need to be made to this vision of Critical Theory as foundational to any contemporary critical project. The first is the point that it evidently derives from a distinct political, cultural, and geographical context. To favor this line of work over other forms of critical work – feminist, queer, anti-racist, decolonial, amongst others – is to fall into the trap so widely critiqued in recent times of privileging European, White, male, and straight epistemologies over many others (Kubota, 2019; Pennycook & Makoni, 2020). Feminist work has a long history too. It may not carry the label 'critical' as its first priority – it has a more obviously nameable critical focus – but it works along similar principles of social critique, and is often engaged in a dialogue with Marxist thought. Feminist theory and activism has both a long tradition of its own that doesn't need to claim origins in Critical Theory, as well as a wide variety of political standpoints, ranging from forms of liberal inclusion to more radical positions. As Arruzza, Bhattacharya, and Fraser (2019) remind us, forms of neoliberal feminism that focus only on equal representation in the workplace miss the point that feminism needs to be simultaneously anti-capitalist, eco-socialist, and antiracist.

Likewise, a critical focus on sexual identity can range from the more liberal movement for marriage equality to far more radical projects questioning forms of sexual identity that are seen as tied to capitalist and colonialist forms of knowledge (Milani & Lazar, 2017). As the wave of recent decolonial and southern theory insists, any critical project also needs to delink from these traditions of Western/Northern critical theory (Mignolo & Walsh, 2018). This is to understand the particular *locus of enunciation* from which Critical Theory emerged, the alternative modes of thought that have been submerged by such frameworks, and the foundational role that concepts of race have played in the development of Western/Northern thought: "Since the beginning of the eighteenth century, Blackness and race have constituted the (unacknowledged and often denied) foundation … from which the modern project of knowledge—and of governance—has been deployed" (Mbembe, 2017, p. 2).

Another important addition is a sense of self-reflexivity or problematization. As Dean (1994) suggests, the version of *critical* in Critical Theory is a form of critical modernism, a version of critical theory that tends to critique "modernist narratives in terms of the one-sided, pathological, advance of technocratic or instrumental reason they celebrate" only to offer "an alternative, higher version of rationality" in their place (Dean, 1994, p. 3). A considerable amount of work in critical applied linguistic domains arguably operates with such modernist narratives, developing a critique of social and political formations but offering only a version of an alternative reality in its place. This version of critical modernism, with its emphasis on emancipation and rationality, has a number of limitations. In place of Critical Theory, Dean (1994) goes on to propose what he calls a *problematizing practice*. This, he suggests, is a critical practice because "it is unwilling to accept the taken-for-granted components of our reality and the 'official' accounts of how they came to be the way they are" (p. 4). Thus, a crucial component of critical work is always turning a skeptical eye toward assumptions, ideas that have become "naturalized," notions that are no longer questioned. Dean (1994) describes such practice as "the restive problematization of the given" (p. 4).

Drawing on work in areas such as feminism, anti-racism, queer, and decolonial theory, this approach to the critical seeks not so much the stable ground of an alternative reality but rather a more constant questioning of all categories. From this point of view, critical applied linguistics is not only about relating microrelations of applied linguistics to macrorelations of social and political power; neither is it only concerned with relating such questions to a prior critical analysis of inequality; rather, it is also concerned with questioning what is meant by and what is maintained by many of the everyday categories of both critical theory and applied linguistics: Language, learning, communication, difference, context, text, culture, meaning, translation, writing, literacy, assessment, and so on. Such a problematizing stance in any critical applied linguistics needs to retain a constant skepticism, a constant questioning of the givens of applied linguistics, a problematizing stance that must also be turned on itself. As Spivak (1993, p. 25) suggests, the notion of *critical* also needs to imply an awareness "of the limits of knowing." One of the things we need to guard against in critical theory, typified by some modernist approaches to knowledge and politics, is an excessive assurity about its own rightness, a belief that an adequate critique of social and political inequality can lead to an alternative reality.

This is also why it is crucial to build in a sense of *positionality* or the *locus of enunciation*, that is to say a way of making explicit the personal (embodied), geographical, historical, and ideological positions from which ideas are articulated (de Souza 2019; Diniz de Figueiredo & Martinez, 2019). This is not merely a process of localization, or of providing biographical details, but also one of resisting the universalizing tropes of the West and the epistemological racism at the heart of applied linguistics. A problematizing stance needs to maintain a greater sense of humility, to be aware of the limits of its own knowing. This self-reflexive position also suggests that critical applied linguistics is not concerned with producing itself as a new orthodoxy, with prescribing new models and procedures for doing applied linguistics. Rather, it is concerned with raising a host of new and difficult questions about knowledge, politics, and ethics.

Hope, Praxis, and Activism

Critical applied linguistics also needs to operate with some sort of vision of what is preferable. (Table 1.3) Critical work has often been condemned for doing little more than criticize things, for offering nothing but a bleak and pessimistic vision of social relations. It is important for critical work, and particularly in an *applied* field (implying change), that we can articulate a grounded vision for how we think things would look better: "Social action must be animated by a vision of a future society, and by explicit judgments of value concerning the character of this future society" (Chomsky, 2013, p. 139). It is also important that such a vision does not slide back into utopian visions of alternative realities, or overemphasizes the transformative potential of critical work. The ideas of *preferred futures* and *radical hope* offer us a slightly more restrained and plural view of where we might want to head. Such preferred futures, however, need to be grounded in ethical arguments for why alternative possibilities may be better. This is why Roger Simon's (1992) classic critical pedagogical book, *Teaching against the grain*, was subtitled *Essays towards a pedagogy of possibility* and why bell hook's (2003) key work, *Teaching Community*, was subtitled *A pedagogy of hope*.

We need not only a language of critique but also an ethical vision and a sense of radical hope (Lear, 2006), if critical projects seeking change are to have meaning. And "to make a discussion of radical hope meaningful … language is critical – absolutely critical – and increasingly so" (Pearson, 2011, p. 226). Pearson is here talking both specifically of the importance of Indigenous Australian languages and more generally of "the greatest gift for a child in Australia" being "another language, a mother tongue, a language of the heart that is not English" (p. 226). We shall return later (Chapter 3) to discussions of language politics, but here we might usefully add that radical hope concerns language in many ways, not only for mother tongues and other languages but in terms of articulating an alternative vision of what can be done. As Heller and McElhinny (2017) point out, it is in the context of hope that questions of desire also become important. Desire here brings together issues of hope and

Table 1.3 The Critical in Critical Applied Linguistics

Central Components	Combining Concerns	Contrast with Mainstream Views
Critical social inquiry	Domination, disparity, discrimination, difference, and desire	A focus on inequality rather than logical problem-solving
Critical theory and beyond	Marxist, feminist, anti-racist, Queer, decolonial, and other theories	A focus on struggle rather than a consensual view of social relations
Hope, praxis, and activism	Ethical and political vision for activist work toward social change	A focus on social change based in collaborative relations

transformation, and sits alongside the other critical dimensions of domination, disparity, discrimination, and difference.

Critical applied linguistics has to have at least two further elements if it is to be of wider significance. For a field that calls itself 'applied,' applied linguistics has been rather slow to articulate a careful vision of how theory and application work. A number of common tendencies have been unhelpful on this score: Many book titles add 'theory and practice' after the main title, which tells us little about their supposed relationship. In other work, there is a tendency to suggest pedagogical or other applications that are not grounded in particular contexts of research or practice (see Clarke, 1994). The promotion of language teaching curricula around the world without adequate grounding in the local educultural context has long seemed more like neocolonial intervention than research-based advice (Pennycook, 1989; Phan, 2017). At the same time, it is also common from the more applied end of work to dismiss 'theory' as irrelevant, as of no consequence to a context of practice. All such versions of (critical) applied linguistics need to be resisted. At the very least, we have to theorize practice in much greater depth (Pennycook, 2010), consider applied linguistics as a theory of practice – applied linguistics is "the practice of language study itself, and the theory that could be drawn from that practice" (Kramsch, 2015, p. 455) – or move toward the more politically-oriented idea of praxis, as "that continuous reflexive integration of thought, desire and action" (Simon, 1992, p. 49).

While applied linguistics generally has been challenged for its relevance to different contexts of global language use, critical applied linguistics is equally open to such a challenge, in terms of both its critical and its applied linguistic epistemologies. Since much of the work that comes under the rubric of critical applied linguistics has been based on Global North (First World/Western) contexts and theories, it has to have ways to ensure that "the research agenda is formulated in collaboration and consultation with local communities" (Makoni, 2003, p. 135), in order not only to develop a relationship between this field of critical scholarship and local knowledge and practice, but to ensure that such local praxis is part of the enterprise itself. Hale's (2006) distinction between *cultural critique* and *activist research* is useful in this context, distinguishing between alignments developed through knowledge content and alignments based on political affiliation through struggle and dialogue. Critical applied linguistics has to be formed in conjunction with local communities and their knowledge, hopes, and desires; and it has to have an activist orientation (Flores & Chaparro, 2018) and work with a continuous reflexive integration of thought, desire, and action.

Domains of Critical Applied Linguistics

In the first part of this chapter, I approached critical applied linguistics by sketching out some of the key principles of critical work. In this second section, I approach the question differently by giving brief overviews of different domains of critical applied linguistic work. This list is neither exhaustive nor definitive of the areas I cover in this book, but taken in conjunction with the issues raised above, it presents us with two ways of conceiving of critical applied linguistics: Various underlying principals and various domains of coverage. It might be tempting to consider critical applied linguistics as an amalgam of other critical language-oriented domains, such as CDA, critical language awareness, critical pedagogy, critical sociolinguistics, and critical literacy. This is a rather unsatisfactory formulation, however, for a number of reasons. It is important that critical applied linguistics has an identity other than just the sum of other work, while those working in CDA or critical literacy or anti-racist education do not need an overarching framework to bring their work together.

It is also important that critical applied linguistics takes a critical stance toward (rather than an easy acceptance of) other critical work. A number of these areas, furthermore, such as critical pedagogy, have important connections with critical applied linguistics but in general operate across a much wider domain. Some other areas, such as CDA, meanwhile, do not in themselves have a strong applied element. The relation between critical applied linguistics and these related domains is therefore a composite intersection of approaches. I have organized the principal areas of work that I see as intersecting with critical applied linguistics in the table below (Table 1.4). They can be categorized generally as dealing with critical approaches to language (policy, bilingualism, and awareness), difference (multiculturalism, anti-racist education, and classroom discourse), text (discourse analysis, literacy, and translation), and pedagogy (second language education, academic purposes, and language testing). This is by no means a comprehensive list of areas: I have included some less commonly included domains such as translation, while omitting others, such as queer pedagogies. These will be developed in much greater length in Chapters 3 (language), 4 (difference), 5 (text), and 6 (pedagogy).

Critical Approaches to Language

It is sometimes assumed that an area such as language policy and planning (LPP) somehow in itself constitutes a critical domain because of its focus on policy. This is by no means the case. There is nothing inherently critical about language policy; indeed, part of the problem, as Tollefson (1991) observes, has been precisely the way in which language policy has been uncritically developed and implemented. According to Luke, McHoul, and Mey (1990), while maintaining a "veneer of scientific objectivity," language planning has "tended to avoid directly addressing larger social and political matters within which language change, use and development, and indeed language planning itself are embedded" (p. 27). What is omitted in most work on language planning is "an exploration of the complex theoretical relationship between language, discourse, ideology and social organization…precisely the central concerns of neo-Marxist social theorizing, poststructuralist discourse analysis and critical

Table 1.4 Critical Domains

Critical Domains	Key Defining Statements
	Critical Approaches to Language
Critical sociocultural approach to language policy (CSALP)	A critical approach to language policy and planning (LPP) is "committed to the ideals of equity and social justice, acknowledging that, even as LPP is a mechanism for majoritarian control, it can be a site of resistance and transformation" (McCarty, 2013, p. 40)
Critical bilingualism (CB)	CB implies "the ability to not just speak two languages, but to be conscious of the sociocultural, political, and ideological contexts in which the languages (and therefore the speakers) are positioned and function, and the multiple meanings that are fostered in each" (Walsh, 1991, p. 127)
Critical language awareness (CLA)	CLA examines the ways in which education and other institutions "silence diverse languages in White public space by inculcating speakers of heterogeneous language varieties into what are, at their core, White ways of speaking and seeing the word/world, that is, the norms of White, middleclass, heterosexist males" (Alim, 2005, p. 28)
	Critical Approaches to Difference
Critical multi-culturalism (CM)	CM "critically examines how inequality and injustice are produced and perpetuated in relation to power and privilege," exploring "a critical understanding of culture," and involving all students "in critical inquiry into how taken-for-granted knowledge, such as history, geography, and lives of other people, is produced, legitimated, and contested in power struggles" (Kubota, 2004, pp. 37–40).
Anti-racist education	"Inherent in the learning of English would be an intense awareness of the effects of English's colonial and racial history on current-day language, economic, political and social practices." (Motha, 2014, p. 129)
Critical classroom discourse analysis (CCDA)	CCDA draws on critical ethnography as a research tool, has "a transformative function" and "seeks to play a reflective role, enabling practitioners to reflect on and cope with sociocultural and sociopolitical structures that directly or indirectly shape the character and content of classroom discourse" (Kumaravadivelu 1999, p. 473)

Table 1.4 Critical Domains (*Continued*)

Critical Domains	Key Defining Statements
Critical Approaches to Text	
Critical discourse analysis (CDA)	CDA "aims to systematically explore often opaque relationships of causality and determination between (a) discursive practices, events, and texts, and (b) wider social and cultural structures, relations, and processes; to investigate how such practices, events, and texts arise out of and are ideologically shaped by relations of power and struggles over power" (Fairclough, 1995, p. 132).
Critical literacy (CL)	CL "marks out a coalition of educational interests committed to engaging with the possibilities that the technologies of writing and other modes of inscription offer for social change, cultural diversity, economic equity, and political enfranchisement" (Luke & Freebody, 1997, p. 1).
Critical approaches to translation (CAT)	"To shake the regime of English, a translator must be strategic both in selecting foreign texts and in developing discourses to translate them. Foreign texts can be chosen to redress patterns of unequal cultural exchange and to restore foreign literatures excluded by the standard dialect, by literary canons, or by ethnic stereotypes" (Venuti, 1997, pp. 10–1)
Critical Approaches to Education	
Critical pedagogy and second language education (CPSLE)	"Advocates of critical approaches to second language teaching are interested in relationships between language learning and social change" (Norton & Toohey, 2004, p. 1)
Critical English for academic purposes (CEAP)	"The overarching goal of critical EAP is to help students perform well in their academic courses while encouraging them to question and shape the education they are being offered" (Benesch, 2001, p. xvii)
Critical language testing (CLT)	CLT "implies the need to develop critical strategies to examine the uses and consequences of tests, to monitor their power, minimize their detrimental force, reveal the misuses, and empower the test takers" (Shohamy, 2001, p. 131).

theory" (p. 28). Language planning and policy, far from being some inherently critical or political enterprise, has often been just the opposite: An apolitical approach to language that serves very clearly to maintain the social and linguistic status quo.

Mapping the development of LPP, Ricento (2015) argues that it is only with the development of a stronger framework of language and political economy that it has developed a more critical edge. Likewise, McCarty (2013) shows how the field has gradually evolved toward a stance that "critically interrogates the ideological, social-structural and historical bases of LLP, emphasizing the relationships among language, power, and inequality" (p. 39). This is a concern of the fields of sociolinguistics and language policy more generally, which will be central to the discussion in Chapter 3 on the *politics of language*. Sociolinguistics has come in for serious criticism itself both for its clumsy understanding of language variation and more particularly its inability to deal with questions of social inequality (Williams, 1992). As Mey (1985) suggests, by avoiding questions of social inequality in class terms and instead correlating language variation with superficial measures of social stratification, traditional sociolinguistics fails to "establish a connection between people's place in the societal hierarchy, and the linguistic and other kinds of oppression that they are subjected to at different levels" (p. 342).

Taking up Mey's (1985) call for a *critical sociolinguistics* (p. 342), Walsh's (1991) understanding of *critical bilingualism*, Fairclough's (1992) and Alim's (2005) *critical language awareness*, or McCarty's (2013) insistence on a *critical sociocultural approach to language policy and planning*, critical applied linguistics needs to incorporate views of language, society, and power that are capable of dealing with a broad politics of language, including language and political economy (questions of language, social structure, and inequality), critical investigations of the global spread of English, or struggles to reclaim minority languages. A central question for Chapter 3 will be how to steer a path between language framed from within political economy (enabling strong accounts of relations between language and inequality, but tending to be overly focused on questions such as language commodification, and thus to fix and reify language) and language framed from a more flexible position (enabling more grounded accounts of language use and language matters but possibly losing sight of material implications of language disparities).

Critical Approaches to Difference

A second cluster of critical applied linguistic work can be grouped together around the politics of difference. Simply put, these concerns have to do with the ways in which differences – cultural, religious, racial, gendered – matter deeply to people yet are also the stuff of discrimination and governance. It was the problematic ways in which the idea of culture was mobilized, particularly in discourses of multiculturalism, that led to Kubota's (2004) insistence on the need for *critical multiculturalism* based on "a critical understanding of culture" (p. 38) that located any understanding of cultural difference in questions of power and inequality. From a pedagogical point of view, she argues, students need to engage "in critical inquiry into how taken-for-granted knowledge, such as history, geography, and lives of other people, is produced, legitimated, and contested in power struggles" (p. 40). While conservative critics have railed against multiculturalism as either a failed enterprise or a perfidious betrayal of the sanctity of the nation, these more critical approaches insist we need to move beyond superficial accounts of cultural difference and engage instead in an investigation into the ways difference is constructed.

Following these insights concerning discrimination and the social construction of difference, race has finally been recognized as central to any critical understanding of language education, whether as part of an account of the colonial and racial history of the spread of English (Motha, 2014), the racialization of the concept of the native speaker (Kubota & Lin, 2009), or the raciolinguistic assumptions about norms and deviations in language use (Alim, 2005; Alim & Smitherman, 2020; Rosa, 2019). Epistemological racism in applied linguistics has to be confronted (Kubota, 2019). In order to understand how race and gender operate together across domains of applied linguistics – in terms, for example, of the ways in which masculinity and English language teaching are intertwined (Appleby, 2014) – we need forms of critical analysis, such as *critical classroom discourse analysis* (Kumaravadivelu, 1999), that can bring these larger formations of difference into our analysis of education, workplaces, courtrooms, and so on.

A central concern for Chapter 4 will be how to establish a position that avoids the celebration, reification, or eradication of difference. The first position – particularly in terms of what is seen as a celebration of diversity – has been roundly critiqued (Kubota, 2016) for lacking an engagement with a critical understanding of how difference is connected to class and racial disparities. The reification of difference – whether cultural or gendered or racial arguments that define people of different backgrounds – has also come in for strong criticism as a form of 'essentialism' (assuming certain characteristics to be determined by assumed identities). To ignore difference, however, along universalist or liberal forms of accommodation – "we're all the same underneath" – is to equally miss the extent of human divergence: "diversity is the given reality of human social action" (Higgins & Coen 2000, p. 15). Also important, therefore, will be the need to avoid overdetermined arguments that suggest that difference is only a product of powerful discriminatory discourses or of neoliberal interests (arguments that the neoliberal co-optation of difference renders all talk of difference suspect).

Critical Approaches to Texts

Various forms of critical text analysis have played an important role in critical applied linguistics. Critical language analysis, Luke (2002) suggests, can trace its roots back to the work of Vološinov in the 1920s. Summarizing work in CDA, Kress (1990, p. 85) explains that unlike discourse analysis or text linguistics with their descriptive goals, CDA has "the larger political aim of putting the forms of texts, the processes of production of texts, and the process of reading, together with the structures of power that have given rise to them, into crisis." CDA aims to show how "linguistic-discursive practices" are linked to "the wider socio-political structures of power and domination" (p. 85). van Dijk (1993) explains CDA as a focus on "the role of discourse in the (re)production and challenge of dominance" (p. 249). Critical approaches to literacy, which we might see as a pedagogical implementation of CDA, are characterized by "a commitment to reshape literacy education in the interests of marginalized groups of learners, who on the basis of gender, cultural and socioeconomic background have been excluded from access to the discourses and texts of dominant economies and cultures" (Luke, 1997a, p. 143). As Luke makes clear, while approaches to critical literacy may share these political goals, there are a range of different approaches, from Freirean-based critical pedagogy, to feminist, poststructuralist, and text analytic approaches.

Medical contexts and other workplaces have long been a site for critical language, literacy, and numeracy work, both at analytic and interventionist levels. Wodak's (1996) study of hospital encounters looks not only at the ways in which "doctors exercise power over their patients" (p. 170), but also at ways of intervening in this relationship. The critical sociolinguistic work of Eades (2010) sheds light on and attempts to change discriminatory aspects of the legal system, particularly in relation to Indigenous Australians. And the implications of constant workplace restructuring – the *new work order* (Gee, Hull, & Lankshear, 1996) or more recently *neoliberal political economy* (Martín Rojo & del Percio, 2019) – have been of concern for the re-marginalization of women (Poynton, 1993b), the changing requirements of language, literacy, and education (Flubacher & Del Percio, 2017), the inscription into new *scripts of servitude* (Lorente, 2017), and the challenges of multilingualism in blue-collar workplaces (Gonçalvez & Kelly-Holmes, 2021; Hovens, 2020).

Also important are less commonly included critical approaches to texts, such as translation. This has to be seen in relation to the problem that while translation remains central for the majority world of applied linguists, it is much less so within the Anglosphere (Kramsch, 2019). Translation, as Niranjana (1991), Kothari (2005), and Spivak (1993) make clear, is intimately tied to the particular kinds of knowledge and the institutions of language that were produced through colonial technologies. Translation "reinforces hegemonic visions of the colonized" and helps to *fix* colonized cultures, "making them seem static and unchanging rather than historically constructed" (Niranjana, 1991, pp. 125–6). Looking broadly at translation as a political activity, Venuti (1997) argues that the tendencies of translations to domesticate foreign cultures, the insistence on the possibility of value-free translation, the challenges to the notion of authorship posed by translation, the dominance of translation from English into other languages rather than in the other direction, and the need to unsettle local cultural hegemonies through the challenges of translation all point to the need for an approach to translation based on an *ethics of difference*. Studies of translation and interpretation in the workplace – such as Crawford's (1999) study of communication between patients, nurses, and doctors in Cape Town health services – show how the work of translation may be tied to gender, class and race (Black women nurses provide unpaid and unrecognized interpretation between patients and doctors). Key issues for Chapter 5 on the politics of texts include an interrogation of the difficult terrain of discourse, ideology, and material relations, as well as a range of questions about the possibilities and the limits offered by approaches to critical literacies and CDA.

Critical Approaches to Pedagogy

Finally, I will turn in Chapter 6 to critical approaches to language pedagogy and testing. I put these last not because I see them either as the 'applied' end of applied linguistics (everything discussed in this section is applied linguistics) or as less important (all of this matters) but more because I want to resist the implication that language education is more important than other domains of critical applied linguistics. It is, nevertheless, a very significant part of the field and critical approaches to second language education have therefore played a significant role in its development. Crookes (2013) suggests that teachers "have been doing something called 'critical pedagogy' for fifty years (using that term) and for hundreds of years, or perhaps always, under a range of related terms" (p. 1). Connecting forms of critical pedagogy – from Freirean to feminist – to second language education opens up an approach that seeks not just better language learning but also social change (Norton & Toohey, 2004).

More particularly, a range of studies have shown how the reproduction or transformation of social class plays out in language classrooms (Lin, 1999), how the racialized world of schooling has deep implications for the educational possibilities of students (Ibrahim, 1999; Paris & Alim, 2017), how sexual identity is always at work in classroom settings (Nelson, 1999; 2009), and why a feminist agenda has to be part of any critical educational project (Appleby, 2013; 2018; Schenke, 1991, 1996; Sunderland, 1994). Critical educational approaches have also been developed in more specialized areas of language education: *Critical English for academic purposes*, for example, suggests that "current conditions should be interrogated in the interests of greater equity and democratic participation in and out of educational institutions" (Benesch 2001, p. 64) and that "the EAP classroom is a site of power, agency and multiple meaning makings" (Chun, 2015, p. 3). Other domains of the curriculum – from critical needs analysis (Benesch, 1996) to critical textbook analysis (Dendrinos, 1992; Gray, 2010) – have also shed light on the ways educational technologies are linked to wider ideological frames.

Language testing has been one of the most resistant to the development of a critical focus. Clearly, however, critical analysis of tests and their effects, or their potential to bring about change, is as imperative as any other domain. Shohamy's (2001) CLT points to the importance of seeing how tests are deeply embedded in cultural, educational, and political contexts, and demands that we ask not only whether it is a good test but in whose interests it is being used, or in McNamara's (2012, p. 577) terms, not only whether it is *fair* test – the "technical quality of the assessment" – but also whether it is a *just* test – "the values implicit in the construct and the consequences of the use of the test." Key concerns for critical pedagogical approaches will be whether – as some have claimed – they promote a political agenda over the learning needs of students, or whether the critical agenda is clearly tied to the interests of the students. This is why it is important to understand that critical EAP, for example, aims both to enhance students' language abilities and to develop forms of critical analysis (Benesch, 2001). Also important will be broad questions of reproduction and resistance in educational contexts: How can educational institutions do more than reproduce the social inequalities of which they are so much a part?

Conclusion: Toward A Critical Applied Linguistics

In the previous section giving a very brief overview of different domains of critical applied linguistics, I have sought to show the areas this field may cover as well as the shared interests. Many of these areas overlap – critical textbook analysis inevitably uses a form of CDA, and critical studies of language in the workplace may be equally sociolinguistic as they are critical literacy – and this brief coverage is by no means exhaustive. Similarly, the critical concerns of class, race, and gender also intersect at many points, so a study of language policies in urban schools may be as much about race as it is about class (Flores & Chaparro, 2018). These domains nevertheless suggest a broad coalition of interests around the workings of power and the effects of inequality. They aim to draw connections between local uses of language and relations of power at the institutional and broader social levels. They insist that language, difference, texts, and education are all political domains, where different visions of a preferred world are struggled over. This is a call to make one's applied linguistic practice accountable to an agenda for positive social change.

This is not an easy task, however. We will have to get our heads around some quite complex questions: How do we understand relations between language and power beyond an assumption that powerful people control language? How do people resist power in and through language? How do we understand questions of difference in relation to language, education, or literacy? How does ideology operate in relation to discourse, beyond an assumption that the ideologies of the powerful are represented in language? The following chapters, therefore, deal with the politics of knowledge, the politics of language, the politics of difference, the politics of texts, and the politics of pedagogy (see Table 1.5).

Critical applied linguistics, then, is more than just a critical dimension added on to applied linguistics: It involves a constant skepticism, a perpetual questioning of normative assumptions. It demands a restive problematization of the givens of both critical theory and applied linguistics and presents a way of doing applied linguistics that seeks to connect it to questions of gender, class, sexuality, race, ethnicity, culture, identity, politics, ideology, and discourse. And crucially, it becomes a dynamic opening up of new questions

Table 1.5 Themes Across the Book

Areas Covered by Chapter	Key Questions
Chapter 1: Introducing critical applied linguistics: Concerns and domains of the field	What does it mean to be critical? What's the difference between critical thinking and critical theory? How do different critical applied linguistic projects fit together?
Chapter 2: The politics of knowledge: The role of theory; conjunctions between knowledge and politics	How do different ways of thinking about language and politics – universalism, liberal egalitarianism, social justice, modernism, and situated practice – inform critical applied linguistics?
Chapter 3: The politics of language: Language and power; approaches to language policy and global English	How do different perspectives on language – linguistic imperialism, language rights, and language reclamation – help us understand language and power?
Chapter 4: The politics of difference: Constructions of difference; gender, race and identity, queer theory, and performativity	How to establish a position that avoids the celebration, reification, or eradication of difference and instead explores difference in relation to power?
Chapter 5: The politics of texts: critical discourse analysis; critical literacies; voice, access, the word, and the world	How do notions such as discourse and ideology differ and what light do they shed on the meaning of text? Should student voice or access to powerful texts be our focus?
Chapter 6: The politics of pedagogy: Critical approaches to education; theories of social reproduction; critical pedagogy	If education is always a social, cultural, and political space, what room is there for change and resistance? What do different forms of critical language pedagogy propose?
Chapter 7: Doing critical applied linguistics: teaching, research, and activism from a critical perspective	How do we do critical applied linguistics as education, research, or activism that can bring about change? What principles underpin critical applied linguistics?

that emerge from this conjunction. This flexible account of critical applied linguistic practice takes us beyond concerns about its disciplinary or inter/ transdisciplinary status. It helps us see how critical applied linguistic practices, which may appear diverse or undisciplined, are instead the coming together of different language-oriented projects, bodies of knowledge, and *matters of concern* (Latour, 2004). It opens up applied linguistics to an ethical engagement with alternative ways of thinking about language and context from the Global South, so that renewal of applied linguistics comes not via other disciplines but rather through alternative forms of knowledge (Pennycook, 2018b).

As I have suggested, critical applied linguistics has to have an activist dimension, an agenda for social change, but it is not much use having such an agenda unless it is well grounded in carefully thought-through approaches to these concerns. A danger with an anti-theoretical activist sensibility is that it may do little more than add a predetermined political agenda to an already established applied linguistic framework. If it's good politics, it must be good critical applied linguistics. So if we've decided that languages have to be saved as part of a political movement, then we just have to describe the language and encourage people to use it again; or if we want to empower students from minority backgrounds, we just need to introduce a bilingual program, and that will sort things out. Very evidently, such positions are both politically and epistemologically naïve: We have to look at the theoretical claims underpinning the combination of applied linguistics and politics. To those who still feel that none of this is really central to applied linguistics work, I would suggest that surely an approach to issues in language education, communication in the workplace, translation, and literacy that focuses on questions of power, difference, access, and domination has to be an important part of what we do.

The sense of critical thinking discussed earlier—a set of thinking skills—attempts almost by definition to remain isolated from political questions, from issues of domination, disparity, difference, discrimination, or desire. The sense of *critical* that I want to make central to critical applied linguistics, by contrast, is one that takes these as the *sine qua non* of our work. Critical applied linguistics is not about developing a set of skills that will make the doing of applied linguistics more rigorous or objective (though rigor, like careful analysis, remains crucial) but is about making applied linguistics more politically accountable. Indeed, I want to invoke two further meanings of *critical* that are also useful to consider: The notion of *critical* as important or crucial: A critical moment, a critical time in one's life, a critical illness; and critical as used in mathematics and physics to suggest the point that marks the change from one state to another, as in critical angle or critical mass.

To the extent that the critical version of applied linguistics that I am exploring here is crucial, important, and deals with some of the central issues in language use, and to the extent that it may also signal a point at which applied linguistics may finally move into a new state of being, these senses of *critical* also need to be included in an understanding of critical applied linguistics. Gee (1994) offers language teachers a choice: Either to "cooperate in their own marginalization" by seeing themselves as just language teachers with no connection to broader social and political issues or to accept that they "stand at the very heart of the most crucial educational, cultural, and political issues of our time" (p. 190). With its wider scope – language policy, health workers, law courts, language survival, multilingualism, cultural difference, and minority language education – critical applied linguistics sits at the juncture of some major critical concerns of our time: Language and migration, discrimination, and unequal educational opportunity.

It might be objected that what I am sketching out here is a problematically normative approach: By defining what I mean by *critical* and *critical applied linguistics*, I am setting up an approach that already has a predefined political stance and mode of analysis. There is a certain tension here: An overdefined version of critical applied linguistics that demands adherence to a particular form of politics is a project that is already limited; but I also cannot envision a version of critical applied linguistics that can accept any and every political viewpoint. It has been mistakenly claimed that critical applied linguistics "takes an individualist approach to the solution of language problems" (Davies, 1999, p. 127). Such a claim rests neither on the politics nor the practices of the field. To advocate a libertarian, individualist politics, particularly in the Global North, where individualism has become tied to a populist conservative agenda, could not be a critical project. Critical applied linguistics has to have a contextual politics and to be critical of political advocacies that support any conservative status quo.

The way forward here is this: On the one hand, I am arguing that critical applied linguistics must necessarily take up certain positions and stances; its view of language cannot be an autonomous one that backs away from connecting language to broader political concerns, and furthermore, its focus on such politics must be accountable to broader political and ethical visions that put inequality, oppression, and compassion to the fore. On the other hand, I do not want to suggest a narrow and normative vision of how those politics work. Critical applied linguistics is not about the mapping of a fixed politics onto a static body of knowledge but rather is about creating something new. It draws of necessity on a wide range of intellectual and political inspiration (see Figure 2.1). As Foucault (1980b) puts it, "the problem is not so much one of defining a political 'position' (which is to choose from a pre-existing set of possibilities) but to imagine and to bring into being new schemas of politicisation" (p. 190). That is the political challenge of critical applied linguistics. It is a collaborative, emergent, listening project as well as an activist, transformative, and unsettling one.

2 The Politics of Knowledge

The Place of Theory

In Chapter 1 of the book, I sketched out a preliminary vision of critical applied linguistics based on an overview of key concerns and domains of work. In the following chapters, I will discuss these themes in terms of the politics of language, difference, texts, and pedagogy. In this chapter, I focus on some essential background concerns to do with knowledge, politics, and power. One of the problems with discussing background theories in relation to critical work is that, at least from some perspectives, theory gets in the way of real work. Such an argument may derive from a number of different positions: For those who conflate critical thinking with critical theory, the issue is only of being trained in better thinking skills, so theory is fairly irrelevant. For others, critical work is merely a matter of progressive politics, or even just common sense, in conjunction with a domain of interest, so politics plus applied linguistics will fit the bill. And for others, doing critical work is about getting out there, working in the community, using Twitter, making things happen. Doing theory is a waste of time. Who needs to talk about subjectivity, structure, agency, or social construction, when the real issues are in the streets, communities, and institutions?

Weedon (1987) argues a feminist tradition of hostility toward theory is based on the one hand on the argument that theorizing, and particularly dominant forms of Western rationality, has long been part of patriarchal power and control over women, and on the other hand that women need to draw on their own experiences to guide political action. For Weedon, however, while both positions need to be taken very seriously, they should not constitute an argument against theory, so that "rather than turning our backs on theory and taking refuge in experience alone, we should think in terms of transforming both the social relations of knowledge production and the type of knowledge produced" (p. 7). In other words, it is indeed important for feminism – or southern theory or critical applied linguistics – to question the kinds of knowledge that are available (their provenance, their interests, their limitations), but it is also important to have ways of thinking about social structure, knowledge, politics, pedagogy, practice, the individual, or language. Not a fixed body of impenetrable ideas, but a set of usable, questioning, problematizing concerns that take knowledge and its production as part of their critical exploration.

Roger Simon (1992) raises the question of what he calls a "fear of theory." Rather than an individual reaction or inability to deal with difficult ideas, this is better seen as part of the complex social relations that surround knowledge, language, and academic institutions, which is why education needs to "be directed not so much at the lack of knowledge as to resistances to knowledge" (p. 95). McNamara (2015) points to the difficult relations applied linguistics has in general to domains of theory (particularly in its slow response to ideas from poststructuralism), and Macedo (2019, p. 36) makes a related point about "theory aversion" in applied linguistics, suggesting that the field of language education has often eschewed theoretical engagement, while activists may similarly claim to have no time for theory. Critical activist applied linguists, therefore, may be doubly hampered by antitheoretical stances. Resistance to critical theory may be for at least two very good reasons. We *do* need to stay engaged with all levels of political action, and there *is* a great deal of difficult and unnecessarily abstruse work claiming nevertheless to be somehow politically engaged.

Certainly, many "critical theorists" need to accept a large measure of blame here: Far too little has been done to make critical academic work more accessible or to show, at the very least, pathways that connect theory and practice. Writers in areas such as critical pedagogy have been quite rightly criticized for their bombastic and obscurantist prose (Gore, 1993). And others have suggested that the constant use of words such as *revolutionary* and *radical* is "mere posturing. I personally do not feel the need to dress up what I do in pseudo-revolutionary bluster" (Johnston, 1999, p. 563). There is nevertheless a strong case to be made for a level of engagement with some key issues in critical theory. Not only does critical applied linguistics presuppose a knowledge of many domains of applied linguistics – second language acquisition, translation, sociolinguistics, language policy, language in the workplace, and so on – but also a knowledge of many concepts in critical theory – determinism, structure, agency, discourse, subjectivity, and so on. Although we do not necessarily need to share the same political outlook on various issues, we do need ways of understanding what our differences are, to go beyond tossing around terms such as *oppression, inequality, imperialism, racism, ideology,* and so forth without a clear understanding of how such terms invoke particular understandings of the world.

If we are to take critical applied linguistics seriously, we need to understand the different forms of background knowledge that inform it. By analogy, someone doing research on young children learning to write in school would be expected to have a good grasp of background theoretical work in areas such as literacy, primary education, and child development; similarly, someone looking critically at early literacy outcomes in relation to class, gender, or race would be expected to have a good knowledge of early literacy and how forms of social difference operate in educational settings. In order for this to work in this book, I have tried to avoid stuffing this chapter with a heavy dose of critical theory. Important concepts are instead woven into the chapters along the way in order to make them as accessible and meaningful as possible (the politics of pedagogy discusses ideas of reproduction and resistance, for example, while the politics of language explores issues around rights and revival). I have also tried not to present a fixed body of immutable knowledge so much as a flexible range of ideas that are open to constant critique. These must also be accountable to political and educational practice. In the rest of this chapter, I examine different positions on the relation between language and politics, or more specifically an account of ways in which the politics of language is denied or dealt with across linguistics and applied linguistics.

All Language Is Political

A key focus of critical applied linguistics is to ask broad questions about language and power. Whether in the early work on language and gender, such as Robyn Lakoff's (1990) *Talking Power: The Politics of Language*, or critical discourse analysis, such as Norman Fairclough's (1989) *Language and Power*, or much more recent work such as Claire Kramsch's (2021) *Language as Symbolic Power*, or van Splunder's (2020) *Language is Politics*, power is central to the analysis, as it is in many of the background texts they draw on, from Pierre Bourdieu's (1991) *Language and Symbolic Power*, to Michel Foucault's (1980b) *Power/Knowledge*. These writers start from the position that language, as Joseph (2006, p17) puts it, "is political from top to bottom." Languages themselves are social and ideological constructs; how we use language with others is shaped by social relations; how we interpret what others say is deeply influenced by social, cultural, gender, and racial identities; "power relations between people are expressed through and reflected in language. Therefore, *language is politics*" (van Splunder, 2020, p. 9, emphasis in original).

We cannot, therefore, study language without acknowledging the politics of the enterprise. This has to be our starting point. But then we have to ask what this means. In order to develop the argument that we cannot escape political arguments in our work, it is worth exploring the idea of politics a bit further. The term *politics* occurs throughout this book; indeed, it is organized around the politics of language, difference, texts, and pedagogy. This notion of politics is not concerned with formal political domains (governments, elections, or state institutions) but rather with the workings of power. Areas of interest such as *language policy* are sometimes taken to represent the political focus of applied linguistics because they have to do most often with governmental decisions about the use and status of languages. Yet politics has to do with far more than policy making. The notion of politics under discussion here takes as its central concern questions of power, and views power as operating through all domains of life. Power is at the heart of questions of domination, disparity, discrimination, difference, and desire. It is, generally speaking, some notion of power that underlies all critical or political analyses. The notion of power sits at the heart of the term *empowerment*, and if we are to salvage anything useful for this bland and overused term, we need to know what version of power we are dealing with. So what is power? And, crucially, how does it relate to language?

One of the difficulties with the notion of power is that it is used so widely to mean so much (or so little). Consider, for example, some of its popular contemporary uses: Power dressing, power to the people, money is power, the power of love, power corrupts. There are the rich and powerful, the power behind the throne, and the vague "powers that be." A liberal democratic view of politics tends to locate power in the government, and thus one political party is "in power" until a different party is voted into power. Most are aware, however, that behind the veneer of politics, there are many others that hold or wield power, anything from a general notion of the state, or the *deep state* (networks of power and affiliation, sometimes dismissed as a 'conspiracy theory'), global capital, transnational corporations, social elites, the media, and so on. Different political visions have different conceptions of how power can be shared, seized, redistributed, or diffused. Does empowerment mean handing over power, making people powerful, helping others to seize, diffuse, share, consolidate, or redistribute power? These questions all imply different understandings of what power is, how it operates, and what strategies we should adopt in the face of power.

It is important to distinguish between notions of power that focus on the individual and more sociological and critical versions of power. If we see power as something an individual has (a person has power over another; she or he is a powerful person), we miss the importance of understanding where power comes from, how it is socially constructed and maintained. At the same time, however, we need to be cautious not to work only with broad social constructs of power lest we lose sight of the workings of power at a more local level. Critical applied linguistics needs ways of understanding how power operates on and through people in the ongoing tasks of teaching, learning languages, translating, talking in the workplace. If, for example, we acknowledge that men generally hold more power than women (they still dominate in many institutions), we need to ask how this operates in and through language, and how it can be changed. Different approaches to language and gender may aim to shed light on different language use in the separate worlds of men and women, focus on the inequitable interactions between men and women, encourage women to use language like men, teach men to learn to listen, and so forth. Is this about sharing power, seizing power, or diffusing power, and do we need to change the society first in the hope that language changes will follow or can we start to change language first (mandate changes in pronoun use, for example) in the belief that this will also change social relations?

In the next section of this chapter, I will explore two common ways in which language and politics are disconnected, or at least supposedly so. In the second half of this chapter, I shall explore different ways of understanding politics in relation to applied linguistics. How do different forms of politics (which, as I suggested, really address questions of power) produce different approaches to critical applied linguistics? For critical applied linguistics, the notion of politics needs to be seen as encompassing not just those areas that are more readily understood as social or political but, rather, all domains of life. How we understand relations between politics, knowledge, and language will greatly affect how we look at critical applied linguistics. Kramsch (2021) distinguishes between two versions of power: The modernist view – including Lakoff (1990) on language and gender, and Fairclough (1989) on critical dis-course analysis – views power as something some people have while others do not: Power is domination and something from which we need to be liberated; the postmodern view, by contrast, views power as running through society in more complex ways: We need to engage with power but we can't escape it. As Blommaert (2005, pp. 1–2, emphasis in original) explains, the point is not to simply be against power, but rather to engage in an "analysis of power *effects*, of the outcome of power, of what power *does* to people, groups and societies, and of *how* this impact comes about." It is to various different ways of looking at this that I now turn.

Linguistics Without Politics

Radical Politics, Reactionary Linguistics[1]

It is common to deal with questions of language without engaging with broader political concerns. How is such a thing possible? In this section, I shall explore two particular constellations of linguistics and politics to show how this happens. The issue centrally is where one sees language as happening, "where in the great spectrum of human communication and expression we are to find 'language'" (Finnegan, 2015, p. 2). Many linguists, particularly from a more theoretical perspective, view language primarily as a system, as linked to cognition (which in turn is seen as happening in isolation within the head), and "the politics of language as at best an after-effect, a sideshow, a trivial epiphenomenon, neither worthy of nor susceptible to serious study" (Joseph, 2006, p. 2). The first position I want to explore here is one that combines an overtly radical political position with a view of language that denies its politics. Noam Chomsky's work is the clearest example of such a stance, espe-cially since he is a public intellectual known both for his linguistic and for his political work.

The central question that arises from this tradition is how such political work can be reconciled with its absence in linguistic analysis. Politically, Chomsky defines himself as an anarcho-syndicalist or libertarian socialist, a radical tradition that draws on the thinking of Pierre-Joseph Proudhon ("prop-erty is theft"), Mikhail Bakunin, Emma Goldman, and others, who opposed the role of the state in human governance: Liberation cannot come through formal politics but by direct local action. Current versions of this position tend to share a Marxist analysis of capitalism while eschewing Marxist analyses of state power and proletarian revolution in favor of "a federated, decentralized system of free associations, incorporating economic as well as other social institutions" (Chomsky, 1974, p. 169). Central goals "are to overcome the elements of repression and oppression and destruction and coercion that exist in any existing society," to oppose "centralised autocratic control of ... economic institutions" and to work toward "direct participation in the form of workers' councils or other free associations that individuals will constitute themselves for the purpose of their social existence and their productive labor" (Chomsky, 1974, p. 169).

It is a pity that the idea of *anarchy* (without government) has become conflated in popular (and academic) discourse with violence and extremism, making it hard to argue a case for what remains a significant, if hard to achieve, political position (Day, 2005; Kuhn, 2009). It is hard not to agree with Chomsky's general assertion that "every form of authority and domination and hierarchy, every authoritarian structure, has to prove that it's justified" (Chomsky, 2013, pp. 32–3). So preventing a child from crossing a busy street may be an easily justifiable use of parental authority, but generally "people have the right to be free, and if there are constraints on that freedom then you've got to justify them" (p. 33). Given the difficulties in establishing what he is *for*, Chomsky is probably most widely regarded for his powerful critiques of what he is *against*, particularly critiques of American and international foreign policy and the role of transnational corporations and the media (Herman & Chomsky, 1988). The focus on the USA and its politics has led to critiques that his program is too focused on American power in the world and that while he urges solidarity with the South, he is "unhelpful in leading us to learn from the South" (de Sousa Santos, 2018, p. 221). Nonetheless, Chomsky has clearly and convincingly articulated a powerful political position over many decades: How does it square with an apolitical linguistics?

The aspects of Chomsky's worldview that are of interest here comprise rationalism, realism, mentalism, creativity, and freedom. He is committed to rationalism, as opposed to empiricism, in research, and rationality as the key guiding principle for thought. His realism means a belief that "the constructs and entities he develops deal with real features of the world, just as the constructs of chemistry or biology do" (Smith, 1999, p. 137). Mentalism refers both to his emphasis on the innateness of linguistic (and other) competencies and to his attempt to "understand the workings of the human mind within the framework of the natural sciences" (Smith, 1999, p. 143). Finally, his libertarianism centers on his belief that humans should be free from constraint. Although Chomsky disavows any "direct connection" between his political and linguistic work, both derive, he suggests, "from certain assumptions and attitudes with regard to basic aspects of human nature" (Chomsky, 1979, p. 3). Central to both streams of work, therefore, is his belief in universal human nature, of which the innate capacity for language is one aspect: "It is the humanistic conception of man that is advanced and given substance as we discover the rich systems of invariant structures and principles that underlie the most ordinary and humble of human accomplishments" (Chomsky, 1971, p. 46).

Chomsky's quite radical "vision of a future social order" is "based on a con-cept of human nature" (Chomsky, 2013, p. 140). If humans have no innate structures of mind, he argues, then they are infinitely open to the malevo-lent influences of political and ideological control. What we need by contrast is an understanding of the "intrinsic human characteristics" that allow for intellectual development, moral reasoning, and so on. And this is where an understanding of language is important since it "can provide some glimmer-ings of understanding of rule-governed behavior and the possibilities for free and creative action" (p. 140). Chomsky therefore provides what is in essence a rule-governed biological antidote to political control. As Newmeyer (1986) explains, although a view of innateness is often seen as politically suspect from a critical standpoint, Chomsky "sees such a conception in an entirely positive political light: Our genetic inheritance – our human nature – prevents us from being plastic, infinitely malleable beings subjugable to the whims of outside forces" (p. 76). For Chomsky, he continues, "universal grammar unites all peo-ple, it does not divide them" (p. 77). "The normal, creative use of language," explains Chomsky (2013, p. 138), "which to the Cartesian rationalist is the best index of the existence of another mind, presupposes a system of rules and genera-tive principles" that are the bedrock of his linguistic project. Thus, for Chomsky, "there are two intellectual tasks." The first is to develop a "humanistic social theory" based on "some firm concept of the human essence or human nature." The second is to "understand very clearly the nature of power and oppression and terror and destruction in our own society" (Chomsky, 1974, p. 172).

It is important to understand this position. While for many applied lin-guists, Chomskyan linguistics are seen as largely irrelevant (there is no interest in language use; though see Macedo, 2019, for a different view), his politics raise a slightly different quandary for critical applied linguistics. Although it is largely pointless to critique Chomskyan linguistics for not being of much use to applied linguistics (it is a wholly different kind of project), it is useful to point to some of the conundrums his broad worldview presents. Put another way, while we know that his treatment of what he sees as "Plato's problem" – how can we know so much with such limited input? (Smith, 1999) – has largely floundered (Evans, 2014) and the pursuit of language universals has been discredited (Evans and Levinson, 2009), we need to consider what is lost when "Orwell's problem" – how can we remain so ignorant in the face of such contrary evidence? – is pursued without an adequately political approach to language. Chomsky's divide between his linguistics and his political work means that the former is seen as conceptually difficult, while "the analysis of ideology" requires nothing but "a bit of open-mindedness, normal intelligence, and healthy skepticism" (Chomsky, 1979, p. 3). This is unfortunately insuffi-cient as a linguistic response to social inequality: As discussed in later chapters (particularly Chapters 3 and 5), unless we deal adequately with the politics of language – through critical approaches to language policy or discourse analysis –

we deprive ourselves of crucial political tools. Rule-governed language behavior and its creative correlate do not provide us anything like a political antidote to Orwell's problem.

The humanist or universalist position that underpins the search for underlying commonalities (from human nature to universal grammar) is also politically problematic. Locating freedom as an intrinsic property of human nature avoids rather than confronts political power. It is against such claims that many writers from the Global South have objected that invocations of universality are always parochial claims for shared Euro-American traits, "Eurocentric hegemony *posing* as universalism" (Appiah, 1993, p. 58). As Foucault (1974, p. 187) pointed out in his debate with Chomsky over the issue of human nature, "these notions of human nature, of justice, of the realisations of the essence of human beings, are all notions and concepts which have been formed within our civilization, within our type of knowledge and our form of philosophy, and that as a result form part of our class system." So while Chomsky's anarcho-syndicalist politics should be welcome within a critical applied linguistic project, his separation of language and politics and his insistence on human nature leave us at a problematic impasse. His failure to see that "the dichotomy between science and politics is political, rather than scholarly, and therefore prey to the politics of the imperial global North" (de Sousa Santos 2018, p. 223) renders his overall project deeply suspect.

Liberal Egalitarianism

While both Chomsky's politics and linguistics make him something of an outlier, there are a number of more common positions that also disconnect language and politics, or at least appear to. These comprise a diversity of political views and a range of approaches to language that generally disavow a connection between the two. Although they may espouse any number of different approaches to research (from positivistic to more hermeneutic approaches), they take such knowledge production to be an autonomous realm that is not connected to more general political views. Arguing that applied linguistics should remain detached from politics, Widdowson (2001) suggests that it is the disinterested stance of rational inquiry rather than politicized orientations to applied linguistics ("hypocritical applied linguistics" in Widdowson's terms) that brings a true critical stance to applied linguistics. For Widdowson, there are no grounds on which we can choose between different political or ethical visions, and thus by taking a political stance, we are imposing our own version of reality, using rather than diffusing power. Again, like Chomsky's position, this is in need of some explanation.

Various factors contribute to this view that applied linguistics should stay clear of politics. This disjuncture between language and politics has been aided by the structuralist orientation toward language that has for so long dominated the field. Structuralism focuses on systems as entities in themselves, trying to establish how the structure of a system is made up of interrelated constituent parts. The proper focus of linguistics from this point of view, as Saussure (1922) argued long ago, is not the moves made in a chess game but the rules that define those moves. As it slotted into the longer history of positivist thought in the social sciences – the modeling of studies of humans around the natural sciences – structuralism became part of an intellectual movement that challenged the elitism, evolutionism, and progressivism of earlier models of the social world. Structuralism as it developed in linguistics, sociology, and anthropology helped move thinking away from a hierarchical view of values with primitive languages, cultures, and societies on the bottom and developed languages, cultures, and societies on the top. Instead, it urged us not to judge or evaluate from some external position but rather to describe from the inside. What mattered was how the internal structure of things worked, not their external relations. Not only were linguists then able to explore the complex inner workings of languages (showing indeed that so-called primitive languages were highly complex), but they were also able to argue that all languages were equal in that they served the needs of their speakers equally.

Such a view, despite all the disclaimers, is a political view, one that espouses a broad *liberal democratic egalitarianism*. So embedded has it become for many academic linguists that it goes unnoticed. It is only when linguists have to explain their *descriptive* (rather than *prescriptive*) orientation, their belief that all dialects are equal, that standard language is just another dialect, or when they encounter those who object to such egalitarian views, that the underlying politics come to the fore. Burnett (1962, p. 221) launched an attack against structural linguistics on behalf of anyone "who cherishes the English language for its grace and beauty, its combination of precision and flexibility," decrying "the social philosophy of the Structural Linguists" for the most insidious kind of "cultural vandalism." While the damage done by advertising and "mudflows of jargon" was considerable, he complained, it was the work of the Structural Linguist that did the most damage, particularly by "incapacitating the coming generation" in schools. The "paradoxical aspect of their assault on the English language" he concluded, "is that they claim to be motivated only by the purest democratic principles."

While this is easily recognizable as a reactionary diatribe against linguistic democracy, and an appeal to those values – aesthetic and hierarchical evaluations of languages – eschewed by the nonjudgmental linguist, he nonetheless rightly names the democratic principles that underpin structural linguistics. Honey's (1997) later reiteration of a similar position (under the title *Language is Power*) – with its attacks particularly against William Labov for his egalitarian approach to African-American Vernacular English – was met with a strong counterreaction from linguists (see for example Watts, 2011, for discussion). Labov (1970, p. 184), it is worth recalling, had taken aim at those "verbal deprivation theorists" who considered Black English vernacular (BEV) to be inferior to standard English, a position that still needs to be countered (Aveneri,

Graham, Johnson, Riner, & Rosa, 2019; Johnson, 2015). Labov suggested by contrast that all "linguists agree that nonstandard dialects are highly structured systems." While Honey's (1997) arguments in favor of standard English (as superior to other dialects of English, and as the means by which the disadvantaged could progress; arguments to which we shall return) are at best linguistically and politically naïve, they likewise shed light on the unspoken assumptions of liberal egalitarianism (it takes someone opposed to views on equality to make this evident).

For Honey (1983, pp. 24–5), "pseudo-scientific judgements about all varieties of language being 'equal'" confine children to their local context and "slam the door on any real opportunity for social mobility." While his advocacy of "standard English" as the solution to this problem misses the point that judgements about the language varieties we speak are never confined to language alone (they are racial, gendered, and classed), his point about claims to equality echoes those of more critical scholars. As Giroux (1983, p. 229) explains, any discussion about working-class language or standard language in educational contexts has to deal with the wider formations of unequal distribution of power. It may be true that "working-class language practices are just as rule-governed as standard English usage" but to claim that "*all* cultures are equal is to forget that subordinate groups are often denied access to the power, knowledge, and resources that allow them to lead self-determined existences." A similar issue arises with the stoush between Braj Kachru and Randolph Quirk, Kachru claiming that his World Englishes framework is engaged in a sociolinguistic enterprise to describe different varieties of English, Quirk decrying this as a form of "liberation linguistics" (Seidlhofer, 2003). Kachru replied that Quirk's view was a 'deficit' view of language users, a debate to which we return in Chapter 6.

From studies of Black English to descriptions of learners' interlanguages, from research arguing that home literacy practices of children from disadvantaged backgrounds are not so much deficient as different from those of middle-class homes and schools to work aiming to save endangered languages, linguists, sociolinguists, and applied linguists have argued their case for equality, that "every human language is as rich and complex as the next" (MacSwan, 2020, p. 327). As Milroy (1999) points out, linguists' views on the equality of languages are not so much "innocent linguistic pronouncements" as they are "overtly and deliberately ideological, and it is disingenuous to pretend otherwise" (p. 20). Hidden behind the claim to critical distance and politically disinterested academic inquiry are a set of largely unexamined liberal democratic assumptions about language equality, with structuralism supporting liberal pluralism (all structures are equal) and liberalism supporting structural isolation (if all structures are equal, why look elsewhere for inequality?). While a conservative critique decries the liberal egalitarianism of (socio)linguistics, a more critical stance also finds fault with the liberal politics that wishes for equality where there is none.

Rampton (1995b) has suggested that we should be wary of spending too much time criticizing liberalism when it is conservativism that is most obviously opposed to a critical standpoint. The problem with liberalism, however, is that by appealing to a middle-of-the-road, commonsense, middle-class philosophy, that is arguably very much a product of ways of thinking in the Global North, it claims the constant middle ground of "reasonableness" and thus detracts from the possibility of more sustained critique. With its claims to scientificity (description) that obscures its underlying politics, and a tendency always to deal with internal structures rather than external connections, this mainstream position denies its own politics and the politics of language more broadly. It may usefully promote the view that all dialects are equal, but in doing so it fails to attend to the broader context in which they are not. We need to understand how languages are political.

Applied linguistics has been dominated by this insipid egalitarianism that does not help us in framing questions of inequality, language, and power. This denial of its own politics, this refusal to take into account broader social and political concerns, makes this an ostrich-like (head in the sand) approach to applied linguistics: It is not so much critical approaches to applied linguistics that are hypocritical (as Widdowson, 2001, has claimed) as it is this denial of politics that is hypocritical. Many liberal democratic approaches to applied linguistics do in fact propose transformative goals but are generally unable, without clearer understandings of the relations between language and power, to do more than discuss differences and decry deficits. As Williams (1992) describes the problem, there is "evidence of an overriding desire to support the underdog, accompanied by a sociological perspective which reflects the power of the dominant" (p. 226).

For Widdowson (2001), the problem in part is that we cannot decide between different political options. This may be true to the extent that we cannot decide between competing positions in terms only of our linguistic or discourse analytic tools. As van Leeuwen (2018) makes clear, critical discourse analysis can use its analytic tools to reveal various things about texts, but in order to *evaluate* them, it needs to be able to arrive at *moral* and *political* conclusions about forms of inequality, and for this it has to look elsewhere (for further discussion, see Chapter 5). But that is exactly the point: Applied linguists, to be worthy of the name, have to get their hands dirty, have to take a stance, have to make decisions about what is going on. It is not enough for Eades (2010), for example, to show that Indigenous Australians face injustices before the law because of the linguistic operations of the legal system, or for Baugh (2018) to merely point to raciolinguistic discrimination in everyday life: It is imperative to call this out and attempt to change the system (as both have done over many years). Or as van Leeuwen (2018, p. 13) puts it, discussing in particular debates around marriage equality, "So long as suffering continues, there is work to be done."

Language and Power from Different Perspectives

Social Justice

While the two positions described above – a radical politics with a reactionary linguistics and a liberal democratic approach to language – generally deny a relation between language and politics, other approaches make this relation more explicit (for a summary, see Table 2.1). A *social justice* point of view is not an easily defined orientation but at the same time is a common rallying call for critical work. A number of recent books – Piller's (2016) *Linguistic diversity and social justice*, Hastings and Jacob's (2016) *Social Justice in English Language Teaching*, and Aveneri, Graham, Johnson, Riner, and Rosa's (2019) *Language and social justice in practice* – make social justice an explicit frame for their work. The benefits of the idea of social justice is that it appeals in a broad way to a sense of fairness that is hard to disagree with. If one feels uncomfortable with the critiques of capitalism and inequality that are at the heart of a neo-Marxist framework, social justice suggests a more positive way of thinking. The problem with the idea of social justice, however, is that it is also a rather vague term whose lineage is principally in liberal democratic principles. The idea of social justice draws its inspiration typically from the liberal tradition of justice in the work of Rawls (1971). This is useful insofar as it introduces an element of moral philosophy to the discussion. Rawls insisted on getting

Table 2.1 Relations Between Knowledge and Politics

Framework	Epistemology and Politics	Relation to Language	Usefulness for Critical Applied Linguistics
Radical politics, reactionary linguistics	Anarcho-syndicalism with nativist and technicist language analysis	Disconnects the political from the scientific analysis of language	Useful politics, unhelpful linguistic universalism
Liberal democratic linguistics	Structuralist linguistics; liberal democratic egalitarianism	Argues for language equality while denying its own politics	Impractical decoupling of language and politics
Social justice and language	Liberal moral philosophy	Suggests ways of dealing with group language rights	General appeal but limited critical foundations
Structure, ideology, and power	Neo-Marxist politics and scientific analysis; macro structures of domination	Language reflects society: Mapping language and inequality	Significant critiques limited by a priori assumptions
Situated practice	Poststructuralist and other situated frameworks	Language as already political but analysis local	Problematizing stance may lead to malleable politics

beyond utilitarian arguments ('the greatest good for the greatest number') and instead argued for a position based on the principle that people could minimize their potential disadvantage rather than maximize their advantage (he argues from a position in which people don't know in advance what social advantages and disadvantages they may have). This means that people should have on the one hand the maximum amount of individual liberty (as long as it doesn't impinge on others') and that any social organization ideally would favor the least advantaged.

This is doubtless an appealing line of thinking, stressing freedom of the individual alongside an emphasis on social justice. It has informed various lines of thinking of relevance to critical applied linguistics, particularly via the work of Kymlicka (2001) on multiculturalism and minority rights, arguments taken up and developed by May (2001) and others as a counter to language rights frameworks that have been less carefully thought through in relation to individual and group rights (an issue to which we return in the next chapter). As Joseph (2006) remarks, however, we need to ask serious questions about Kymlicka's acceptance of the nation state, privileging of indigenous rights and "national minorities" over immigrant rights (Haque, 2012) (a tempting moral argument but one that deems newly arrived people to have fewer rights), and his defense of language purification (as largely harmless). To ignore the relation between language purification and its dangerous nationalist and racist connections is to overlook serious political concerns (Joseph, 2006). Kymlicka's argument that individual freedom requires a cultural context of choice is a "liberal articulation of a romantic understanding of the value of language" (de Schutter, 2016, p. 52). Although this line of thinking shows the importance of language to political theory, Ives (2015, p. 65) takes this "individualistic liberalism" to task for its inability to deal with the politics of language adequately.

This tradition of social justice that draws on the liberal moral philosophy of Rawls (1971) has been further critiqued for being color blind, since "whites do not recognize their privileging *as* privileging, as differential and unfair treatment" (Mills, 2017, p. 47). With its emphasis on the individual and lack of concern with groups based around class, race, or gender – "taking a propertied white male standpoint as given" – "modern mainstream Anglo-American epistemology was for hundreds of years from its Cartesian origins profoundly inimical terrain for the development of any concept of structural group-based miscognition" (Mills, 2017, p. 49). It is not that *social justice* cannot be invoked as part of a critical project, but rather that it is not an adequate grounding for a critical enterprise. Nor does this mean that to invoke social justice is necessarily to take up a standpoint of *White ignorance* (Mills, 2017), but rather that there is not enough in this tradition of liberal thought to safeguard against it.

As Mills (2017, p. 147) argues, the inability to deal with race in any meaningful way "is structural and symptomatic of white political philosophy in general." The problem, in part, is the development of "ideal theory," the dominant mode of political philosophy that has produced a White vision of the world (Mills, 2014). We may be reminded here of other idealist abstractions, such

as Chomsky's (1965, p. 3) "ideal speaker-listener in a completely homogeneous speech community." While Chomsky's strange construct is often critiqued
from a sociolinguistic or applied linguistic point of view for not being related
to real language use, this critique potentially misses the point that such idealistic abstractions are dangerous misrecognitions of the world. Following Mills'
critique of social justice – "How theoretically useful is it… in the philosophical
investigation of social justice to start from a raceless ideal so remote from reality?" (Mills, 2017, p. 148) – the more important critique is to ask what purposes
can be served by abstractions of language that avoid fundamental questions of
race, class, gender, and other formations of inequality?

To be clear, I am by no means critiquing the books cited at the beginning
of this section. It is quite possible to ground one's views of social justice in a
range of different ways. Piller (2016), for example, develops her idea of social
justice from Nancy Fraser's (1995; 2005) focus on economic redistribution, cultural recognition, and political representation. This leads to an exploration of
the relations between linguistic diversity, economic inequality, cultural domination, and unequal political representation. And while Aveneri, Graham,
Johnson, Riner, and Rosa (2019, p.5) make reference to the Rawlsian tradition, they develop a sharper critical focus on "access, equity, power, privilege,
and marginalization." Others affiliating themselves with social justice draw on
alternative traditions. And yet, as Dominguez (2017) remarks, "social justice
as it is widely construed has remained colonial" (p. 232) in that it seeks to
make inequitable forms of subjectivity – colonized ways of being and doing
and valuing – available to all. Social justice as a framework in itself seeks a
kind of balance, a liberal form of equality, without the critical dimension to
address, for example, colonial forms of knowledge. Social justice, according to
Gounari (2020, p. 14), has become a bit like 'critical thinking,' "an educational
niche, a teachable competence, a set of skills and values to be transmitted in
the classroom, rather than an exploration of an uncharted and problematic
terrain that would push students to understand themselves in the world and
name the perpetrators of social injustice." Social justice can be an appealing
way of framing a critical project – it certainly has the advantage of being more
welcoming to those who are unsettled by strident critical views – but in itself it
is a vague and largely liberal idea that cannot provide an adequate theoretical
or political grounding for critical applied linguistics.

Structure, Ideology, Science and Power

The different constellations of language, power, and knowledge that come
together across a range of critical applied linguistic work are in fact a tan-
gled web of different agendas, from feminist to antiracist, from decolonial to
neo-Marxist (and, of course, many combinations of these), and from ethnographic to discourse analytic, interpretive to positivist. To simplify things a bit,
however, I will deal first of all with approaches that take a broadly neo-Marxist
and modernist approach to power and combine this with an argument in favor

of critical work as scientific work. They may share with aspects of the radical project described earlier a belief in rationality, realism, and scientific endeavor, including the old Marxist divide between science and ideology; but they differ fundamentally in their emphasis on the political analysis of language use. This position is one held by many of those who have worked in critical applied linguistics over the years. Phillipson (1992) explains the aim of his book *Linguistic Imperialism* (to which we return in Chapter 3) as "contributing to 'rational, scientifically-based discourse'" on the global spread of English, in the hope that "an adequate, theoretically explicit foundation for analysing the issues has been provided" (p. 75). Here, then, is an analysis of language and imperialism based on scientific analysis. From this point of view, language – or at least language policy – is deeply political and the goals of one's work as a critical applied linguist are to uncover the structural operations of power and the ideological operations by which they are obscured.

Let us unpick this position a bit further. A useful place to start is Mey's (1985, p. 342) *critical sociolinguistics,* which "seeks to recognize the political and economic distortions that our society imposes on us." The aim is to "explain the differences between *oppressed* and *oppressor* language by pointing out that the different classes have unequal access to societal power" (p. 342). Of particular importance here is the emphasis on distortion (ideology distorts reality), oppressed and oppressor language (some have power, others don't), and class (the cornerstone of inequality lies in socioeconomic relations). Combining this Marxian framework with scientific analysis, Mey (1985, p. 343) goes on to explain that "sociolinguistics as a *critical* science bases itself on the assumption that the moving force of our society is capital's need to accumulate profits." Scientific analysis can overcome ideological distortion. This, we might say, is the classic position of critical language studies, from linguistic imperialism to critical discourse analysis, making language and ideology reflexes of the primary capitalist distortions of the social order.

Fairclough's CDA operates from a similar viewpoint, arguing that "social order … is the political objective of the dominant, 'hegemonic,' sections of a society in the domain of language as in other domains" (Fairclough, 1992a, p. 48). For Fairclough (1989, p. 33), the state is the key element in "maintaining the dominance of the capitalist class, and controlling the working class" through an alliance of capitalists and those with shared interests who form the *"dominant bloc."* While other relations such as gender and race are also important, "class relations" have "a more fundamental status than others" (Fairclough, 1989, p. 34). As a form of political analysis, then, this is a fairly traditional neo-Marxist position, with the strengths and weaknesses such a position brings. On the good side, this work has always made clear its political stance, has emphasized the importance of a political approach to language, and has made material relations of inequality fundamental to the analysis. The re-emergence of political economy as a key ingredient in any critical applied linguistics (Block, 2014, 2018a; O'Regan, 2021), and particularly with the critical attention to neoliberalism, grounds this work in crucial understandings of fundamental inequalities. And with ideology as the distortion of what is real, discourse analysis has a ready-made goal in ideology critique.

This kind of analysis also has various shortcomings. For many sociologists, while Marxist thought has been important for a focus on class and material conditions, the tendency toward oversimplified accounts of oppressed and oppressors mean there are "too many flaws and inadequacies in Marxist thought for it to supply an overall grounding for sociological analysis" (Giddens, 1982, p. 167). A constant critique has also been that the insistence that class or socioeconomic relations are more fundamental than any others overlooks the ways in which gender and race, for example, are both intertwined with class and equally bound up with the distribution of material resources and discriminatory practices (Flores & Chaporro, 2018). Marxism has "enabled bourgeois men to analyse society from the point of view of the industrial proletariat but it has subsequently been shown to have occupied a position that was both masculinist in content and Eurocentric in context" (Barrett, 1991, p. 161). The common version of ideology in this framework, furthermore, that makes critical language studies an analysis of the distorting meanings of a dominant group has also been critiqued by other critical scholars, for its treatment of ideology as "conspiratorial, as the conscious production of an individual or group whose objective is the subversion of some other group" (Williams, 1992, p. 244). These issues will be taken up in much more depth in later chapters, particularly Chapter 5.

Two final concerns are the focus on scientific analysis and the proposals for alternative visions. Drawing on the framework of CDA developed by herself and Norman Fairclough, Ruth Wodak (1996) suggests that a key principle of CDA is that it is "a socially committed scientific paradigm. CDA is not less 'scientific' than other linguistic approaches" (p. 20). Kress (1990) likewise insists that that while their "activity is politically committed, it is nonetheless properly scientific, perhaps all the more so for being aware of its own political, ideological, and ethical stance" (p. 85). These arguments are understandable both in terms of the era and context when they were written ('scientific' in various European contexts can also mean little more than 'academic'), and as a defense against critiques that critical work is not good academic work. But this appeal to science, at least in contemporary times, rather uncomfortably adheres to a hierarchy of knowledge production that places the scientific at the summit.

Finally, there are difficult concerns here (as in all critical work) about what alternative vision or strategies for change we are left with. Two positions present themselves: Either a basic materialist position, which suggests that to change relations in language we need to change social relations of power, or a focus on removing ideological obfuscation, leading to emancipation through awareness. Mey (1985, p. 352) argues the former position: "In the final perspective, what we're dealing with, strictly speaking, is not linguistic oppression as such, but rather, *societal* oppression that manifests itself linguistically" (p. 352).

It is on similar grounds that Block (2018c) insists that the focus on critical work ultimately has to be on the redistribution of wealth in society. We have to change the society first in order to change language. The dual problems with this position are that it renders language only a reflection of society, which is an impoverished and inaccurate understanding of the social role of language (Cameron, 1990), and it leaves us as critical applied linguistics with little ground for action other than a radical restructuring of society. I'm all for a radical restructuring of society – I'm more with Chomsky on this one than insipid proposals to vote for social democrats – but I also want a domain of linguistic activity that matters in its own right.

A more optimistic argument is that by making people aware of forms of linguistic or ideological oppression, there are possibilities for forms of emancipation. Awareness, therefore, becomes a sort of political enlightenment that can lead to empowerment, which if turned into social action may become emancipation. Critical language awareness aims to "empower students by providing them with the opportunities to discover and critically examine the conventions of the academic discourse community and to enable them to emancipate themselves by developing alternatives to the dominant conventions" (Clark, 1992, p. 137). This at least provides an alternative to the assumption that only prior social change can have any effect, but it operates with several problematic assumptions about pulling away the veil of obscurity imposed by ideology, and as Kearney (1988, p. 386) notes, it is "unlikely that any amount of 'knowledge' about the falsehood of our experience is going to help us think or act in a more effective or liberating way." Critical forms of education that do little more than "explain the intricate mechanisms of our enslavement" do not necessarily give us useful ways forward. Lewis (2018) makes a related point about the limited possibilities for change offered by 'error correction' (showing why certain beliefs about language are wrong). Discourses of emancipation, as Usher and Edwards (1994, p. 27) note, despite their "emancipatory intentions, their desire to enlighten, may be implicated with the will to power and may, therefore, have oppressive consequences."

This constellation of views – and as I have tried to make clear, they do not necessarily sit together, but have here been combined for convenience – that bring neo-Marxist analyses of the social order together with a focus on ideology, science, and emancipation present a far more useful frame for analysis than the disjuncture between language and politics discussed in the first part of this chapter. This common approach nonetheless has various limitations: While insisting on the importance of relating language to social and political concerns, it all too often presents a material version of power located only in class relations; it views ideology as the obfuscations of dominant class interests; it assumes that scientific analysis of reality can help us escape from these ideological falsities; and thus, unless we can change society first, we can at least hope for emancipation through awareness. In the following section, I shall present and critique a slightly different way of approaching these questions.

Situated Practices

The final position I want to consider – and as I have tried to make clear these are constellations of ideas and by no means compartmentalized frameworks – we might call a postmodern or poststructuralist approach. As Kramsch (2021) explains, in contrast to the modernist versions of power concerned centrally with forms of domination of one group by another, postmodern accounts of power tend toward a more multifaceted diffusion of power through the social world. My comments in the previous section suggest a need to question critical work based on a modernist emancipatory framework in which power is held by the oppressors (the dominant bloc) and maintained by ideology, and in which emancipation can be brought about as a result of awareness of the operations of ideology. This type of emancipatory modernism is close to the project of Critical Theory as developed by Habermas (1972). Patti Lather (1991) suggests we need to add a fourth category to Habermas' technical, practical, and emancipatory knowledge, a category that includes poststructural and postmodern approaches to knowledge.

The term *postmodern*, however, has been greatly compromised by decades of attacks from both conservative commentators and critical theorists. In a nutshell – we shall return to these debates at various points – the postmodernist refusal of grand narratives (the rejection of overarching theories and explanations, such as structuralism or Marxism) are seen as leaving it open to forms of epistemological, ethical, and political relativism. The argument, simply put (which it often is), is that postmodernism suggests that 'anything goes,' all is relative, there is no place from which we can make ethical and political judgements. This is a rather crude misunderstanding of what postmodernism has aimed to do from those who want to maintain a sure footing for their own position (that is, not to adopt a questioning stance about their own knowledge and politics). Thus, to make the obvious point that languages are social constructs (what else could they be?) all too easily brings accusations of taking up a poststructuralist or postmodernist position (as if this constituted a critique in itself), which is "strongly associated with deconstructivism" and "largely defined in opposition to the classical ideals of the Enlightenment and modernism" (MacSwan, 2020, p. 326).

It is such assumptions about the Enlightenment and the Global North that Southern Theory (de Sousa Santos, 2018) has sought to challenge. Postmodernism can also be seen as part of this challenge "as European culture's awareness that it is no longer the unquestioned and dominant centre of the world" (Young, 1990, p. 19). Such a view of postmodernism links it specifically to a politics that seeks to question the canons of Eurocentric knowledge, a stance of great significance in the context of applied linguistics, particularly when linked to its global role in relation to the teaching of major languages such as English. Despite the resistance to large-scale theories and the insistence on complexity and localized forms of knowledge, postmodernism cannot be simply dismissed as a form of relativism. As Lather (1992) argues, following Haraway (1988), relativism and universalism sit as complementary poles within a modernist frame of knowledge. If challenges are made to objectivist or universalist frameworks of knowledge, the counterargument simply involves accusations of relativism or nihilism, which, Lather (1992) suggests are "an implosion of Western, white male, class-privileged arrogance – if we cannot know everything, then we can know nothing" (p. 100). A useful postmodernism works with a notion of *situated knowledges* (Haraway, 1988) that should not be equated with relativism: "The relativism of modernity needs to be distinguished from the partiality and particularity of the postmodern moment" (Usher & Edwards, 1994, p. 223). Postmodernism, then, questions the whole polarity between universalism and relativism, suggesting instead that knowledge, action, and value are always specifically located.

There are doubtless various problems with a strong 'post' position: It would be unwise to suggest that it somehow offers an instant solution to the concerns raised earlier about the old-world solidity of neo-Marxist approaches, or the vagueness of social justice. A tendency to overemphasize discourse, for example, has made it open to the critique that it does not deal with real, material social relations. Kubota (2016) has critiqued what she sees as poststructuralist, postmodernist, and postcolonialist approaches to diversity for their lack of political grounding and ultimate collusion with neoliberalism. While many such critiques are based neither in a well-informed understanding of these 'post' positions nor in a clear articulation of the neoliberal cooptation they claim – as Canagarajah (2017) makes clear, they tend to conflate quite different ways of engaging with diversity – they do point to the ways that such a position can appear to lose its grounding, may appear to revel in abstractions rather than stay grounded in questions of racism, class oppression, and so on.

It is worth recalling, however, that for Weedon (1987; 1997), whose *Feminist practice and poststructuralist theory* influenced many applied linguists, the project was to find a "theory of the relation between language, subjectivity, social organization and power" (1997, p. 12). Weedon's (1997, p. 31) *feminist poststructuralism* has always been a political project, drawing on feminism, antiracism, and aspects of Marxist discourse, such as the "material nature of ideology, or, in poststructuralist terms, discourse, the importance of economic relations of production, the class structure of society and the integral relationship between theory and practice." The crucial difference, she explains, is that this position "does not assume in advance that discourses and the forms of social power which they legitimize are necessarily ultimately reducible to the capital-labour relationship." A poststructuralist position, therefore, is by no means devoid of politics (as some oddly claim) but rather refuses to assume *a priori* what such relations are and how they operate. Such a stance has important ramifications for research, seeking not so much to map language and text against a given socioeconomic analysis but rather seeking to understand social and political relations through language analysis. From this point of view, language is *part of* the social and indeed an active element in its construction, rather than a reflection of prior social categories.

While there is often both a rather unfortunate anti-intellectualism and a peculiar politics (critical stances allied with populist conservativism) in many critiques of postmodernism or poststructuralism, I do not particularly want to spend time defending this territory. It doesn't matter what we call it, as long as we understand the grounded, perspectival, or *situated* aspect of this position: The insistence on locality and the prominence of the locus of enunciation (from where we speak). It is these concerns that have reemerged both through the growth of linguistic ethnography (and a determination to understand language use in multifaceted, local ways) and a rejuvenated southern politics that has insisted that the universalist claims that are incessantly critical of supposed relativism must in themselves be understood for the particular perspective from which they view the world. So let us call this final position a *situated practice* that maintains that we need to account for the position from which we are speaking, taking both the idea of *situatedness* and of *practice* seriously (Pennycook, 2010). While viewing language as fundamentally bound up with politics, this position nevertheless articulates a profound skepticism about truth claims, and about an emancipatory position outside ideology. It views language as inherently political; understands power more in terms of its micro operations in relation to questions of class, race, gender, ethnicity, sexuality, and so on; and argues that we must also account for the politics of knowledge.

As Cameron (1995, pp. 15–6) explains, following the work of Butler (1990; 1997) and others, rather than treating sociolinguistic categories – class, gender, race, and so on – as fairly fixed givens for analysis, from this perspective they are seen as "relatively unstable *constructs* which are therefore in need of explanation themselves." Language then becomes part of the explanation, since "language is one of the things that *constitutes* my identity as a particular kind of subject. Sociolinguistics says that how you act depends on who you are; critical theory says that who you are (and are taken to be) depends on how you act." It is on such grounds that McNamara (2019) insists on a poststructuralist approach to understanding *subjectivity* through the close study of conversational data, shedding light on the microactions of social life that are part of the wider operations of racist and homophobic discourse. On related grounds, Busch (2017) uses poststructuralist analysis as part of her understanding of *Spracherleben*: The lived experience of language. Pointing to another important aspect of this way of thinking – that the operations of power are multifaceted – García, Flores and Spotti (2017, p. 13) argue that a "critical poststructuralist lens" allows us to see the tensions between language as regulator and enabler.

Drawing on a range of thinkers from Foucault (1980b) and Butler (1990; 1997) to Braidotti (2013) and de Sousa Santos (2018), this approach seeks alternative ways of understanding without recourse to discourses of science or humanism, with their underlying claims to fundamental or essential essences. Whereas, for example, in discussing the notion of justice, Chomsky (1974) argues for "some sort of absolute basis ... ultimately residing in fundamental human qualities, in terms of which a 'real' notion of justice is grounded"

(p. 185), Foucault (1974) argues that "the idea of justice in itself is an idea which in effect has been invented and put to work in different types of societies as an instrument of a certain political and economic power or as a weapon against that power" (pp. 184–5). We could substitute 'language' for 'justice' in this debate and see similar differences: Is language grounded in fundamental human qualities or an invention used for and against the workings of power (Makoni & Pennycook, 2007)? Rather than being grounded in an overarching theory or politics, this approach insists on understanding the contextuality of knowledge, the perspectives of the speaker, and "the knowledges that emerge from social and political struggles and cannot be separated from such struggles" (de Sousa Santos, 2018; p. 2). This, then, is the final constellation of ideas that will inform the discussion in future chapters.

Conclusion: Not Whether But How To Be Critical

I have sought in this chapter to sketch out different configurations of knowledge, politics, and language, from those that see a connection only at the level of human nature to those that argue a liberal democratic case for language without acknowledging it as political, or seek in liberal concepts of justice a means to ground critical projects; from those that seek to map language against a pregiven socioeconomic analysis, to those that insist on locally-understood operations of language and politics. For some, the relation between language and politics is better avoided, while for others it is the cornerstone of their work. I have also sought to make clear that none of these is a tight box of linguistic and political theory: Egalitarian linguists may also seek a critical political agenda while poststructuralist analysis can easily slide into liberal politics. Adopting different perspectives, however, will have major implications for how applied linguistic questions are addressed, as well as opening up new questions for interrogation. Critical applied linguistics draws on a wider array of work than I have outlined in this chapter – feminist, Queer, antiracist, decolonial, and so on – that are discussed in subsequent chapters. A chart of some of the intersecting influences in critical applied linguistics can be seen in Figure 2.1.

If we take a piece of second language discourse, for example, each would likely look at it from a different perspective. For the radical-reactionary position, the task would be to demonstrate how the development of the language user's utterances follows certain underlying and universal principles. By uncovering scientific facts about natural cognitive processes, we can push back against ideological claims about language use. A liberal-egalitarian position meanwhile would be principally interested in showing that there is nothing wrong with the supposedly deviant forms of speech for they are part of the developing grammar of the learner: All language, even that of a learner, is as rich and diverse as any other. All things being equal, the learner will go on developing to become a free and full-fledged member of the target speech community. The social justice perspective, by contrast, is more interested in

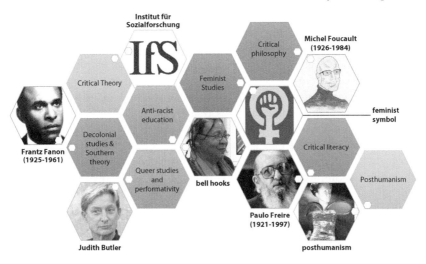

Figure 2.1   Critical Influences

why this person has had to learn this second language to start with: What individual rights are being overlooked by the move away from their first language?

For the emancipatory modernist, however, it is not so much the form of the learner's utterances that are of central interest but rather questions of access and content. All things are not equal. Like the social justice concerns, the issues here have to do with the wider social context of the utterance, and particularly the classist and racist division that relegates second language speakers to a secondary status. What access do people such as this – the individual is less important than their position as migrant, refugee, worker in precarious employment – have to particular uses of language, how might they be positioned, how might they become more aware of the ways in which they are discriminated against, and how then could they find ways to struggle against an inequitable system? The situated practice perspective shares some of these concerns but seeks to understand more local relations of language and power: Is this language use constricting or enabling, part of hip-hop discourse or a performance of a particular style? The social, cultural, and historical location of the speaker matters not because their language use is thereby already marginalized – language reflects society – but because this positioning helps shed light on the conflicting discourses at play.

At the same time, we should not overplay these differences. While a poststructuralist position is critical of *structure* – as an enclosed system within which we conduct our analyses – this does not mean that it cannot therefore deal with, for example, structural racism. The point of the idea (as with other forms of structural discrimination) is that this is not about individuals and their views but a question of institutions, social formations, ideologies, discourses, and so on. We may get at deep-seated forms of discrimination and inequality in different ways, but all critical standpoints view such concerns in systemic terms, whether we look at practices (as sedimented social action), discourses (as formations of power and knowledge), ideologies (as ideas formulated in the interests of the powerful), institutions (as social formations that structure society), or northern epistemologies (as ways the Global North systematically excludes the Global South). These are different perspectives but they all seek to get beyond individualistic and liberal accounts of choice, freedom, and the individual. As Marx (1852, p. 1) famously put it, people "make their own history, but they do not make it as they please; they do not make it under self-selected circumstances, but under circumstances existing already, given and transmitted from the past."

As we pursue different domains – the politics of language, difference, text, and pedagogy – in the following chapters, the greater complexity of different intersecting critical domains will become more apparent. I have attempted in this chapter, in rather compressed and simplified form, to sketch out various configurations of how language and politics may be related. The key question is not *whether* applied linguistics is political but about *how* it should be critical. In Chapters 3 to 6, I will discuss the implications of different ways of doing critical applied linguistics. The next chapter will give more substance to the claims already made in this chapter that language is political from top to bottom, that language use, language rights, language reclamation, and so on are all deeply political endeavors, and need to be grounded in clear political and theoretical positions as well as grounded forms of research and action.

Note

1. In the first edition, I labeled this position 'anarcho-autonomy'. The liberal position outlined later I called 'liberal-ostrichism.' I no longer consider these labels very useful (though the ostrich metaphor did some nice work) and I've attempted here to move away from the over-labelling of positions.

3   The Politics of Language

The previous chapter (Chapter 2) focused primarily on relations between knowledge and politics. It sought to highlight the differences among five broadly-sketched constellations of knowledge and politics: A combination of radical politics and universalist linguistics; a mainstream linguistic egalitarian perspective; a framework based around social justice; a neo-Marxist-inspired position looking at power and ideology; and a situated practice perspective that insists on local forms of knowledge. Since applied linguistics always has to do with language in some form, the development of a political vision of language must form a backbone to critical applied linguistics. The case has already been made in the previous chapter that language is always political (Joseph, 2006; van Splunder, 2020), so I will not reiterate this point here. The question is not whether it is political but how. Questions of language policy, multilingualism, language rights, and language maintenance, where the issue is how languages are dealt with within broad social policies, will be the focus of this chapter. Other questions, such as how difference and identity are constructed and opposed in language, will be the focus of Chapter 4 on the politics of difference. Questions of language and ideology and language pedagogy will be the focus in Chapters 5 and 6.

I focus in this chapter on a number of principal concerns, all of which can be considered exercises in *linguistic decolonization*: In the next section, I look at broad questions to do with the politics of language through a focus on different ways of looking at the global spread of English. In line with the framework developed in the previous chapter, I will frame this in terms of liberal egalitarian, emancipatory modernist, and situated practice approaches to English. As I suggested in the previous chapter, we should not see these as rigidly clear positions but rather as particular constellations of ideas that often go together. It is quite possible to imagine these working in alternative ways, and it is also clear that even ideas that are commonly used together – such as linguistic imperialism and language rights – do not necessarily operate from a coherent theoretical base. The notion of decolonizing language is taken up both in the discussion of postcolonialism and the decolonial option, and also in relation to the importance of decolonizing ideas about language. The conclusion suggests some general ways forward for thinking politically about language.

The Global Spread of English

Liberal Diversity: All Englishes Are Equal

A useful way to open up this discussion is through an exploration of ways of understanding the global spread of English. While there are good reasons to focus our attention on issues other than English – a remorseless interest in English and English language teaching may reinforce the very dominance that is being critiqued – it remains nonetheless – and because so much has been written about it – a useful domain to explore different ways of understanding language and power. Following the discussion in the last chapter, we can categorize these generally as liberal egalitarian approaches emphasizing linguistic diversity, neo-Marxist concerns with English imperialism, and critical approaches that seek to understand the contextual inequalities of English (for a summary, see Table 3.1). It is of course possible to find – particularly in various nonacademic contexts – celebratory accounts of global English. Such views typically explain the spread of English not in terms of global power structures but rather in terms of individual choice, and encourage English speakers to rejoice in the fact that "English is streets ahead and fast drawing away from the rest of the chasing pack" (Hanson, 1997, p. 22).

This view, which I have elsewhere (Pennycook, 1999b) termed a *colonial celebratory* position on English, has been well documented and critiqued (Bailey, 1991; Phillipson, 1992; Pennycook, 1994b, 1998a). Simply put, this is a position that trumpets the benefits of English over other languages, suggesting that English is superior to other languages in terms of both its intrinsic (the nature of the language) and extrinsic (the functions of the language) qualities. I use the term *colonial* in conjunction with *celebratory* here because these celebrations of the spread of English, its qualities, and characteristics have a long and colonial history and form part of what I elsewhere called the *adherence of discourses* (1998a), the ways in which particular discourses adhere to English.

Table 3.1 Frameworks for Understanding the Global Role of English

Frameworks	Political Tools	Strengths and Weaknesses
World Englishes and ELF	Laissez-faire liberalism and liberal egalitarianism	Critique of normative assumptions about English limited by weak analysis of global politics
Linguistic imperialism and unequal Englishes	Theories of imperialism, language ecology, and language rights	Powerful critiques of global inequality limited by focus on causes over effects and political incoherence
Situated power and decolonial options	Contextual studies and post- and decolonial theories	Focus on local contexts of politics and use limited by potential to lose sight of larger picture

An initial decolonization project is simply to counter such glorifications of English. Although at least in academic circles they are less often explicitly stated, such views about the inherent benefits of English nonetheless underpin many current discussions of academic writing, for example (normative assumptions about the pre-eminence of writing in English).

The common line on English in academic circles, however, espouses a more liberal egalitarian view. In one line of thinking – what we might call *laissez-faire liberal idealism* – the main concern is to balance the spread of English with the recognition of first languages. Like Hogben's (1963) proposal for *Essential World English* – in which English serves people around the world as a universal second language "for informative communication across their own frontiers about issues of common interest to themselves and others" (p. 20), while other languages are supported as "a home tongue for love-making, religion, verse-craft, back chat and inexact topics in general" (p. 20) – Crystal (1997) argues for a complementarity between support for the benefits of English as a global means of communication and the importance of multilingualism, a balance between the dual values of international intelligibility and historical identity. On the one hand, we have all the advantages created by the spread of English: Ease of communication, global travel and communication, and so on, while on the other hand, we work to sustain local cultures and traditions. For Hogben (1963) "one language has priority by common consent as the sole medium of informative communication between speech communities" while they retain "their native habits of discourse for reasons which have little or no relevance to the exacting semantic demands of science" (pp. 28–9).

All we need in this way of thinking is to celebrate universalism while maintaining diversity. This vision of complementary language use – English will be used for international purposes while local languages will be used locally – does not take into account the far more complex social and political contexts of language use, the ways it is "sustained by socioeconomic and market forces" or the way the "educational system reproduced and legitimatizes the relations of power and knowledge implicated with English" (Dua, 1994, p. 132). It also problematically leaves other languages as static markers of identity, as well as patronizingly narrow in scope in their dealings with romance, religion, poetry, daily chat, and topics of less global importance. This vision of comfortable complementarity thus fails to constrain "the expanding and strengthening hold of English" while also contributing "to the marginalization" of other languages and cultures (Dua, 1994, p. 133). This lack of critical engagement with English and optimistic hope for linguistic complementarity ultimately contribute, in Phillipson's (1999) view, to what he calls, following Tsuda (1994), a *diffusion of English paradigm*.

The most influential ways of engaging with questions around the global spread of English, however, have been framed within another liberal egalitarian framework, *World Englishes* (Kachru, 1992), and its more recent cousin, *English as a lingua franca* (ELF) (Seidlhofer, 2011). Kachru's influential model of Three Circles – the inner circle where English is widely spoken as a first language, the outer, postcolonial circle where it is used internally as a second or additional language, and the expanding circle, where it is largely used for external, foreign language communication – has certainly given us useful ways of conceptualizing different contexts of language use, and has changed the ways in which we view varieties of English and norms of correctness (giving us multiple Englishes). Although this framework can be seen in terms of a decolonial intent – it aims to throw off the shackles of Inner Circle/native speaker language norms – it is at heart a liberal egalitarian model, aiming to show that just as different dialects are equally complex in their own terms, so varieties of English (at least in the Outer Circle) should be seen as equal to those of the center.

The World Englishes framework posits a new list of standard varieties but tends to overlook difference within regions, or questions of power, class, inequality, and access. Parakrama (1995, pp. 25–6) raises critical concerns about "the smoothing out of struggle within and without language" and thus the tendency toward the "homogenizing of the varieties of English on the basis of 'upper-class' forms." As Martin (2014, p. 53) observes in the context of the Philippines, there are at very least circles within circles, comprising an inner circle "of educated, elite Filipinos who have embraced the English language," an outer circle who may be aware of Philippine English as a variety but are "either powerless to support it and/or ambivalent about its promotion" and an expanding circle for whom the language is "largely inaccessible." For Tupas (2006, p. 169) "the power to (re)create English ascribed to the Outer Circle is mainly reserved only for those who have been invested with such power in the first place (the educated/the rich/the creative writers, etc.)." Whilst appearing, therefore, to work from an inclusionary political agenda in its attempt to have the new Englishes acknowledged as varieties of English, this approach to language is equally exclusionary. Ultimately, concludes Bruthiaux, "the Three Circles model is a 20th century construct that has outlived its usefulness" (Bruthiaux, 2003, p. 161), and for the discussion here it fails in the end to provide an adequate political framework beyond a call for recognition of different varieties. While pluralist approaches to English have opened up an understanding of postcolonial diversity, there has also been a tendency to "romanticize the multiplicity of local language use without sufficiently interrogating inequalities and injustices involving race, gender, class and so on" (Kubota, 2015, p. 33).

The more recent work on English as a lingua franca (ELF) (Jenkins, 2006; Seidlhofer, 2011) has been useful insofar as it does not work with nation-based linguistic models (Indian, Philippine, Nigerian, etc. Englishes). Although it purports to deal with everyday language use – and thus to focus potentially on a less elite version of language than the World Englishes approach – there is still insufficient attention to what we might call 'English from below' or the everyday interactions of non-elites. As O'Regan (2014, p. 540) notes, furthermore, there is a "profound disconnect" between the desire on the one hand to recognize and promote features of ELF (and to argue that the norms for English communication should derive from the majority second language speaker interactions), and the need on the other hand to recognize the structural inequalities of the world which will "always distribute economic and linguistic resources in a way which benefits the few over the many and which confers especial prestige upon selective language forms." While the WE approach has framed its position as a struggle between the former colonial center and its postcolonial offspring, the ELF approach has located its struggle between so-called native and non-native speakers. Yet neither of these sites of struggle engages adequately with wider questions of power, inequality, class, ideology, or access (O'Regan, 2021). The ELF framework, Guilherme (2018) asserts, is Eurocentric, myopic, reductive and uncritical and has been unhelpful for understanding English, other languages, globalization or the politics of knowledge.

Linguistic Imperialism, Language Ecology, Language Rights

A constellation of rather different approaches to these questions opens up clearer concerns around power, inequality, and political economy. Tollefson (1991) distinguishes between work that focuses on individual power, individual motivation, and rational choice and work that seeks to understand the broader social and political conditions in which any such action occurs. Language policy, he argues, "must be interpreted within a framework which emphasizes power and competing interests" (Tollefson, 1991, p. 201). Tollefson goes on to argue for the need to go beyond a general respect for diversity and instead to view access to education and other domains of use of the mother tongue as a fundamental human right: "A commitment to democracy means that the use of the mother tongue at work and in school is a fundamental human right" (p. 211). The notions of language rights, language ecologies, and linguistic imperialism have come together most notably within the work of Phillipson (1992).

Phillipson's (1992; 2009) linguistic imperialism framework places questions of power squarely in the picture, and was developed "to account for linguistic hierarchisation, to address issues of why some languages come to be used more and others less, what structures and ideologies facilitate such processes, and the role of language professionals" (Phillipson, 1997, p. 238). There are various strands to Phillipson's argument: Linguistic imperialism is concerned with the ways in which English is constantly promoted over other languages, the role played by organizations such as the British Council in the promotion and orchestration of the global spread of English (it was far from accidental), and the ways in which this inequitable position of English has become embedded in ELT dogmas, such as promoting native speaker teachers of English over their non-native speaker counterparts, or suggesting that the learning of English is better started as early as possible (a trend that is continuing worldwide, with English language teaching occurring more and more at the primary and even pre-primary levels). Linguistic imperialism "dovetails with communicative, cultural, educational, and scientific imperialism in a rapidly evolving world in which corporate-led globalization is seeking to impose or induce a neo-imperial world order" (Phillipson, 2006, p. 357).

At stake, therefore, in this vision of English linguistic imperialism is not only the ascendency of English in relation to other languages, but also the role English plays in much broader processes of the dominance of forms of global capital and the assumed homogenization of world culture. For Phillipson (2008, p. 38), "acceptance of the status of English, and its assumed neutrality implies uncritical adherence to the dominant world disorder, unless policies to counteract neolinguistic imperialism and to resist linguistic capital dispossession are in force." The issue for Phillipson is *structural power*, the ways that English is promoted through multiple agencies and to the exclusion of other languages. What this obviously lacks is a view of how English is taken up, how people use English, why people choose to use English. As we have seen, critical work often problematizes that notion of choice, arguing that choices are both materially and ideologically constrained.

Phillipson runs the danger of implying that choices to use English are nothing but an ideological reflex of linguistic imperialism. Even when we are suspicious of ideas such as choice – a favorite neoliberal concept – we still have to be cautious about suggesting that all decisions are so structurally or ideologically constrained that they are mere reflections of a global order. What Phillipson shows, therefore, is how and for what purposes English has been deliberately promoted and spread. What he does not show are the effects of that spread in terms of what people do with English. Phillipson takes a fixed view of language (English) and maps it onto a deterministic political framework (imperialism), suggesting thereby not only that the promotion of English supports dominant capitalist and political interests – as O'Regan (2021) shows, this is clearly the case – but also that all English use is equally compromised. It is perhaps the very power of Phillipson's framework that is also its weakness.

While Phillipson usefully locates English within inequitable relations of globalization, there are therefore several limitations to this view. Park and Wee (2012, p. 16) explain that a "problem of linguistic imperialism's macrosocial emphasis is that it does not leave room for more specific and ethnographically sensitive accounts of actual language use." It "dehumanizes the very people it purports to help" (Joseph, 2006, p. 146). In order to equate imperialism with linguistic imperialism, Phillipson has to "materialise language," as Holborow (2012, p. 27) puts it, a position that cannot adequately account for the ways in which English is resisted and appropriated: "The intention is not to *reject* English, but to *reconstitute* it in more inclusive, ethical, and democratic terms" (Canagarajah, 1999a, p. 2). Phillipson's critique of the global spread of English has compelled many to reflect on global inequities in which English plays a role, but his insistence that this should be seen in terms of imperialism has also narrowed the scope of the debate. It is essential, as Blommaert (2010, p. 20) notes, to approach the sociolinguistics of globalization in terms of a "chequered, layered complex of processes evolving simultaneously at a variety of scales and in reference to a variety of centres." We shall return to some of the ways of understanding these processes of resistance, appropriation, and decolonization (Bruthiaux, 2008; Pennycook, 2007), but first we need a short discussion of related frameworks of language rights and ecologies.

Drawing on Tsuda's (1994) distinction between a "diffusion-of-English paradigm" and an "ecology-of-language paradigm," Phillipson and Skutnabb-Kangas (1996) argue that rather than accepting policies that promote the global spread of English, we should work toward the preservation of language ecologies. This notion of language ecology derives from Haugen (1972) and suggests the importance of "the cultivation and preservation of languages" (Phillipson & Skutnabb-Kangas, 1996, p. 441) in a way parallel to how we understand natural ecologies. The notion of language ecologies can be useful since it shows how complex chains of multilingualism may be disturbed by the incursion of literacy or a major language such as English (Mühlhäusler, 1996). The language ecology metaphor, however, can lead toward some very unhelpful ways of thinking about language: A *biologization* of languages as natural species-like objects rather than cultural artifacts; an assumption that while linguistic diversity may be crucial to humans, *enumeration* of language diversity is its most important measure; and an *objectification* of languages as things that adapt to their environment rather than as part of human endeavors to create new worlds (May, 2001; Pennycook, 2004a).

More persuasive has been the related argument in favor of language rights. "We are still living with linguistic wrongs" that are a product of two dangerous myths: A belief in the normality of monolingualism and a concern with the dangers of multilingualism to the security of the nation state (Skutnabb-Kangas, 1998, p. 12). "Unless we work fast," she argues, "excising the cancer of monolingual reductionism may come too late, when the patient, the linguistic (and cultural) diversity in the world, is already beyond saving" (p. 12). What she and Phillipson (Phillipson & Skutnabb-Kangas, 1995; Skutnabb-Kangas & Phillipson, 1994) have proposed, then, are that "universal linguistic human rights should be guaranteed for an *individual* in relation to the *mother tongue(s)*" so that first languages are protected from official languages and language shift, and students gain benefits from educational provision in their first language (Skutnabb-Kangas 1998, p. 22; emphasis in original). This is a more compelling argument for diversity in terms of human rights – a *moral* and *political* argument – than arguments for pluralism for its own sake or as part of a natural ecology.

Powerful as such arguments are, there are also a number of problems. There is a rather strange mix here of the broadly liberal democratic appeal to human rights (as individual rights) and overly simple analyses of social inequalities between "the A-team, the elites of the world, and the B-team, the dominated, ordinary people" (Skutnabb-Kangas (1998, p. 16). This tends to obscure rather than reveal social realities. There are also obvious concerns that "while general proclamations of linguistic human rights may not do much harm, it is doubtful that they can be translated into law" (Coulmas, 1998, p. 72). A more sophisticated line of thinking about minority rights (based particularly around the work of Kymlicka, 1995) has been developed by May (2011; 2017), who argues that "promotion-oriented language rights for language minorities" – that is to say, not just rights tolerating the use of such languages, but rather rights in support of their use in the public domain – may "still be the best means of ensuring the greater recognition and protection of minority languages and their speakers over time" (May, 2017, p. 36).

Arguments in favor of language rights and opposed to language death, however, have been widely critiqued. Wee (2011) questions the idea that languages can have rights, pointing to the reification of languages such a view suggests. The internal conflicts across language varieties may be as important as languages themselves. Mufwene (2016, p. 141) is similarly critical of the idea that language rights could somehow supersede the rights of language users, suggesting that this poses a "wicked problem" for linguists: "what is good for the survival of a particular population in the face of a changing socioeconomic ecology versus what is ideal for the practice of linguistics." Of major concern for Pupavac (2012) are the international forms of governmentality proposed to intervene in local political struggles, an issue that echoes Rassool's (1998, p. 98) questioning of whether "a universalizing discourse on cultural and linguistic pluralism" is an appropriate tool for dealing with linguistic and cultural diversity. As Sonntag (2003) puts it, "the willingness to use the language of human rights on the global level to frame local linguistic demands vis-à-vis global English may merely be affirming the global vision projected by American liberal democracy" (p. 25).

Such critiques raise broader questions about the politics of language and diversity. Coulmas (1998) asks whether the idea that language shift is necessarily so detrimental might be a passing ideological fashion, based as it is on a "nineteenth-century romantic idea that pegs human dignity as well as individual and collective identity to individual languages" (p. 71). Mufwene (2016) notes that these debates about language endangerment and loss have been "marked by a number of disputable assumptions about what languages are and about the terrible price humanity incurs in losing linguistic and cultural diversity as some of them die" (p. 115). This also points to the problem that if, as Sonntag (2003) notes, we frame the issues within Northern political agendas and languages, we miss the point that this may be equally impositional. Put another way, "if we frame the dominance of English by talking of the power of the 'English language' we are casting our concerns in a particular *English* intellectual mould" (Law and Mol, 2020, p. 269; emphasis in original). This is why we need to operate from a framework of *critical resistance* (Hoy, 2004) that demands not just a critical stance toward the world, but also a critical stance toward the ways this is framed.

Ultimately, as Leonard (2017. p.15) argues, we have to ensure that these neocolonial assumptions about language, culture, and preservation, these ways of categorizing and theorizing "Indigenous languages using norms for major global languages," or "Western constructs of what 'language' is when engaging in Indigenous language research, teaching, and advocacy," are put aside, in favour of local control of language reclamation projects. In short, this is about "decolonising 'language'" (Leonard, 2017, p. 32) and decolonizing multilingualism (Phipps, 2019). The constellation of ideas that form around linguistic imperialism, language ecology, and language rights, then, form a powerful and robust critique of the dominance of some languages over others and the threat this may pose to minority languages. As I have stressed elsewhere, these ideas do not necessarily have to occur in conjunction: The neo-Marxist-derived position on imperialism sits at odds with the liberal discourse on rights, and many who argue in favor of language rights and maintenance would eschew the totalizing narrative of linguistic imperialism. Language ecological positions (Stibbe, 2015), meanwhile, particularly taking on board posthumanist and ecofeminist insights (Appleby, 2019), have moved discussions of language and ecology forward considerably.

A theory of imperialism is not a prerequisite to look critically at the politics of language. At the same time, we should be wary of rejecting this dystopian position in favor of the utopian visions of diversity in WE of ELF frameworks. At the very least, if we wish to look at varieties of English, we need to address *unequal Englishes* (Tupas & Rubdy 2015; Tupas & Salonga 2016). Any claim to a variety of English, while at one level a defiance of inner circle norms, is also always a political claim in relation to other varieties, and a claim amid competing social, economic, and political values, a question of *unequal Englishes*, "the unequal ways and situations in which Englishes are arranged, configured, and contested" (Tupas & Rubdy, 2015, p. 3). "Any discussion of English as a global language and its socioeducational implications," Rubdy (2015, p. 43) reminds us, "cannot ignore the fact that far from being a solution to the dismantling of 'unequal power' relations in the world, English is in fact often part of the problem." The notion of *unequal Englishes*, however, only takes us part of the way, since it maintains a pluralist vision of Englishes while pointing to their unequal status. This falls short of grasping the extent of the political and theoretical *delinking* that is necessary to decolonize English (Kumaravadivelu, 2016; Mignolo & Walsh, 2018). More important in relation to the politics of language are close and detailed understandings of the ways in which English is embedded in local economies and relations of power, and it is to this more *situated* understanding of language politics that I now turn.

Situated Language Politics

In line with the framework outlined in the previous chapter, I shall now contrast some of the broad-brush, grand narrative approaches to language politics outlined in the previous section with more situated approaches to language practices. This will then be followed by a broader discussion of strategies of decolonization. We need an understanding of language in relation to power that operates neither with a utopian vision of linguistic diversity, nor with a dystopian assumption of linguistic imperialism. While we ignore Phillipson's warnings at our peril – the idea of linguistic imperialism can be useful for drawing attention to the deliberate policies behind the spread of English – it is important to develop a multifaceted understanding of the politics of language. As Canagarajah (1999b, pp. 41–2) explains, rather than a totalizing assumption of dominance, we need to "find out how linguistic hegemony is experienced in the day-to-day life of the people and communities in the periphery. How does English compete for dominance with other languages in the streets, markets, homes, schools, and villages of periphery communities?"

A theory of imperialism is not the only way to look critically at questions of language politics. More important are close and detailed understandings of the ways in which English is embedded in local economies of desire, and the ways in which demand for English is part of a larger picture of images of change, modernization, access, and longing. It is tied to the languages, cultures, styles, and aesthetics of popular culture, with its particular attractions for youth, rebellion, and conformity; it is enmeshed within local economies, and all the inclusions, exclusions, and inequalities this may entail; it is bound up with changing modes of communication, particularly Facebook, Twitter, and other forms of social media; it is increasingly entrenched in educational systems, bringing to the fore many concerns about knowledge, pedagogy, and the curriculum. We need to understand the diversity of what English is and what it means in all these contexts, and we need to do so not with prior assumptions about globalization and its effects but with critical studies of the local embeddedness of English.

We might still suggest there are many Englishes, but not so much in the terms of language varieties posited by the world Englishes framework, but rather in terms of different Englishes in relation to different social and economic forces. In Iran, for example, English education has been a "site of struggle, in which multiple forces compete" (Borjian, 2013, p. 166) with state and religious opposition to Western forms of modernity attempting to create "an indigenized model of English education, free from the influence of the English-speaking nations" (Borjian, 2013, p. 160). The *indigenization* of English education was not so much a local movement to make English their own, so much as a state ideology to oppose Western influence. In Algeria, by contrast, the growth of English education sits in a different set of complex historical and political relations, involving both French as the former colonial language and postcolonial processes of Arabization. English, as a "new intruder in Algeria's sociolinguistic scenery," suggests Benrabah (2013, p. 124) is caught up in local political struggles around French, Berber, Arabic, colonial legacies, contemporary politics, religion, and economic disparities.

In South Korea "English fever" has driven people to remarkable extremes, from prenatal classes and tongue surgery to sending young children overseas to study. English is a language subject to both neoliberal economic and political practices and "local ideologies and contingencies" (Park, 2013, p. 300). As a new destination for such English language learners, the Philippines markets itself as a place where "authentic English" is spoken, yet its real drawcard is that its English is "cheap and affordable" (Lorente & Tupas, 2014, p. 79). Looking at this local embeddedness in terms of "entanglements of English" in the Philippines (Pennycook, 2020) points to the ways that English is at once a desirable asset for local people – providing access to work in call centers (Friginal, 2009) as well as providing domestic workers with linguistic capital overseas (Lorente, 2017) – a cheap product for wealthier nations in the region, as well as a site of sexual desire in online language classes (Tajima, 2018) and a language that limits educational provision in other languages (Lorente, 2013). It is tied up with a range of local and global forms of inequality (in terms of class, race, and gender) (Reyes, 2017).

Understanding such local entanglements of English – that include both the effects of global political and economic forces and local circumstances of social relations – requires meticulous studies of English and its users, as well as theories of power that are well adapted to contextual understandings. Language education (the focus particularly of Chapter 6) is never just about some linguistic system with a label (English, Chinese, Greek, or Darug) but rather is involved in economic and social change, cultural renewal, people's dreams and desires. As Motha and Lin (2014, p. 332) contend "at the center of every English language learning moment lies desire: Desire for the language; for the identities represented by particular accents and varieties of English; for capital, power, and images that are associated with English; for what is believed to lie beyond the doors that English unlocks." These involve particular constructions of desirability, in terms typically of heterosexuality and race, with White Western men playing a distinctive role in and around English language education (Appleby, 2013; Takahashi, 2013).

To understand language and power in relation to English, therefore, we need to incorporate an understanding of desire (for all those things promised by English) alongside domination (the contingent and contextual effects of this spread), disparity (the inequitable forms of access to English, other languages, and the goods on offer), discrimination (the many exclusionary images and accounts of others embedded in English discourses), and difference (the cultural politics with which English is entangled). These complicities of language and power will be explored further in relation to the construction of social and cultural difference in Chapter 4, and in relation to the politics of pedagogy in Chapter 6. While grand narratives of language politics – linguistic imperialism and language rights – can give us insights into the global operations of languages, they miss the local working of language politics, for which we need ways of understanding the contextual operations of language. As I have been arguing, furthermore, this also requires a decolonial move.

The Decolonial Imperative

As the discussion above suggests, we need to account for the ways in which people react to forms of power, resisting, appropriating, challenging, and changing. People are not mere respondents to the dictates of social structure and ideology but rather are social actors who also resist sites of oppression. These two ways of thinking – Canagarajah (1999b) characterizes them as a *reproduction orientation* (concerned with how power and inequality are reproduced) and a *resistance perspective* (concerned with how people oppose and resist forms of power) – will reoccur at various points in this book (they are important themes in the critical analysis of education, for example, in Chapter 6). The question, when faced with a dominant language such as English, is how "in everyday life, the powerless in post-colonial communities may find ways to negotiate, alter and oppose political structures, and reconstruct their languages, cultures and identities to their advantage" (Canagarajah, 1999b, p. 2). It is to this context of colonial, postcolonial, and decolonial studies that I now turn.

Colonialism and Postcolonialism

I have suggested several times in this chapter that we need to think in terms of decolonizing language. This means addressing the colonial matrix of power that has been central in the creation of both the global inequalities around languages discussed above and the ways in which languages are understood. When Canagarajah (1999b) talks of "post-colonial communities," he is largely referring to the historical fact of having been formerly colonized. In this sense, a postcolonial perspective can inform an historical understanding of language and education. As Rampton (1995a, pp. 325–6) reminds us, there has been a "noticeable failure to address colonial and post-colonial language relationships" when we consider language use in school settings in England in relation to the countries of origin of many of those children (colonial ties with South Asia, West Africa, and the Caribbean). Neglecting such analysis runs the danger of losing a "purchase on the ways in which British discourse about language, foreigners and education have been shaped within particular positions of power."

The term *postcolonial* also carries the sense, however, of opposition, of undoing – as far as this is possible – some of the wrongs of colonialism. In order to understand what is at stake in the decolonial imperative, we need to make a few brief observations about colonialism. In simple terms, we can understand colonialism on the one hand "as a particular phase in the history of imperialism, which is now best understood as the globalization of the capitalist mode of production, its penetration of previously non-capitalist regions of the world, and destruction of pre- or non-capitalist forms of social organization." (Chrisman & Williams, 1994, p. 2). Many of the origins of the current state of global neoliberalism can be understood in terms of the colonial stage of the broader processes of imperialism. As Nandy (1983, p. 1) observes, on the other hand, "It is becoming increasingly obvious that colonialism – as we have come to know it during the last two hundred years – cannot be identified with only economic gain and political power."

For Nandy, colonialism is also a "state of mind in the colonizers and the colonized" (Nandy, 1983, p. 1). As Thomas (1994) puts it, "colonialism is not best understood primarily as a political or economic relationship that is legitimized or justified through ideologies of racism or progress. Rather, colonialism has always, equally importantly and deeply, been a cultural process" (p. 2). In terms of the various critical standpoints I am trying to outline in this book, this by no means questions the significance (or brutality) of the political and economic activities at the heart of colonialism. The issue it raises is the relation between such activities and the ideologies that attended them. Put simply, was the racism that was at the heart of the colonial endeavor developed as a justification for colonial practices or did it also have a partly autonomous coexistence? In many ways, of course, the two are not easily or usefully separable, and it is no coincidence that discourses around race in Europe expanded massively as European empires expanded. The question remains, however, whether we see racist discourse as a secondary product of the political economy of colonialism or as an equal actor in the imperial drive.

Wherever we wish to stand on this point, it is important to appreciate not just how Europe engaged in colonialism but how colonialism *produced* European culture, ideology, and philosophy. Colonialism was the very context in which much of European culture and knowledge was developed. According to Fanon (1961, p. 371), "L'Europe a pris la direction du monde avec ardeur, cynisme et violence" (Europe undertook the leadership of the world with ardor, cynicism, and violence). This is the same Europe "qui jamais ne cessa de parler de l'homme, jamais de proclamer qu'elle n'était inquiète que de l'homme, nous savons ajourd'hui de quelles souffrances l'humanité a payé chacune des victoires de son esprit" (p. 372) (where they were never done talking of Man, and where they never stopped proclaiming that they were only anxious for the welfare of Man: Today we know with what sufferings humanity has paid for every one of their triumphs of the mind).

Fanon's "situated thinking, born of a lived experience that was always in progress, unstable, and changing," (Mbembe, 2017, p. 161) is central to many strands of critical thought, "aimed at smashing, puncturing, and transforming" colonialism and racism (p. 162). Fanon also makes clear the relation between the European enlightenment, with its "grand projects and universal truth-claims" (Young, 1990, p. 9), and the project of European colonialism: "Humanism itself, often validated among the highest values of European civilization, was deeply complicit with the violent negativity of colonialism, and played a crucial part in its ideology" (Young, 1990, p. 121). The fact that ideas about "human nature, humanity and the universal qualities of the human mind as the common good of an ethical civilization" (Young, 1990, p. 121) occurred at the same time as European colonialism always renders claims to humanity and universal qualities suspect (at least when uttered by scholars from the Global North).

Fanon's work remains a cornerstone for a great deal of more recent work under postcolonial or decolonial labels: His deeply political work was always, as Mbembe (2017) reminds us, situated and flexible, yet in ardent opposition to the deep-seated effects of racism and colonialism. Two significant upshots of this work are that many lines of Euro-American thought have their origins in colonial relations, and that critical work has to be able to develop a decolonial stance. As Singh (1996, p. 5) remarks, "Cultural, racial, and moral differences established by colonialism continue to have broad ramifications for the way in which marginal, subordinated races, cultures, economic groups, and sexualities are defined and figured as 'others' in relation to dominant privileged categories." Some of these concerns will be the focus of the next chapter, concerned with ways in which 'difference' has been constructed. For critical applied linguistics, however, an equally central concern is how ideas about language were constructed within colonial relations.

Western academic knowledge and disciplines such as anthropology, linguistics, and economics developed during and as part of the colonial process (Cohn, 1996). The development of an understanding of language and of speakers of languages has therefore to be understood in the context of a particular kind of mapping of linguistic assumptions onto other speakers. According to Monaghan (2012, p. 52), "before anthropologists and linguists came along," Indigenous communities in South Australia "engaged in fluid speech practices and arguably did not have, or indeed need, the concept of a formalised language." As Errington (2001, p. 24) explains, colonial authorities and missionaries "shared a territorial logic that was similarly inscribed in colonial linguistic work, presupposing mappings of monolithic languages onto demarcated boundaries." Once they had established these bounded confines, they assumed the existence of "ethnolinguistically homogeneous groups" in terms of 'tribes' or 'ethnicities' (p. 24). Linguists can therefore be understood as a "rather special group of colonial agents who adapted European letters to alien ways of talking and, by that means, devised necessary conduits for communication across lines of colonial power" (Errington, 2008, p. 4). As a result, the description of languages was intimately linked to the wider colonial emphasis on human hierarchies. The writing and codifying of speech inscribed certain notions of order, hierarchy, and bounded fixity (Makoni & Pennycook, 2007).

In order to try to undo this colonial-linguistic legacy, we need strategies of decolonization. The sometimes ambiguous *postcolonialism* – both a material state after the end of colonialism and a political and cultural movement that seeks to challenge the received histories and ideologies of colonialism (Loomba, 1998; McClintock, 1994) – developed a specific interest in understanding how different texts – novels, travel writing, anthropological texts, colonial documents, maps, and images – were central to the discursive production of colonies and colonized peoples. Edward Said's (1978) work on *Orientalism* is often seen as paradigmatic here as it sought to show how the 'Orient' was a product of European writing. Postcolonial studies have come in for criticism (particularly from critical social scientific orientations), however, because of both the 'post' label (implying colonial relations might be over) and because of its modes of analysis that have more to do with literary theory than political economy. For a number of Indigenous Australians, the idea of postcolonialism obscures the point that they still live under colonial conditions

(Heiss, 2003). Other scholars are skeptical of the term on the grounds that it is a "convenient invention of western intellectuals which reinscribes their power to define" (Smith 1999, p. 14).

Kubota (2016, p. 481) argues that postcolonialism "favors Eurocentric textual analysis and European theorists but overlooks social, economic, and political struggles experienced by the underprivileged." The focus, she suggests, has been too much on discursive construction – from Said onward, Foucauldian discourse analysis has been a key tool of postcolonial studies – and not enough on the racial, social, and economic struggles faced by colonial and postcolonial people. Key postcolonial concepts such as *hybridity* were developed to avoid a colonized versus colonizer dichotomy, to escape essentialist accounts of either colonial imposition or colonized resistance, and to show how colonized people had taken up and appropriated colonial languages and cultures for their own uses. This is a key position in the World Englishes movement, with its argument that "creativity in world Englishes" is based on "various types and levels of hybridity, both linguistic and cultural." This is a "type of hybridity in which African and Asian interculturalism and linguistic innovations and experimentation play a vital role" (Kachru, 2009, p. 463).

The focus on hybridity, however, as a way to overcome these essentializing tendencies, has also been widely critiqued for offering only an endpoint of diversity rather than a more substantial commitment against inequality (Lorente & Tupas, 2014). Kubota (2016) takes the current emphasis on notions of diversity, plurality, flexibility, and hybridity in applied linguistics to task for its lack of engagement with socioeconomic disparities and racial discrimination. Postcolonial theory, she suggests, along with the resultant celebration and romanticisation of diversity and plurality in applied linguistics is complicit with neoliberal ideology, emphasizing diversity at the expense of equality (cf Flores, 2013; though see Canagarajah, 2017, for a more complex understanding). Thus, even though postcolonial studies have arguably long had as a central agenda the identification, dismantling, and overcoming of the regimes of truth produced by colonialism, and even though it has been an important tool for academics in the Global South to reorient curricula away from Northern norms, and while many of the thinkers it has drawn on – from Fanon to Said and Spivak – remain key thinkers in anticolonial movements, the focus of postcolonial studies on discursive rather than political economic formations (as well as its establishment in comfortable Northern academic institutions) have rendered it suspect as an adequate critique of global relations in the wake of colonialism.

La opcíon descolonial

The notion of the *decolonial option* – *la opcíon descolonial* (Mignolo, 2011) – has sought to fill this space, building particularly around a different lineage of South American scholarship such as Dussel's (1977) *Filosofía de Liberación* (liberation philosophy). Central to this work has been Quijano's (1991; 2007) distinction between colonialism (colonial economic and political structures) and coloniality[1] (*colonialidad*), "long-standing patterns of power that emerged as a result of colonialism, but that define culture, labor, intersubjective relations, and knowledge production well beyond the strict limits of colonial administrations" (Maldonado-Torres, 2007 p. 243). This work seeks to reinvigorate the focus on the continued effects of colonial power, arguing for the need to find alternative ways of thinking beyond universal, modern, Western, colonial ideologies, and to work toward new ways of thinking (Mignolo & Walsh, 2018). Mignolo "flatly rejects the assumption that rational and universal truths are independent of who presents them, to whom they are addressed, and why they have been advanced in the first place." (Mignolo, 2011, p. 99). The assumption that one can speak from an anonymous, generalizable, universal position has to be rejected in favor of an understanding of the place from which we speak, the locus of enunciation (De Souza, 2019; Diniz de Figueiredo & Martinez, 2019).

In Maldonado-Torres' words, the *decolonial turn* "introduces questions about the effects of colonization in modern subjectivities and modern forms of life as well as contributions of racialized and colonized subjectivities to the production of knowledge and critical thinking" (Maldonado-Torres, 2007, p. 261–2). The decolonial option, then, offers another way forward in thinking about the effects of colonialism (coloniality) and capitalism on the world, and with the collaboration of Mignolo and Walsh (2018), it has managed to bring a more grounded and pedagogical focus on *praxis* to the discussion. Two ways this line of thinking have been taken up in applied linguistics can be found in Kumaravadivelu's (2016) call to decolonize TESOL and in García's (2014; 2019) insistence that *translanguaging* has a decolonial potency. Drawing on the work of Mignolo (2011) and others, Kumaravadivelu (2016) makes a strong case for a *grammar of decoloniality* that would get beyond studies that attempt patronizingly to show that the non-native teacher can teach as well as their native speaker counterparts. As Kumaravadivelu, has long argued, what we need – rather than the colonial discourses of methods, native speakers, English-only classes, and so on – are "context-specific instructional strategies that take into account the local historical, political, social, cultural, and educational exigencies" (Kumaravadivelu, 2016, p.81). Here, again we see a turn toward the local, the situated, and the specific within a broader politics.

While for some, the focus on *translanguaging* (to which we shall return) does little more than substitute new, and perhaps infelicitous, terminology for perfectly good notions such as bi- or multilingualism, for others such as García (2014), the notion is tied to the broader decolonial struggle. García and Li Wei (2014) connect their own thinking on translanguaging to Mignolo's (2000) *bilanguaging*, which aims at "redressing the asymmetry of languages and denouncing the coloniality of power and knowledge" (p. 231). For Cushman (2016, p. 236), a "translingual approach to meaning making evokes a decolonial lens" through its attempt to question the ideological assumptions that support certain languages, genres, and modes. While Jaspers (2018) may be quite right in questioning the idea that translanguaging is transformative in itself, for García (2019, p. 166), it is part of a project to "denounce the coloniality of power that keeps named languages as walls and barriers to opportunities."

Conclusion: Challenging Politics and Language

This chapter has considered one of the central topics of any form of critical applied linguistics: The ways in which languages operate in relation to power. This is a question not only of language policies, rights, and maintenance, but also of how we think about language itself. By focusing in part on the global spread of English, I have tried to show that different ways of thinking in both linguistic and political terms lead to different outcomes. An insistence on linguistic equality, drawing on conventional linguistic doctrine, has brought us World Englishes and English as a Lingua Franca, and their arguments that English is the property of all, that ownership of English no longer rests in the hands of its so-called native speakers, that English is locally inflected, no longer encumbered by conventional decrees, no longer tied to particular speakers and places. These are important insights, but they lack a more incisive understanding and critique of the global power structures within which English (or any other language) operates. As Williams (1992) puts it, these frameworks may aim to support the disenfranchised, yet they do so with perspectives that reflect the ideologies of the dominant.

The framework that makes language politics central to its formation is the linguistic imperialism and language rights constellation (though imperialism and rights sit rather uncomfortably with each other). Phillipson and Skutnabb-Kangas (1996) argue that English goes hand in hand with processes of "ideological globalization ... transnationalization ... and Americanization and the homogenization of world culture ... spearheaded by films, pop culture, CNN, and fast-food chains" (p. 439). Globalization, however, if understood as complex economic and cultural processes, needs a more intricate vision than one simply of homogenization of world culture (Featherstone, 1990). The "new global cultural economy has to be understood as a complex, overlapping, disjunctive order, which cannot any longer be understood in terms of existing center-periphery models" (Appadurai, 1990, p. 296). As Blommaert (2010) has made clear, in order to understand the sociolinguistics of globalization, we need not only a critical focus on the inequitable structures of global capital but also a clear focus on the multifaceted and intersecting layers of mobile linguistic "*resources*, of the real bits and chunks of language that make up a repertoire, and of real ways of using this repertoire in communication" (p. 173).

Approaches that insist on linguistic or cultural imperialism, on Americanization, and on mass consumer culture taking over the world as part of Western economic and political domination fail to account for cultural and linguistic practices that are produced in resistance, as neither reflecting dominant practices nor based entirely in local ways of doing things, but rather as alternative or *third* spaces (Kramsch, 1993). As studies of the global take-up of forms of popular culture (viewed in critical rather than pejorative terms), such as hip-hop, have shown, rather than assumptions about homogeneity, we need instead to consider how people take up, use, change, appropriate, and transform cultural and linguistic practices (Alim, Ibrahim, & Pennycook, 2009; Pennycook, 2007). The global genre of hip hop is thus "infused with local meaning and values by speakers who 'remix' language varieties" that in a South African context, for example, may include "African-American English (AAE), South African Englishes, Kaaps (a variety of Afrikaans), and local registers such as Sabela and Tsotsitaal in order to navigate local physical spaces, and hip-hop activities and interactions" (Williams 2017, p. 1).

The implication of these arguments is that we have to work contextually, we have to think in terms of situated practices. Canagarajah's (1999b, p. 76) critical ethnographies of resistance focus on the ways the Tamil community in Sri Lanka "appropriates English to dynamically negotiate meaning, identity, and status in contextually suitable and socially strategic ways," thereby modifying "the communicative and linguistic rules of English according to local cultural and ideological imperatives." Once we start to pursue such questions in terms of local contexts of language, it becomes clear that we need to consider English not so much in terms of some inevitable commonality but rather in terms of *worldliness* (Pennycook, 1994b), referring to the ways language is always in the world but not reducible to its worldly circumstances, or in terms of *entanglements* of English (Pennycook, 2020) to show how English is bound up with local and global effects of culture, power, and economy.

This brings us to a key area of contemporary discussion around the politics of language. If we are concerned with questions of language and opportunity, or of language support and maintenance, we have to ask what kinds of applied linguistic action may help people achieve certain goals. While some of this will be saved for a later discussion (Chapter 6) of language, politics, and pedagogy, the question that remains concerns the visions of language and politics with which we work. As Ndhlovu (2018, p. 118) puts it, while the invocation of "high-sounding metaphors of human rights, anti-imperialism and biodiversity resonate with contemporary international conversations around social justice and equity issues," they do not achieve much because "standard language ideology remains ensconced as the only valid and legitimate conceptual framework that informs mainstream understandings of what is meant by 'language'." From this point of view, we will not be able to change conditions of linguistic inequality on political grounds alone; it is only by also challenging linguistic paradigms that we can change the operations of language in terms of disparity and discrimination.

One of the difficulties here hinges on the ambiguity of the phrase 'standard language ideology.' For many linguists, this refers to the promotion of standardized language over other varieties, which, from a liberal egalitarian point of view is inappropriate: All varieties are equal in their own (structural) terms, so none is better than any other. From a more critical linguistic point of view, however, 'standard language ideology' refers to this very view, the institutionalized linguistic vision of language equality. We may wish equality of languages where there is none, but unless we grapple with a broader set of linguistic inequalities, we may fail in our political goals. This takes us back to discussions around attempts to shift both the political and linguistic terrain. Some of this can be traced back to Rampton's (1995a) focus on *language crossing*, "the use of language varieties associated with social or ethnic groups that the speaker does not normally 'belong' to" (p. 14). Such a view of language use depends on a nonessentialist stance, a refusal of static categories of *ethnicity* and *belonging*, and an understanding of the possibilities of using language against the grain, of taking up and using a language that has been a tool of oppression, colonialism, or rigid identity and turning it against itself.

For some, such as MacSwan (2020, p. 321), translinguistic approaches that question standard language ideologies (what he calls a "deconstructivist perspective") are "at odds with a civil rights orientation, the backbone of language education policy in the United States." From this point of view, we need to operate with languages as commonly conceived in order to argue for language rights, the argument being that if standard language ideologies are the common currency, these are the terms in which we should operate. There are similarities here with the 'language of power' arguments discussed in Chapter 5: If we can identify what is powerful, then that is what we should teach. For others, however, grasping the challenges to linguistic orthodoxies presented by translinguistic perspectives opens up new alternatives for language activism. Language revival, as Zuckermann (2020) makes clear, is never about bringing the same language back to life: It always involves change and the influence of other languages. Indigenous language practices in Arnhem Land (North Australia) are characterized "by diversity, flexibility, fluidity, and the depth and nuance of linguistic repertoires." Such "translingual practices" are the "ordinary and unremarkable …stuff of everyday communication in peripheral communities" (Vaughan, 2020, p. 99). From this perspective, language activism is best carried out with ways of understanding language that accord with local practices rather than assumed language definitions.

Some of these tensions can be partly resolved by recalling Spivak's (1993) notion of "the strategic use of essentialism." As Spivak points out, the "critique of essentialism" should be understood not as an exposure of our or others' errors but as "an acknowledgment of the dangerousness of something one cannot not use" (p. 5). Notions such as language rights and linguistic imperialism are powerful and can be very effective for pointing out issues of great moral and political concern. Putting such terms onto the applied linguistic agenda and into the applied linguistic vocabulary is important. Strategically used, they can be significant tools in critical applied linguistic struggles, but we also need to acknowledge the dangerousness of these terms that we cannot not use. Using essentialism strategically is at least one way to do one's politics. As Rajagopalan (1999, p. 201) suggests, the notion of linguistic imperialism derives from a way of thinking based in "an intellectual climate of excessive nationalist fervor… an intellectual climate where identities were invariably thought of in all-or-nothing terms." This reinforces the point that without a form of *critical resistance* (Hoy, 2004) that is critical of both the world and the terms in which we make these criticisms, without a decolonial option (Kumaravadivelu, 2016; Maldonado-Torres, 2007) that can delink us from the normative terms of the debate, we will not be able to engage adequately with the politics of language.

In conclusion, a critical applied linguistic approach to language needs social, political, and economic analyses that locate language within a critical exploration of inequality. It is imperative that we develop useful, subtle, and situated analyses of language and power. Part of the process of developing critical applied linguistics has to be in the ways we work both with and against critical concepts such as class, patriarchy, or imperialism. Such analyses need to take us beyond determinist or pessimistic visions that leave little space for change: Critical applied linguistics needs forms of enquiry that can lead to forms of action. We need not only large-scale theories of society but also ways of thinking about change, resistance, and alternatives. It is important to have a vision of language that not only reflects but also produces and therefore can alter social relations. As Cameron (1990) argues, a position that suggests that language merely reflects society suggests that the only domain for change must be social change: We need instead a way of thinking about language that suggests that change in language may also produce change in society, whether that be in terms of gender relations, racism, or language policy. Otherwise, both our analysis and our pedagogy remain paralyzed.

Note

1. In the first edition of this book, drawing on other sources, I made a distinction between postcoloniality (conditions following colonialism) and postcolonialism (theoretical attempts to deal with the colonial legacy). Since this is rather different from Quijano's (2007) formulation (colonialism is the fact, coloniality the legacy), I have removed this discussion to avoid confusion.

4   The Politics of Difference

I suggested in Chapter 2 that different ways of approaching difference had to be an important part of any critical applied linguistic discussion. There are a number of concerns at stake here: For some, it is better to view difference as only "skin deep": We are all the same underneath. This humanist or universalist position is a nice liberal egalitarian ideal, but it fails to engage either with the very real differences that are part of being human, or with the very real differences that are constructed by humans about each other. Particular ways of considering difference also overlook how difference works: Categorizations of difference in some positivist social science traditions – notable particularly in Second Language Acquisition (SLA) studies – tend toward simplified classifications such as 'sex' (M/F) or 'socioeconomic status' that do little to help us understand what may lie behind lives lived along certain gender and class lines. From this point of view, the search is generally for universal patterns of cognition, so social difference is nothing more than a variable that may affect the ways we think. Other studies, meanwhile, have sought to take cultural differences seriously but have done so along lines that render culture or nation or gender or race or sexuality a static pattern of beliefs and behaviors that predetermine the way we do things.

This problem of *essentialism* has received considerable critical attention. As Spack (1997) has observed, TESOL and applied linguistics is full of generic labels such as *foreign, other, different,* or *limited* to describe the learners in language classrooms. García (2019, p. 152) makes a related point that the division of languages into *second, first, foreign, heritage,* and so on is "a construction of western powers, and especially their schools, to consolidate power and create governable subjects." When students are described in cultural terms, this tends to be done in terms of an "archaic view of culture" in which "a fixed profile of particular traits for a particular cultural group" (Spack, 1997, p. 768) is repeated over and over again. This view of cultural *fixity* is part of a long history of colonial othering (see also Chapter 3) that has rendered other cultures fixed, traditional and exotic, whereas the cultures of the Euro-American center are assumed to be dynamic, contemporary, and transparent (Pennycook, 1998a). Possibly the *locus classicus* of this work remains the cultural thought patterns created by Robert Kaplan (1966) in which "Oriental" students think in spirals while Westerners think in straight lines. Drawing on the work of Said (1978), Susser (1998) points to the considerable Orientalism in applied linguistic writing on Japan, "a pervasive discourse that shapes our descriptions and then our perceptions of Japanese learners and classrooms" (p. 64). Kubota (1999) points to the ways in which concepts such as *individualism, self-expression, critical thinking,* and *extending knowledge* have been linked to Western cultures while their supposed counterparts – *collectivism, harmony, indirection, memorization,* and *conserving knowledge* – have been attributed to Asian cultures.

In this chapter, I argue for the importance of a politics of difference for critical applied linguistics, a view that difference is constructed and engaged with amid questions of power (Kubota, 2004). An important part of this discussion acknowledges that lines of difference are produced through human frames of reference: Physical differences that may mark human dissimilarities (height, hair color, body shape, accent, and so on) only take on significance in so far as they are combined in particular ways, along particular lines of historical discrimination, and these may change according to changing circumstances. A good example is Ibrahim's (1999) study of how a group of immigrant African youths "become Black" as they engage with possible forms of language and identity in their school in Canada. They may already be differentiated along lines of language, culture, ethnicity, nationality, and so on, but "faced with a *social imaginary*" in the racialized world of North America, a framework in which they are already defined as Black, they start to identify with certain linguistic and cultural forms, such as "*Black stylized English* (BSE), which they accessed in and through Black popular culture" (Ibrahim, 1999, p. 351). Their identification as Black (an identification that was not necessarily salient as they grew up) then becomes a resource for particular ways of walking and talking, and particular forms of engagement with popular culture (such as hip hop) and politics.

In this chapter, then, we will focus on forms of difference – typically along lines of class, race, gender, and sexuality – and why they matter for any critical applied linguistic project. We will look at second language learning, identity, and subjectivity in an attempt to understand why it is so important to understand the ways in which language learner identifications matter. We will consider the ways in which difference (particularly gender and race) is constructed, but is no less real as a result. A focus on gender in particular will help consider how different ways of thinking about gender and power – in terms of domination, difference, and performativity – bring us to different ways of thinking about language and difference. The ways that forms of difference operate in conjunction – commonly called *intersectionality* – will also be important, before we return to a theme flagged earlier (see introduction): Whether a focus on "recognition" (the struggle to recognize forms of difference) should be subservient to the greater goal of "redistribution" (the reallocation of wealth within a more just political economy) as some have argued (Block, 2018c). I will argue, by contrast, that, as Fraser (2000) suggests, the issue is one of thinking through how the recognition of difference can be thought of in social terms (issues of social participation) rather than as an isolated question of cultural respect.

Difference, Identity, and Language Learning

Of all the domains of applied linguistics that have most resisted a critical engagement with social context, SLA has been the most determined. Lantolf suggests that SLA "presents a lopsided and uncritical view of both itself and the scientific tradition from which it arises, and it precipitously dismisses those who would challenge it" (Lantolf, 1996, p. 716). The problems here have been a rigidly cognitivist orientation to language learning (it is something that just happens in the head), coupled with a positivist research tradition that allows for a focus on cognition in isolation, and an unwillingness to discuss other ways of thinking about learning. Much of this came to a head in the mid-1990s, when skirmishes between those arguing for a much wider set of options (Block, 1996; Firth & Wagner, 1997) – "letting all the flowers bloom" (Lantolf, 1996) – were met with a rearguard action to let as few flowers bloom as possible (Gregg, Long, Jordan, & Beretta 1997). Nothing very productive can be gained from revisiting these debates (see Seidlhofer, 2003, for a summary), but they mark a particular moment in applied linguistics when studies of language development bifurcated.

What was for a long time considered mainstream SLA research proceeded in its narrow focus on the "linguistic–cognitive" dimensions of additional language learning (Ortega, 2014, p. 33), assuming that language was a set of grammatical and lexical items learned in sequential order and that this learning was something that occurred in the head. This cognitive-information-processing model, with its computer-oriented metaphors – input, output, language data, attention-getting devices, and so forth (Johnson, 2004) – has continued on much the same path with its rather particular assumptions about the internal divisibility of languages into structural constituents and an external divisibility into demarcated languages. Humans, meanwhile, could be divided internally into minds and bodies, and externally into creatures separated from other animals and the world around them (Pennycook, 2018a). This strange way of thinking about language and humans led to a vision of language development where the brain operated more or less independently of the body as a kind of computing machine, a cognitive sandwich (Waters, 2012) which processed language input before emitting forms of output.

A range of alternative approaches, however, tried to bring *sociocultural* factors back into the picture, insisting that learning could only be understood in its social and cultural contexts. McKay and Wong's (1996, p. 603) study of adolescent Chinese immigrant students in the United States insists that instead of the "generic, ahistorical, 'stick figure' of the learner painted in much literature on second-language learning learners," they need to be understood as complex social actors, with "a multitude of fluctuating, at times conflicting, needs and desires" operating in "complex social environments that consist of overwhelmingly asymmetrical power relations and subject the learners to multiple discourses." Norton Peirce (1995) took SLA research to task for the unhelpful dichotomization between learners and contexts, the uncritical theorizing of social contexts, and the failure to look at questions of power and access. For Rampton (1995b), work in SLA "could probably benefit from an enhanced sense of the empirical world's complex socio-cultural diversity" (p. 294). Gebhard (1999) argues for a "sociocultural perspective" on language development that takes as a starting point "an understanding that the origin and structure of cognition are rooted in daily social and cultural practices in which an individual participates" (p. 544). From this point of view, SLA is seen as "an institutional phenomenon shaped by cultures and structures at work in educational systems" (p. 545) and "schools are structured cultural spaces that play a role in the distribution of discourse practices and the production and reproduction of social orders" (p. 554).

Sociocultural theorists of language learning (Johnson, 2004; Lantolf, 2000) have insisted that cognition is always social to start with, and that to understand language development, we have to focus on interaction and activity (Lantolf and Thorne, 2006). Alongside these *sociocultural* approaches – drawing to various degrees on Vygotskyan social psychology and its materialist origins (Holborow, 1999) – another sociocultural endeavor was Norton Peirce's (1995, p. 579) insistence on understanding the "language learner as having a complex social identity that must be understood with reference to large and frequently inequitable social structures which are reproduced in day-to-day social interactions." As she developed this notion of social identity, Norton (1997, p. 420) insisted that power and social institutions were central to understanding "the relationship between the individual and the larger social world, as mediated through institutions such as families, schools, workplaces, social services and law courts." Critiquing the SLA tendency to box up social difference into a series of "variables," Norton (2000, p. 13) goes on to suggest that ethnicity, gender, and class are not so much background variables bur are rather "in complex and interconnected ways, implicated in the construction of identity and the possibilities of speech."

As work along these lines suggests, "in educational practice as in other facets of social life, identities and beliefs are co-constructed, negotiated, and transformed on an ongoing basis by means of language" (Duff and Uchida, 1997, p. 452). As others argue, we have to grasp the dynamic interplay between "fixed identity categories that are applied to social groupings" – such as race, gender, ethnicity, and language – and the ways people "think of themselves as they move through the different discourses in which these categories are salient" (Thesen, 1997, p. 488). Norton's (2000) view of identity draws on poststructuralist accounts of subjectivity, referring to the ways in which our identity is formed through discourse. Identities, from this perspective, are multiple, a site of struggle, and change over time. As Lather (1992, p. 101) explains, subjectivity is seen "both as socially produced in language, at conscious and unconscious levels, and as a site of struggle and potential change." Poststructuralist theories of the subject emphasize that neither background nor experience alone can account for identity; rather it is constructed through a web of class, race, gender, language, and social relations. From this point of view, the person takes up different subject positions within different discourses, and language – or discourse – is a crucial element in the formation of subjectivity.

Performing Subjectivities

While this perspective brought social categories of gender, race, sexuality, and ethnicity into the picture, and insisted that language learning could not be understood without an account of institutional power, it has also been taken to task for not going far enough in exploring how discourse and identity operate. As Thesen (1997) points out, Norton's reliance on "single identity markers" such as "*primary caregiver* or *multicultural citizen*" (p. 505) still leave us with rather fixed identity options. Price (1996, p. 336) suggests that for all the focus on discourse, society, and power, this view of identity "rests ultimately on an appeal to individual capacities and does not explore far enough the way the individual subject/learner is implicated in social and discourse practices." This question hinges on how it is that we actually "take up" subject positions, how it is that we actually become subjects of and subject to discourses. From a poststructuralist point of view, which downplays questions of agency, and questions the individual/social divide (McNamara, 2019), any suggestion that people deliberately choose between discourses runs counter to the whole idea that we are the products of discourse. For Price (1999) and McNamara (2019), the struggle here is to understand how in the ongoing production of discourse – in conversations, for example – subjectivities are performed. We shall return to questions of performativity later in this chapter.

Once we start to see identities not so much as fixed social or cultural categories but as a constant ongoing negotiation of how we relate to the world, then we have to acknowledge that second language classrooms, speech therapy sessions, literacy in the workplace, or the process of translating have a great deal to do with questions of identity formation and transformation. If we take seriously the idea that engagement in discourse is part of the continuing construction of subjectivity, then language classrooms (Morgan, 1997), academic writing (Clark and Ivanič, 1997), and many other fields of applied linguistics are deeply concerned not only with language learning or writing conventions, but also with questions of identity, which in turn are related to social categories, institutions, and questions of power. From this point of view, engagement with particular languages and cultures must also be about identity formation. Identities or subjectivities are constantly being produced in the positions people take up in discourse. So the question of possibilities, of what different possible forms of difference we create, acknowledge, or oppose, is a crucial one whether viewed from the point of view of students, teachers, or researchers.

From its narrow focus on fixed forms of identity and language learning as solely a cognitive activity, "signs indicate that SLA as a field is willing and able to make space for social views of language learning" (Ortega, 2018, p. 65). The work of the Douglas Fir Group (2016), for example, aims to incorporate social dimensions to the standard SLA framework through an interdisciplinary approach, a new, rethought SLA" that can "contribute to the development of innovative and sustainable lifeworld solutions that support language learners in a multilingual world" (Douglas Fir Group, 2016, p. 39). Ortega (2019) sees some hope in both the World Englishes model (see Chapter 3) – for providing a more pluralistic vision of language – and the DFG model for opening up social considerations of language learning, and enabling a push toward "considering multilingualism as the central object of inquiry and embracing social justice as an explicit disciplinary goal" (Ortega, 2019, p. 24).

These changes are generally positive (even if making "space for social views of language learning" is a somewhat limited starting point), though in relation to a wider critical applied linguistic agenda, there is evidently a long way to go: The 'multilingual turn' (May, 2014; Ortega, 2014) in socio- and applied linguistics is doubtless to is to be welcomed, but it is less a critical orientation than a recognition of where we should be starting from. The pluralistic model of World Englishes is likewise better than monological views of language, but, as discussed in Chapter 3, frames issues in liberal egalitarian terms, and thus lacks a political engagement with difference. A commitment to social justice is also an overdue change but social justice perspectives, as discussed in Chapter 2, generally lack a clear analysis of inequality.[1] For Kramsch and Zhang (2018), the "utopian" model of language learning in the DFG framework, with its transdisciplinary perspectives, and put-everything-in compromises, still feels out of touch with classroom realities or questions of power and difference. Alongside considerations about developing simple models to describe complex practices (rather than these complex models to account for simple ideas) (Yunkaporta, 2019), approaches to SLA need to engage in much more comprehensive ways with questions of gender, sexuality, and race (Flores & Rosa, 2019).

Language, Gender, Sexuality, and Difference

For obvious reasons – clear forms of linguistic discrimination and ample numbers of people (especially women) in the field ready to examine these concerns – the relations among gender, language, and power have received considerable attention and offer some clear ways in which we can distinguish different ways of looking at the politics of difference. Forms of discrimination against women in and through language are widely attested: Women are stereotyped as talkative, while at the same time, they are frequently silenced or ignored; many languages have a range of derogatory terms for women; it is also common for apparent male/female terms ('stud' and 'slut' being a well-known example in English) to suggest radically different moral evaluations of sexual behavior; women are often relegated to private rather than public language domains; women's use of language frequently bears signs of lower social status; women's ways of talking are not accorded respect; male norms and terms (nouns, pronouns, and so on) are generally taken as the norm, as representative of humans, while women are subsumed within these categories (Pauwels, 1998). Clearly, language is an important site of the reproduction of gendered inequality, but to understand how gender and sexuality may relate to a range of issues in applied linguistics, we need to consider carefully what models of language, power, and identity we are using. It is to questions of difference in terms of language, gender, and sexuality that I therefore turn in this section.

Dominance, Difference, and Performativity

An obvious starting point is the observation that men have more power than women, and this is reflected in language (or silences): "Men's language is the language of the powerful," as Lakoff (1990, p. 205) puts it in her key early work. "It is the language of people who are in charge in the real world. Women's language developed as a way of surviving and even flourishing without control over economic, physical or social reality." (p. 205). Studies of language and gender have long divided the field into two camps: Dominance or difference (see Table 4.1). As Coates (1998, p. 413) explains, research based on a *dominance* perspective "interprets the differences between women's and men's linguistic usage as reflexes of the dominant-subordinate relationship holding between men and women." In this view, language use between people of different genders reflects different social power. Although this has the advantage of making research on language and gender from the outstart a political question, it has the drawback of making women's language nothing but a negative reaction to the language of men. As discussions of power in this book have already highlighted, all-or-nothing accounts of power, a description of the powerless in terms of a *deficit* (for further discussion see Chapter 6), and the assumption that language reflects reality lack an adequate sociolinguistics of difference.

Table 4.1 Dominance, Difference, and Performativity

	Dominance	*Difference*	*Performativity*
Gender and power	Men have power; women lack power	Men and women are socialized separately	Gender and sex are produced rather than pregiven categories
Gender and language	Men's language is more powerful than women's	Men and women use language differently and misunderstand each other	People perform gendered identities through language
Possibilities for change	Change society (and power) or teach women to use powerful language	Teach men and women to understand their competitive and cooperative ways	Show how genders are performed, not essential, parts of identities

Already in Lakoff's (1990, p. 205) comment "and even flourishing," we can see a reluctance to relegate the disempowered to a state of helplessness. Similar concerns emerged in the discussion in the previous chapter of resistance to English in and through the language. Research from the *difference* perspective "sees the differences between women's and men's linguistic usage as arising from the different subcultures in which women and men are socialized" (Coates, 1988, p. 413). In this view, men are socialized with men, and women with women, and the miscommunication between the two is a form of cultural miscommunication. This position has been popularized by the work of Deborah Tannen (1990) in books such as *You Just Don't Understand: Women and Men in Conversation.* The advantage of this approach is that it has been able to look at women's language as a cultural behavior (and thus as different) and not as a social reflex. The disadvantage is that it tends to remove the political dimension from the equation, focusing on difference as a result of differing socialization rather than unequal social power.

The move to understand women's language as separate but different has therefore been a move to "celebrate women's ways of talking" (Coates, 1998, p. 413). As critical reviews of Tannen's work (Cameron, 1995; Troemel-Ploetz, 1991) suggest, however, a view that locates gender relations merely in terms of miscommunication between two subcultures is a dangerously apolitical view of language and gender, largely removing questions of power from the picture. And since, as Cameron (1995) makes clear, suggestions for change based on this difference model of language tend simply to celebrate difference and thus ignore all the inequitable gendered relations of society, any proposal for change "based on the 'difference' model is a good deal less radical than its exponents imagine" (p. 198). This line of thinking also deteriorated into populist books on gender difference, such as Gray's (1992) *Men are from Mars, Women are from Venus,* painstakingly debunked by Cameron (2007). At the very least, the dominance position has needed greater complexity, while the difference position has needed more politics (and more complexity).

While this distinction has enabled useful discussions about language, gender, and power, both orientations have tended to offer static and stereotyped descriptions of gendered language. Johnson (1997) points to two main problems with much of this work on language and gender. On the one hand, both the so-called dominance and difference models "are characterized by almost exclusive *problematization of women*" (p. 10) with little attempt to understand men as anything other than an "all-purpose male oppressor" who "talks too much, interrupts and generally dominates conversations with women" (p. 11). On the other hand, there is an "implicit assumption that men and women are binary opposites, and that speech constitutes a symbolic reflection of that opposition" (p. 11). Such assumptions detract from any serious study of language and gender, enabling a search for linguistic correlates that "verify presumed oppositions between male and female language usage" (p. 11). Once one goes looking for such correlates, it is not hard to interpret them in favor of such preconceived assumptions of difference (Cameron, 1997).

This takes us back to a recurring theme throughout this book that unless we problematize assumptions about power and dichotomous ways of thinking (men–women; dominant–dominated; oppressed–oppressors; haves–have-nots; emancipated–unemancipated), we fail to unravel the very questions we are seeking to understand. Once we appreciate the ways in which social lives and questions of gender, class, ethnicity, age, health, knowledge, education, and so on intersect, it is evident that we need to understand the operations of power in a nonreductive way. Discussing the range of contradictory advice to women as to whether they should therefore use language as men do or accept and value their own language as different, Cameron (1995) suggests that in "this whole contradictory discourse, the most important common factor is simply the idea of an eternal opposition between 'masculine' and 'feminine' styles." Thus, any kind of change "based on the a priori acceptance of an all-pervading gender duality will end up being co-opted to reactionary ends, because the starting assumption is itself reactionary" (p. 200).

Circular arguments about language and gender have been confronted by challenges to the male-female binary, notably through questions around sexuality, performativity, Queer theory, and the rise of the LGBTIQA+ movement in recent years. According to Butler (1990), gender is not a noun, something we do or have, but rather "gender proves to be performative—that is constituting the identity it is purported to be. In this sense, gender is always a doing, though not a doing by a subject who might be said to preexist the deed" (p. 25). Gender, then, is "the repeated stylization of the body, a set of repeated acts within a highly regulatory frame that congeal over time to produce the appearance of substance, of a natural sort of being" (p. 33). If the gender-as-difference position may be seen, in terms of the frameworks outlined in Chapter 2, as a liberal egalitarian view (all would be well if only we could understand each other better), and the gender-as-dominance position as a modernist view of power in the hands of the powerful (Kramsch, 2021), Butler's (1990) argument sits more comfortably within a view of situated practices: Gender is not a pregiven category, an essence of men and women, but rather an effect of repeated social practices, since "language *produces* the categories through which we organize our sexual desires, identities and practices" (Cameron & Kulick, 2003, p. 19) (figure 4.1).

Relating Butler's thinking to questions of language and gender, Cameron (1997) argues that the focus needs to be not so much on gender differences as the difference gender makes. This view has major implications not merely for questions of gender and sexuality but for all understandings of difference, identity, and power. Indeed, Cameron (1995) suggests that for gender here, "we could substitute any apparently fixed and substantive social identity label" (p. 16). The question then becomes not how language use reflects pregiven gender/sex differences but how the construction of difference is related to the production of dominance. Rather than assuming, as in traditional approaches to sociolinguistics, that "people talk the way they do because of who they (already) are," we need to turn this round and consider that "people are who they are because of (among other things) the way they talk" (Cameron, 1997, p. 49). The point then becomes, echoing Butler's rethinking of Austin (1962) (how to do things with words), how to do gender with language: "What is important in gendering talk is the 'performative gender work' the talk is doing; its role in constituting people as gendered subjects" (Cameron, 1997, p. 59).

For those who see in Butler's idea of performativity too easy a pulling-on and taking-off of identity, Butler (1993) explains that these are not voluntary acts of gender performance but highly regulated practices: "performativity is neither free play nor theatrical self-presentation; nor can it simply be equated with performance" (Butler, 1993, p. 95). As Butler conceives the term, it gives us important ways of understanding the local contingencies of identity formation. This can then help us understand the discussion earlier about identity, when Price (1996) questions Norton Pierce's (1995) views of how people take on identities: It's not so much a question of choosing a discursive position as of engaging in discourse that produces our subjectivity. The notion of performativity (Cameron, 1997; Pennycook, 2004b; 2007), therefore, gives us a useful way forward in seeking to avoid simplistic assumptions about how men and women talk, suggesting instead that it is in the situated practices of social engagement that language and gender co-construct each other.

Beyond Inclusivity: Engagement and Intersectionality

Understandings of gender and sexuality have been undergoing major shifts over the last few decades (at least in some parts of the world), as ideas such as *marriage equality* gain ground (though it is largely an inclusive idea of equality, and arguably a conservative move toward social conformity). Back in the early 1990s, when the first symposium was held at a TESOL conference on lesbian and gay concerns in English language teaching (for those of us who attended that first event, it was an exhilarating but perilous moment), there had been minimal attention to questions of sexual orientation in the field. As Nelson (1993) suggested (in her paper from that forum), there remain many basic attitudes in second language education that need to be shifted, including a general assumed heterosexism; a belief that questions of sexual preference have no place in ESL; a belief that students from other countries would find questions of sexual orientation too controversial and that dealing with such questions would be moving into unjustifiable tampering with people's social lives; a sexist acknowledgment of gay men in ESL but ignorance of lesbian teachers; and a tendency for straight teachers to assume gay and lesbian issues are not their concern and should only be addressed by gay and lesbian teachers themselves.

As Nelson convincingly argued, all these assumptions need to be questioned. Gay and lesbian teachers and students are denied the possibility of expressing and using those parts of their identities linked to their sexual orientation: "Because of heterosexism, those of us who are involved in gay culture often feel we must hide any expression of that culture" (Nelson, 1993, p. 144); students often have many and interesting things to say about sexuality; it is the responsibility of all teachers to bring questions of sexuality to bear on their work for we all have sexual orientations. Jewell's (1998) study of a transgendered student in an ESL class shows how she struggles to find possible spaces to speak and roles to identify with: "For Jackie, sexuality is fundamental to social identity. Like her, some people actively promote a gay or transgendered identity, but this is clearly not reflected in ESL textbooks and their rigid consideration of sex-roles and relationship possibilities in society" (p. 9). More generally, Jewell suggests "precisely because there are gay students in our classes, we need to incorporate their stories, experiences and ideas into the classroom dialogue, so that they, too, feel as worthy and represented as any other student in that space" (pp. 6–7).

There is a danger, however, that such arguments remain at the level of what Britzman (1995) terms "pedagogies of inclusion" (p. 158). Liberal-egalitarian stances may well move beyond positions of tolerance (it's OK to be gay) toward a position of inclusion (let's make sure questions of sexuality are part of the curriculum) but may still lack the tools for a deeper engagement with difference. Schenke (1996) has strongly criticized what she calls "the tired treatment of gender and 'women's lib' in many of our ESL textbooks" (p. 156). In place of these worn-out, liberal, issues-based approaches, she proposes what she calls a "practice in historical engagement," a focus on "the struggle over histories (and forgetting) in relation to the cultures of English and to the cultures students bring with them to the classroom already-knowing" (p. 156). From this point of view, then, questions of difference, identity, and culture are not merely issues to be discussed but are about how we have come to be as we are, how discourses have structured our lives. Questions of gender or race, therefore, make up the underlying rationale for the course. "Feminism," Schenke argues, "like antiracism, is thus not simply one more social issue in ESL but a way of thinking, a way of teaching, and, most importantly, a way of learning" (p. 158).

As Misson (1996) argues with respect to homophobia, and Fazal Rizvi (1993) in the context of racism, to develop antihomophobic or antiracist education requires much more than simply some rational, intellectual explanation of what's wrong with racism and homophobia. 'Error correction' does not take us far enough (Lewis, 2018). Rather, we need an engagement with people's investment in particular discourses, that is, in questions of *desire*: "Our subscription to certain beliefs is not just a rational or a socially-determined thing, but we invest in them because they conform to the shape of our desires" (Misson, 1996, p. 121). As discussed in Chapter 2, a major challenge for critical work is both how it theorizes power and how it views ways of disentangling from relations of power. A problem with modernist approaches to critical consciousness is the assumed pathway from challenging ideology (which masks the truth), to awareness (understanding ideological obfuscation) and emancipation (the possibility of conducting oneself outside of such falsehoods) (Table 4.2).

This view presupposes notions of ideology and rationality that do not easily accord with an appreciation of how we live our lives. Critical education that aims to change how things are needs to engage with people's desires (Fuery, 1995) rather than just hope to change people's minds. A similar point was

Table 4.2 Inclusivity, Awareness, and Engagement

	Liberal Inclusivity	*Critical Awareness*	*Situated Engagement*
Focus	A pedagogy of inclusion and tolerance of diversity	Bringing awareness of difference and inequality	Understanding difference as it is produced in practice
Mode	Representations of diversity in texts, curricula, and classrooms	Increased awareness leading to empowerment or emancipation	Genealogical and narrative accounts of difference and desire

made in Chapter 3 with respect to people's desire for English and the goods it claims to deliver: To understand and undo relations of language, gender, race, and sexuality, we need to consider issues of desire (preferences and investments in ways of being) alongside domination (the very apparent relations of power between men and women as they are played out in everyday contexts), disparity (the inequitable access that men and women have to material and cultural goods), discrimination (the evident and ongoing forms of discrimination that are embedded in language and discourse), and difference (the ways in which gendered differences are produced in interaction).

Rather than an *inclusionary* approach, this requires an *engagement focus* in language education and other areas of critical applied linguistics. Identifications along gender, race, class, sexuality, disability, and so on are so fundamental to identity and language that they can never just be things we add on to the curriculum for discussion. Narrative or memory work in pedagogy and research suggest that telling stories is about accounting for how our bodies and desires got here. As we work to engage critically, poetically, historically, hermeneutically, and narratively (Kearney, 1988), we need to find ways of engaging with lives, bodies, and desires. The idea of *engaged pedagogy* derives in part from bell hooks' (1994) pedagogical approach that addresses questions of class, race, and gender and seeks *transgressive* ways of teaching (Florence, 1998). For hooks (1994), the inclusion of questions of race, gender, and class in discussions is all too superficial in that it fails to take into account the student histories and subjectivities. This engagement focus, then, links questions of identity, politics, and language directly and sees different formations of identity as intertwined.

For Schenke (1991), a feminist pedagogy of ESL can be engaged through "a *genealogical* practice in memory work." Similar to Butler's (1990) call for "a *feminist genealogy* of the category of women" (p. 5), Schenke is arguing against an essentialized notion of women and instead seeking to work from a feminist perspective that acknowledges the complex interrelations between constructions of gender and other socially and culturally constructed forms of identity or subjectivity. From this point of view, there is no neutral, nurturing, womanly space outside relations of power, only the need to constantly work through and against certain operations of power. As with Nelson's (1999) understanding of the interrelations between sexuality, gender, and cultural difference, or Ibrahim's (1999) interweaving of questions of race, gender, and popular culture, Schenke is here getting at the multiplicity of concerns in any pedagogical moment.

This takes us to another important contemporary theme: *Intersectionality* (Crenshaw, 1991; Arrighi, 2007), the point being that these dimensions of class, race, and gender cannot in any useful sense be taken on their own: Class constantly intersects with race (institutional racism has very obvious socioeconomic implications), gender with class (structural inequalities in the job market), and so on. This may be about a handwritten "Trans Black Lives Matter" sign at a Black Lives Matter rally or the educational intersections of class, race, and gender. As bell hooks (1989; 1994; 1996) has long argued, forms of domination and discrimination are interconnected: Rather than a hierarchy of discrimination, we need to see gender, race, and class together. Acknowledging the interlocking layers of discrimination and disempowerment has been a common theme in critical scholarship for a long time, without necessarily being named in this way. Tara Goldstein's (1996) study of how class, language choice, and gender interact on the shop floor of a factory in Canada was clear about this, as was Crawford's (1999) study of communication in Cape Town (RSA) health services, where the relationship between patients, nurses, and doctors is interwoven with issues of power in language, culture, translation, race, and gender. Such studies acknowledge that race, class, and gender operate not in isolation but rather as a "trilogy of oppression and discrimination" (Knapp, 2005, p. 255).

The adoption of Crenshaw's (1991) term *intersectionality* has constantly reminded us of the importance of seeing how categories such as gender, race, and class are both internally divided – the forms of discrimination and oppression encountered by women are not uniform and White women's experience may be very different from those of Black women – and interconnected. Developing the idea of *intersectional sociolinguistics*, with a particular focus on sexuality, Levon and Mendes (2016, p. 12) argue that we need to avoid intersectionality becoming the mere meeting point of identities. It is more useful, they suggest, to explore the ways in which social systems operate together, constantly examining "how a practice related to sexuality may also be related to gender, race/ethnicity, social class, and so on, and critically interrogating why it is that these categories are linked in this way." We need to understand how social practices and lived experiences are related to language use in the social production of interlocking forms of difference and identification.

Queer Theory

This line of thinking also makes it clear that we cannot assume "a universal basis for feminism, one which must be found in an identity assumed to exist cross-culturally" or a corresponding "universal or hegemonic structure of patriarchy or masculine domination" (Butler, 1990, p. 3). This is by no means to downplay questions of gender and inequality but rather to seek out the ways that local actions produce gender effects – she gives the example of the *girling* of a newborn baby being held up in the air as someone announces "it's a girl" – and to question assumptions that gender follows from sex (e.g., male bodies lead to masculinity) and that desire (sexuality) follows from both. Such an understanding of gender and desire has been crucial for Queer theory in its attempts to go beyond *gay/lesbian* labels and instead to work with more flexible understandings of identity (Zita, 1992). Thus, as Jagose (1996) explains, Queer theory challenges the type of identity politics implicit in labels such as *gay* and *lesbian*, and while acknowledging the gains achieved by mobilizing around such categories (and see the discussion in Chapter 3 of strategic essentialism), seeks to move into a more complex understanding that "questions that those descriptors are self-evident" (p. 126).

Queer theory may at times appear contradictory, both embracing "'minority' sexual identities" and troubling "the very notion of sexuality as a basis for identity" (Nelson, 2009, p. 22). In this first sense, we might see the term as one of inclusivity, of embracing different forms of sexual identity; in the second sense, "sexual identities are being conceptualized in a poststructuralist sense – that is, as processes rather than properties" (Nelson, 2009, p. 23). While a "lesbian and gay framework has been very useful politically in mobilizing for civil rights, it may be less useful pedagogically" (Nelson, 1999, p. 373). A related point was made in the previous chapter (Chapter 3): While a framework of language rights may be useful for mobilizing for certain language policies, it may be less useful for understanding language or for educational projects. Nelson goes on to argue for the importance of using Queer theory since it "shifts the focus from gaining civil rights to analyzing discursive and cultural practices, from affirming minority sexual identities to problematizing all sexual identities" (Nelson, 1999, p. 373). Thus, she argues, "queer theory may provide a more flexible, open-ended framework for facilitating inquiry, particularly within the intercultural context of ESL, than lesbian and gay theory does" (p. 377).

Queer theory has thus opened up a number of avenues for both intellectual inquiry and political activity. Queer linguistics, in Milani's (2013) view, in order to engage with the "complexity of *sexed* meanings in public texts," requires multimodal forms of analysis. As Thurlow (2016) goes on to argue, a process of *queering* discourse studies (for further discussion, see chapter 5) requires a much greater engagement with questions of affect, performance studies, and other ways of getting at how language is part of a wider range of semiotic, embodied, and affective practices. A *queer framework*, Nelson (2009, p. 25) argues, presents many possibilities for engaging questions of sexual identity in language classrooms since "sexual identities are conceptualized as performative and communicatively produced." This turns the "teaching emphasis away from gay inclusion per se and toward sexual-identity inquiry" (Nelson, 2009, p. 25).

Queer theory, according to Thurlow (2016, p. 6), has two main themes, on the one hand, making visible "the lives of marginalized sexual identities" and surfacing "more complex, nuanced ways of thinking about sex/sexuality." On the other hand, Queer theory "also disrupts and challenges the received 'here-and-now' wisdoms of academic theory and promotes a more self-reflexive, openly subjective role for the scholar." It is this intersectional engagement with identity and transgressive challenge to institutional norms that I have been trying to get at in this section: Identities are social categories that are largely imposed on us but which we come to identify with. They are a constant site of struggle as we try to work with the identities we are given ("becoming Black" in Ibrahim's, 1999 terms). From a critical applied linguistic point of view – whether we are looking at identity, critical discourse studies or language education – these are not just ways of being to be discussed or included, but categories of social difference to be investigated and engaged with (Table 4.2).

Conclusion: Embodiment and Recognition

By raising the issue of the politics of difference, this chapter deals with a number of significant themes for critical applied linguistics. Looking at identity as something we perform through language rather than as something reflected in language helps get away from preordained categorizations of identity. The notion of performativity (Pennycook, 2004b) is therefore important since, as Jagose (1996) puts it, "debates around performativity put a denaturalising pressure on sex, gender, sexuality, bodies and identities" (p. 90). This emphasis on performativity and the lived experiences of language users has also enabled the return of the body to language studies. Where once language was conceived centrally in terms of an abstract system in a cognitive sandwich, more recent work has insisted on the salience of language as embodied. It is precisely against the removal of the body that so much critical, and especially feminist, work has fought, arguing that academic work on language has floated in a disembodied state that has been able to ignore exactly all those embodied aspects of life – gender, sexuality, ethnicity, and disability – that matter. In recent years, the body has reemerged as a place where our subjectivities are generated and embodied, helped by Foucault's (1980a, 1980b) contention that the body may be a more useful focus for studies of power than some notion of ideology. Bourdieu's (1991) notions of *habitus* and embodied cultural capital are also useful here since Bourdieu insists our cultural habits are not mere cognitive apparitions but rather are written onto our bodies.

As Threadgold (1997) suggests, at this point we can see how a social order is "*both* imbricated in language, textuality and semiosis *and* is corporeal, spatial, temporal, institutional, conflictual, and marked by sexual, racial and other differences" (p. 101). Our investment and desire in beliefs and ways of doing things are not some rational, intellectual inclination, as many views of ideology, awareness, and emancipation seem to imply, but rather part of what our bodies have become. As Ibrahim (1999) shows, as the youths he studied become Black, they learn both *the talk* and *the walk*. Taking bodies properly into account starts to redress the historical imbalance that has placed language, cognition, identity, and learning as cranial than corporeal, while relegating the body and the senses to the physical. Recent shifts to encompass an understanding of the body, senses and material artifacts have brought much greater attention to "touches, sights, smells, movements, material artefacts" and "shared experiences, dynamic interactions and bodily engagements" to go beyond the narrow story of cognition and language in the head (Finnegan, 2015, p. 19). Although sociolinguistics has been better than its logocentric linguistic cousin in acknowledging various roles for the body – studies of nonverbal communication (Kendon, 2004), for example, or the challenge to rethink the divide between Sign and gesture (Kusters & Sahasrabudhe, 2018) – the body has often been conceived as "secondary to language rather than as the sine qua non of language" (Bucholtz and Hall, 2016, p. 174).

In their call for "an embodied sociocultural linguistics" (p. 174), Bucholtz and Hall argue not only for making more salient bodily aspects of communication commonly acknowledged but often peripheralized, such as voice ("the embodied heart of spoken language" p178), but also for understanding how the body is discursively constructed, and how recent thinking has sought to understand how the body is "imbricated in complex arrangements that include nonhuman as well as human participants, whether animals, epidemics, objects, or technologies" (p. 186). It is not just that bodies produce and are deeply involved in language – questions of voice and gesture may be far more significant than the peripheral role they have often been given as language supports – but also that language produces bodies: "language is a primary means by which the body enters the sociocultural realm as a site of semiosis, through cultural discourses about bodies" (Bucholtz and Hall, 2016, p. 173).

Butler's (1990; 1997) insight that bodies are a discursive rather than a biological product – that while biology may give us certain features, it is their social and cultural meaning that render them significant – brings to the fore an understanding that discourse and materiality are not easily separable (contra those who insist that discourse is a noncorporeal category) and that "race and gender are socially constructed" (Haslanger, 2012, p. 5). Since this idea is often misconstrued – that something is socially constructed is taken to mean it's not real – it is important to understand this neither as an antirealist claim – race and gender are socially constructed and we need to understand the "reality of social structures and the political importance of recognizing reality" (p.30) – nor a causative claim – race and gender are not brought into existence by social factors but are categories embedded in social relations rather than biological differences (pp. 86–7). The important goal for Haslanger is to understand differences that are socially constructed but not recognized as such – gender and race being obvious examples – and then to find ways to *resist* this reality.

This brings us finally back to a discussion of recognition. As already discussed in the introduction, one key way of framing questions of justice and inequality has been Fraser's (1995; 2000) arguments for redistribution and recognition (see e.g., Piller, 2016). Simply put, distributive justice refers to the equitable (re)distribution of resources, while recognition justice refers to the equitable recognition of different groups. There are two corresponding forms of injustice: Maldistribution and misrecognition. Revisiting these arguments,

Fraser (2000) has been concerned that the rise of recognition politics – struggles to recognize difference and identity along lines of class, gender, race, sexuality, ethnicity, and so on – has started to *displace* struggles for redistributive justice (the redistribution of economic goods) and to *reify* identities: "the idea that one could remedy all maldistribution by means of a politics of recognition is deeply deluded" (p. 112). This increased concern with what has been disparagingly termed "identity politics" has been critiqued from all corners of the political spectrum: From conservatives for promoting forms of racial, sexual, and gendered rights that intervene in the neoliberal project of individualism and corporate ownership; from liberals for denying freedom of speech in the critique of discriminatory language; and from the left for focusing on forms of difference when it's ultimately political economy that matters.

The problem has been that cultural theorists – "reversing the claims of an earlier form of vulgar Marxist economism" (Fraser, 2000, p. 111) – have overreached themselves in their belief that a more equitable society can be achieved by forms of recognition before anything else. This has led some (Block 2014; 2018c) in critical applied linguistics to argue for a reversal of this misguided prioritization of recognition. There are also problems, however, with an overemphasis on redistributive goals. First, as critical applied linguists, our capacity to engage with questions of recognition – the role of sexuality in language classrooms, for example, or raciolinguistic discrimination in the workplace – is greater than our ability to change the functioning of the economy. We need to be clear, therefore, whether we see our (critical) applied linguistic work itself as activist work, in which case what we write and teach is what we do (and in which case we are more able to intervene in terms of recognition), or whether we see our work more in terms of meta-discourse about applied linguistics (in which case, arguing for redistributive goals may make more sense).

Second, an argument that political economy matters more than other forms of difference runs the danger of overlooking questions of intersectionality discussed above, and of assuming that questions of race or sexuality are not also issues of material inequality. Block (2015, p. 3), argues, for example, that "social class is unlike dimensions of identity like gender, race, ethnicity, nationality, sexuality, and religion in that it is first and foremost about the distribution and redistribution of material resources." Flores and Chaparro (2018, p. 380) take this view to task – in the context of language and schooling in Philadelphia – for overlooking "the racialized experiences of language-minoritized communities" and the point that "race is also rooted in distribution and redistribution." An argument can indeed be made, at least in contexts such as the USA, that race is a more fundamental marker of inequality than class. Finally, the way forward is not to constantly cast recognition and redistribution against each other but, as Fraser has always argued, to see both as needing to be transformative.

The difference between more normative identity politics and a more transformative approach to recognition can be seen in the difference, discussed in the previous section, between gay-identity politics, which demands only the recognition of this identity, and Queer theory, which, by contrast, questions the "homo–hetero dichotomy so as to destabilize all fixed sexual identities" (Fraser, 1995, p. 83). In response to her subsequent concern that the focus on recognition has come to believe in recognition for its own sake, Fraser (2000, p. 113) insists that the central issue is "social subordination," the ways that people are prevented from "participating as a peer in social life" (p. 113). This means that misrecognition is not a "free-standing cultural harm" as if not recognizing people's identity claims was the only harm being done, but rather "an institutionalized relation of social subordination." Viewing recognition from the point of view of status entails an examination of "institutionalized patterns of cultural value for their effects on the relative standing of social actors" (Fraser, 2000, p. 113). Misrecognition is perpetrated and perpetuated through "the workings of social institutions that regulate interaction according to parity-impeding cultural norms" (p. 114), such as marriage laws that exclude same-sex partnerships, racial profiling by the police, or the denigration of 'single mothers' by educational or welfare institutions.

To conclude, the point here is that forms of difference matter deeply, and critical applied linguists have to have a way of getting our heads around this without surrendering questions of social and cultural difference – sexuality, disability, race, gender, class, or ethnicity – to a view that the recognition of such identities is the endpoint of any analysis. This is about changing social subordination while also facing the ethical imperative to engage with the profundity of human difference. Only through an attempt at *engagement* can we take up the challenge for an ethical response to another (hooks, 1994; Kearney, 1988). It is about finding a way out of the problems of celebrating difference (as if this were a goal in itself), essentializing difference (as if we know how difference operates at local levels) or eradicating difference (as if difference is better overcome). If we acknowledge that questions of identity and power are closely linked to language and are therefore key concerns for critical applied linguistics, it is important to consider research and pedagogical responses to forms of difference. Any critical project has to have a transformative vision. As this chapter has suggested, real transformative action involving language (the goal of critical applied linguistics) is not best conceived in terms of raising critical awareness in the hope that emancipatory projects will flow from this. This is also why critical applied linguistic teaching and research, as Thurlow (2016) insists, has to be about affect, desire, performance, and bodies. This will of course have implications for how we think about research, pedagogy, and activism (Chapters 6 and 7).

Note

1. To reiterate a point I made in Chapter 2, skepticism about the possibilities of social justice frameworks is not intended as a critique of the work of colleagues who are placing questions of social inequality and racism squarely on the SLA table. It is also important to acknowledge that while social justice remains a rather nebulous way of focusing critical concerns, it is less likely to scare people away.

5 The Politics of Text

Of all the domains of critical applied linguistics, it is perhaps critical discourse analysis/studies (CDA/S) that has become best known, with its own journal (*Critical Discourse Studies*) and common inclusion, at least as a methodology, in research approaches. Indeed, it has become fairly common to make reference to 'critical discourse analysis' as part of a research project as if this in itself renders a project more broadly critical. This chapter will look critically at CDA/S – evaluating its strengths, assumptions, and weaknesses – before moving on to look at related educational textual concerns, such as critical literacy. Whereas Chapter 3 looked at critical approaches to language from what we might call an *external* perspective – How do we understand the social distribution of language? What kinds of language policies can help or hinder language use? – this chapter turns to an *internal* perspective on the meanings and uses of texts. While the focus will also be on how broader social and political forces relate to the production and reception of texts (the internal/external division is only a partially useful one), questions here will typically focus on issues of discourse and ideology: How is it that texts come to mean as they do? How can we understand the ways in which ideologies operate through texts? How do readers interpret texts, and what effects may this have?

We shall turn first to CDA/S in an effort to show how various strands of textual analysis relate to the broad configurations of knowledge and politics outlined in Chapter 2. Central concerns here are whether we see power as something that some people have while others do not, or whether we see it as a more diffused set of operations; whether we see ideology as a distortion of the truth that is realized in discourse (so critical discourse analysis attempts to unmask the truth behind the curtain of ideological distortion), or whether we see discourses as ways of viewing the world (so critical discourse analysis seeks to understand how the world is discursively constructed). The second part of the chapter looks at critical literacies – as a form of applied critical discourse analysis – and focuses in particular on a debate between access-oriented and inclusivity-oriented approaches to literacy. The issue here is whether the focus of critical literacy is primarily on providing the tools for engagement (powerful language) or enabling students to voice their concerns (powerful voices). The conclusion will look at ways these debates can be resolved.

Critical Discourse Analysis

Although CDA/S appears to have achieved a form of disciplinary solidarity for itself, it can also be seen as a fairly broad constellation of approaches. Fairclough and Wodak (1996) distinguish eight different approaches to CDA, including *French discourse analysis* (Foucault, 1979; Pêcheux, Conein, Courtine, Gadet, & Marandin, 1981), with a focus particularly on broad discursive formations; *critical linguistics* – particularly the work of Fowler (1996), Fowler, Kress, Hodge, and Trew (1979), Hodge and Kress (1988), Kress and Hodge (1979), and Kress and van Leeuwen (1990) – with its origins in *social semiotics* (Halliday, 1978); *sociocognitive studies* aiming to account for the relation between language use (discourse) and social relations, particularly in van Dijk's (1993a, 1993b) work on racism in discourse; the *discourse-historical method* of Ruth Wodak (Wodak, 1996; 2015; Wodak, de Cillia, Reisigl, & Leibhart, 1999) with its focus on anti-Semitic discourse in Austria and elsewhere; and various other approaches looking at discourses of Nazism or the Far Right (Jäger & Jäger, 1993). Wodak (1996) also lists eight principles of CDA, pointing to the relations between discourse and power, discourse, and society, discourse and social change, and so on.

It is not useful in this chapter to delve into these different ways of approaching CDA. Broadly speaking, we can say that CDA/S arose as a way of analyzing texts and power, or, more specifically, looking at discourse not so much in terms of structural explanations (how do the internal structures and functions of language use make it coherent?) but rather in terms of its social relations (how do we understand the social assemblage of texts?). Fairclough (1995) explains the central goal of CDA/S as *denaturalizing ideologies*, that is, showing that what we assume – background knowledge or common sense – is in fact always an ideological representation of a particular social group that can be revealed by critical analysis. The basis for understanding these social groups, particularly in the work of Fairclough (1989), is a fairly orthodox neo-Marxist interpretation of power, grounded in a critique of capitalism: "The abuses and contradictions of capitalist society which gave rise to critical theory have not diminished, nor have the characteristics of discursive practice within capitalist society which give rise to critical discourse analysis" (Fairclough, 1995, p. 16).

He goes on to argue that "most analysis is with social relations of domination *within* a *social system* which is capitalist, and dominated by—but not reducible to—relations of class" (p. 18). By assuming that "that there is a one-to-one relationship between ideological formations and discursive formations" (Fairclough, 1995, p. 40), CDA/S aims to make these ideological systems and representations transparent and to show how they are related to the broader social order. As Roderick (2017, p. 4) explains CDA/S has, from the outset, "sought to reveal how macro-social relations of domination are enacted through but also obfuscated in the production of texts." Apparently simple on one level – the social order is reflected in discourse – these arguments also require a fairly complex chain of relations: Ideological positions can be uncovered in texts; ideologies are the (naturalized) views of powerful social groups;

by reproducing their ideologies, these groups are able to reproduce social relations of power; and by making the textual representation of their ideologies transparent, CDA can help dismantle these relations of power.

In a series of books and articles, Fairclough (1989, 1992b, 1993, 1995) has developed and enlarged this view of CDA/S. Probably the best known element of his work is the development of what he calls his "three-dimensional" model of CDA (Fairclough, 1995, p. 98), incorporating on one level the analytical procedures of description, interpretation, and explanation, and on another level, the different levels of text, text production and reception, and the larger sociopolitical context. As others who have employed this model (e.g., Janks, 1997) observe, using it flexibly (rather than in some linear fashion) allows for multiple points of entry into texts and their contexts. A great deal of useful work has been done under the broad label of CDA/S, which more generally has insisted on a political view of language, a commitment to academic work that is unashamedly critical, and an obligation to work toward social change via critical language work. At the same time, this work raises some key issues for critical applied linguistics concerning ways in which power, text, and meaning are related. In the following section, therefore, we will look in closer detail at the notions of discourse, ideology, truth, and power.

Ideology, Discourse, Truth, and Power

In the summary above of different approaches to CDA/S, we can see a distinction between discourse as language use and discourse as a broad organization of ideas (similar, in fact, to the notion of ideology). Various attempts have been made to distinguish between these two versions of discourse, Fairclough (1995) suggesting that *discourse* as an abstract noun refers to "language use conceived as social practice" and that *discourse* as a count noun refers to "ways of signifying experience from a particular perspective" (p. 135). Discourse, in this view, refers to language use, and like, for example, *syntax*, is a general aspect of language, while discourses in the plural refer to ways of understanding the world. Gee (1996) makes a related distinction between small *d* discourse (language use) and big *D* Discourse (worldview). Gee's distinction has proved popular over the years, though big *D* Discourse has shifted somewhat in recent accounts to refer to "ways to enact and recognize socially meaningful identities" (Gee 2015, p. 106; Gee, 2018, p. 110). It draws attention to the distinction between a notion of discourse as language in use, which then has to be related to wider forms of social organization (and particularly ideology), and a poststructural understanding of discourse (Discourse), which already suggests ideological formations: We can talk of colonial, medical, management, neoliberal discourses, and so on.

Ideology or Discourse?

Whether the two ideas of discourse are really as far apart as sometimes claimed (I asked a number of years ago whether they might indeed be incommensurable;

Pennycook, 1994c) or whether they could be more easily understood together, depends on various ways in which one approaches questions of language and ideology: If, as argued in Chapters 2 and 3, all language is political, then discourse cannot be separated from ideology, and Discourse cannot generally be considered without a focus on language (broadly understood). The distinction nonetheless leaves us with a number of concerns about how we understand relations among language, discourse, and ideology. CDA/S has generally operated with discourse referring to language use (discourse analysis) and ideology referring to knowledge formations (the critical part of the analysis). This approach makes sense for those coming from a linguistic background for whom language and discourse are elements that need to be related to larger concerns such as society and ideology. But for cultural and critical theorists more generally, a major point of debate has been not so much to relate discourse to ideology but rather to choose between the two as competing terms. As Mills (1997) suggests, "for all cultural and critical theorists there has been intense theoretical difficulty in deciding whether to draw on work which is based around the notion of ideology or work which refers to discourse" (p. 29). This is not therefore just a set of terminological options, but rather a much deeper set of issues to do with language, power, and society.

Simply put, the difficulties with the notion of ideology rest on two principal concerns: Whether it is seen as a misrepresentation of reality (ideologies are false) and whether it is seen as necessarily dependent on prior assumptions about a socioeconomic base (see the discussion in previous chapters about assumptions about the essential core of material relations in neo-Marxist thought). Foucault (1980b) rejected the notion of ideology because it "always stands in virtual opposition to something else which is supposed to count as truth" (p. 118). It is not so much that work in CDA/S is not aware of this problem concerning its truth claims but rather that by often adhering to a traditional view of ideology, it seems to have few ways of escaping this dilemma. Thus, Wodak (1996), for example, suggests that ideologies are "often (though not necessarily) false or ungrounded constructions of society" (p. 18). For many in mainstream CDA, it is therefore assumed that discourses "are 'distorted' by power" (Wodak, 1996, p. 17). Van Dijk (1993b) argues that CDA "implies a political critique of those responsible for its *perversion* in the reproduction of dominance and inequality" (p. 253, emphasis added). For Fairclough (2001, p. 134; emphasis added), the issue is one of "*misrepresentations* which clearly contribute to sustaining unequal relations of power." We have an ideal *order* that is distorted, disordered, or perverted by the operations of power.

Much of this way of thinking draws explicitly on Habermas' (1998) belief in "rationally motivated consensus" based on an *ideal speech situation* (McCarthy, 1978, p. 325): "systematically distorted communication occurs when the universal, pragmatic norms of the ideal speech situation become subordinated to privileged interests, producing asymmetrical power relationships and resulting in a false consensus about the validity claims made" (Wodak, 1996, p. 30). This grounding in Habermasian communicative rationality, leads to a "tacit acceptance of a logocentric conception of both communication and ethics" (Roderick, 2017, p. 7), or put another way, it assumes given norms of social and communicative behavior that become distorted when power intervenes. While this particular tradition of critical work is rather poorly understood in the Anglosphere (Forchtner, 2011), and while the idea of idealization is often misunderstood (idealizations are critiqued for being precisely that, missing the point that they are used as idealizations for particular rational thought experiments), such idealizations – like Chomsky's ideal language user or Rawls' vision of justice (see Chapter 2) – can lead all too easily to unexamined norms of language, society, communication, or justice that overlook the gendered or racialized preconceptions that underpin them (Mills, 2017).

As Threadgold (1997, p. 112) puts it, Habermas' "post-Marxist masculine and modernist anxiety about order, arrangement and keeping everything in its assigned place—perhaps especially women" does not bode well for those that do not fit this vision of a well-ordered world. This rationalist approach to order and disorder is of course by no means the only way critical discourse studies are understood. Fairclough's (1989) views on order and disorder are quite different: *Orders of discourse*, from his perspective, are the discursive equivalent of the social order, that is to say an inequitable order that needs to be opposed. For Fairclough (1995), the problem CDA needs to address is the order in society and discourse imposed by capitalism; for Wodak, the problem to be addressed is the institutional disorder of discourse. Either way, the concern of these writers is to unwind the distorting effects of power, either by a return to order or through a restructuring of the social order.

The first major difficulty with CDA/S, therefore, concerns questions of ideology and discourse. One of the key problems with this position is that it leaves CDA/S practitioners in the difficult position of claiming to be able to discern truth from falsehood with discourse analytic tools. Such truth claims – backed either by a view that discourse analysis is scientific and therefore true, or by a wider appeal to shared beliefs about the world with a compliant readership – leave the discourse analyst in an awkward position (Patterson, 1997). The challenge for ideology critique is whether there can be any nonideological position; or to raise the question differently, what is the locus of enunciation of the analyst? Too much work of this sort assumes a patronizing principle that people are ideological dupes from whose eyes the clear-sighted analyst can remove the blindfolds of ideological obfuscation (Latour, 2004). This is not, it should be noted, an argument that we cannot deal with questions of truth and reality – all truth is discursively constructed so we can have no purchase on reality – but rather a critique of the position that claims for itself insights into reality that override everyone else's. This also raises the question of the basis of the critical element of CDA/S: As van Leeuwen (2018, p. 8) remarks, CDA/S is not only concerned with analysis of discourse but also its evaluation, which requires "some kind of moral commitment from the analyst." In short, these are not simply questions of analysis, but also of ethical judgement.

Table 5.1 Key questions for Critical Discourse Analysis/Studies (CDA/S)

Truth and falsehood	Is discourse the realization of ideological falsehoods or the construction of different realities?
Analytic goals	Is CDA/S concerned with unmasking the truth or understanding the making of reality?
Production, reception, and context	Can the discourse analysis determine meaning without taking production and reception into account?
Language and power	Is the goal to explore diverse operations of power or to show preconceived operations of power in discourse?
Scope of discourse	Can standard versions of discourse do the work needed for a critical analysis?
Locus of work	How can CDA/S become sensitive to wider decolonial imperatives?

Language, Location, and Materiality

These common ways of doing CDA/S lead to various other problems that are of interest for a general discussion of critical applied linguistics (see Table 5.1). One of these has to do with the problem of whose meanings get to count in any analysis. In the first instance, this question of textual meaning can be taken up in terms of production and reception: Although CDA/S often includes processes of reception in its model (Fairclough's framework promises equal weight to both), neither the production of texts – who produced the text under what conditions for what purposes? – nor their reception – how is the text interpreted by people under particular conditions and in particular locations? – is given much space.[1] Both processes are frequently overdetermined by ideological and infrastructural assumptions: The 'media,' for example, produce texts in the interests of the powerful, which in turn are read by compliant readers. One of the problems of CDA/S, Blommaert (2005, p. 35) suggests, is that it only starts once some analyzable text has come into being, and "stops as soon as the discourse has been produced," that is to say CDA/S tends to put too much emphasis on the text itself, while ignoring what happens before, around, or after it.

There is an authoritarian strain in this way of interpreting texts (McCormick, 1994) suggesting both the absolute meanings conveyed by ideologically constructed discourses and the unconditional capacity of the analyst to read the hidden meanings behind the text. This failure to problematize its own reading practices – and thereby to realize that what is found in the text is not some pregiven textual or ideological reality amenable to careful analysis but has rather been read into the text from particular positions – is not overcome, it should be noted, by arguing that all texts are open to all and any interpretations, in the liberal egalitarian formulation proposed by Widdowson (1998). Blommaert has suggested that critical analysis needs to get beyond "the old idea that a chunk of discourse has only *one* function and *one* meaning" (Blommaert, 2005, p. 34) and if we want to "understand contemporary forms of inequality in and through language," we should look not only inside language but outside (in society) as well (Blommaert, 2005, p. 35). Blommaert's point is that in order to understand how texts operate socially, culturally, and politically, it is never enough just to develop good tools for text analysis. We need instead ethnographic accounts of the making and purpose of texts, their roles once circulating in social spaces, and the positions from which people read and understand them (Blommaert, 2005, p. 16).

This concern is in part a result of a limited view of discourse. The problem with CDA/S is not, according to Jones (2007, p. 362), "its assumption that discourse is political but with its conception of discourse." As Jones makes clear, the melding of orthodox structuralist approaches to language and discourse (the common use of systemic functional grammar is a good example) with a wider political form of analysis may broaden the spectrum of what is to be examined, but it does not sufficiently broaden the ways in which language is understood. As Luke (2002) explains, there is a good fit between forms of structural linguistics, forms of ideology critique and structural neo-Marxist social analysis since they rely on similar assumptions about text, systematicity, and rationality. Taking such insights further, Thurlow (2016, p. 23) points to the tendency to look at what is present rather than absent, at stability and uniformity rather than the transitory, ephemeral, and intangible or invisible. The "insistence on the primacy of words and writing" Thurlow (2016, p. 4) suggests, overlooks bodies, affect, objects, and other forms of materiality.

The narrow view of discourse also relates to a narrow view of the scope of CDA/S, linked in part to the concern with socioeconomic questions. Although in the work of Wodak (2015) and others we at least see a move away from a focus on discourses in English, and on socioeconomic questions (her work on anti-Semitism in Austria and the new Right in Europe has been important here), CDA/S has also been taken to task for employing "western worldviews, values, concepts, models, analytic tools, topics of interest, and so forth, as universal and exclusive standards" (Shi-Xu, 2015, p. 1). CDA/S has, it seems, had only limited relations to postcolonial or decolonial thinking. As Resende (2018) remarks, CDA cannot be seen as a methodology that can be used without regard to its production and location of critique; like many other domains of applied linguistics, it needs to be decolonized.

CDA/S should no longer "restrict critical analyses of discourse to highly integrated, Late Modern, and postindustrial, densely semiotised First World societies" (Blommaert, 2005, p. 35). Put another way, CDA/S needs to move away from its rather obsessive focus on neoliberalism in contemporary societies in the Global North, and its use of discourse analytic tools that have also evolved in such contexts, and embrace instead other languages, other contexts, and other tools. CDA/S, Shi-Xu (2015, p. 1) argues, "forms a hegemonic discourse, reproducing old-fashioned colonialist knowledge and excluding alternative visions." This is a recurrent concern with old-school critical work (and one that other critical work does not escape easily): It operates with universalizing tropes of critical thought and fails to engage with more serious concerns about knowledge production, coloniality, and the need for a decolonizing project not *directed by* the old-guard of CDA/S but rather *directed at* their modes of analysis and generalization (Pennycook & Makoni, 2020).

Questions of materiality take us to another problem with much of CDA/S, namely the assumption that language/discourse reflects reality (see Chapters 2 and 3), and that this reality is to be found in the material conditions of socio-economic disparity. This was Foucault's (1980b) second objection to the notion of ideology: "ideology stands in a secondary position relative to something which functions as its infrastructure, as its material, economic determinant" (p. 118). Foucault was objecting to the idea that ideology is necessarily the product of other social and economic factors. For Fairclough (1989), because ideologies are always linked to the maintenance of inequitable relations of power and because ideologies are most commonly expressed in language, it is in language that we must search for the means by which power is maintained. This kind of formulation can be appealing but it locates power as an already given entity maintained through the ideological operations of language. As I shall argue in the next section, we need ways of exploring rather than assuming the workings of power.

Different Versions of Power

While the big-D/little-d distinction that has become quite common in discourse analysis may, on the one hand, overemphasize a distinction between language and worldview, it may, on the other hand, fail to attend to the differences that underpin ways of thinking about power in relation to ideology or discourse. Big-D Discourse generally derives from a poststructuralist approach to language and power. At its heart, this is not so much a question of terminology but whether ideology is seen as a falsification of reality, or whether we adopt the idea that discourses produce reality and are, therefore, competing versions of the truth. As Mills points out, "much of Foucault's work on discourse has been an open discussion and dialogue with the term ideology, and in some sense the term discourse has been defined in dialogue with and in reaction to the definition of ideology" (Mills, 1997, p. 32). Poststructuralist notions of discourse operate from a position that discourses do not imply truth or falsehood (they construct what is thought of as true, but not in relation to something else that is false). This of course leads to the rather difficult position – often criticized as being relativist – that we can't actually decide between truth and falsity (there are only rival constructions of the truth). The issue, Foucault (1980b) suggests, is not to try to construct a category of scientific knowledge that can then claim some monopoly on the truth but rather to see "historically how effects of truth are produced within discourses which in themselves are neither true nor false" (p. 118). We will return below to some of the implications of this position, but let us consider first Foucault's understanding of power.

Table 5.2 Structuralist and Poststructuralist Versions of Power

Structuralist (neo-Marxist) Version of Power	Poststructuralist (Foucauldian) Version of Power
Power is a preexisting condition of society	Power needs to be explained, not assumed
Certain groups (the powerful) have power; others (the powerless) do not	Power is not owned or possessed but operates through society
Power is a product of socioeconomic relations	Power does not have some ultimate location or origin
Power exerts external effects on different domains	Relations of power are not outside but part of other relations
The role of critical work is to reveal from the outside the workings of power	There is no position from which one can arrive at the truth outside relations of power
Power represses, controls, excludes powerless people and ideas	Power is not merely repressive but is also productive
Power is exerted through ideology in discourse	Discourse is the conjunction of power and knowledge

Power, it is worth reminding ourselves (when poststructuralism is rather strangely critiqued for being unconcerned with questions of power), was a central aspect of Foucault's work, not as some undifferentiated whole that was linked to class, state, sovereign, or culture but as operating constantly on and through people. Foucault (1991, p. 148, my italics) saw power not as a given totality that explains how things happen but rather as *"that which must be explained."* There are a number of ways in which this view of power differs from structuralist and neo-Marxist accounts (see Table 5.2). First of all, power is not something owned or possessed but rather something that operates throughout society. For Foucault (1980a), power is not the institutional control of citizens within a state, or a mode of ideological control, or even "a general system of dominance exerted by one group over another" (p. 92); rather, power refers to the "multiplicity of force relations immanent in the sphere in which they operate" (p. 92). Thus, "power is not something that is acquired, seized, or shared, something that one holds on to or allows to slip away; power is exercised from innumerable points, in the interplay of nonegalitarian and mobile relations" (p. 94). Power does not have some ultimate location or origin, whether social or economic relations, the power of a sovereign, or the power of a state. Power operates everywhere. As Kramsch (2021 p. 72) explains, a poststructural position insists that "the sources of symbolic power are not singular but multiple, not unitary but diverse, not permanent but changing and conflictual."

As a result, power relations are not somehow external to things such as knowledge or sex but are part of them. Power does not control from outside; it is not something linked only to coercion or repression but rather something that inhabits our interactions: "Power comes from below; that is there is no binary and all-encompassing opposition between rulers and ruled at the root of power relations" (p. 94). This also means that there is no position outside power and no position from which one can arrive at the "truth" outside relations of power. This takes us back to the discussion above of CDA/S approaches to discourse, where ideology (falsehood) is infused with power (a result of dominant views of the world) and truth sits outside such power (the revelations of the analyst). For Foucault (1980b, p. 131) truth isn't "outside power, or lacking in power.... Truth is a thing of this world." Each society "has its own regime of truth, its 'general politics' of truth: That is, the types of discourse which it accepts and makes function as true."[2]

For Foucault, then, power is not merely repressive but is also productive: "Far from preventing knowledge, power produces it" (Foucault, 1980b, p. 59). It also always engenders resistance. "Where there is power, there is resistance" (Foucault, 1980a, p. 95). And so finally, returning to questions of discourse, this is where power and knowledge meet: "power and knowledge directly imply each other" (Foucault, 1979, p. 27). This is not the version of power and knowledge commonly used elsewhere (knowledge = power) but rather an understanding that knowledge and power are discourse, which "produces reality; it produces domains of objects and rituals of truth" (Foucault, 1979, p. 194). So "it is in discourse that power and knowledge are joined together" (Foucault, 1980a, p. 100), which gives to discourse a role in making the world (hence the idea of Discourse as a worldview) rather than reflecting the world.

This version of power and discourse is very different from the version in Critical Theory and CDA/S. For many, Foucault's work suggests a dangerous and irrational relativism that goes against emancipatory possibilities: If emancipation cannot be achieved by a rational revelation of the truth (which has been obscured by ideology), and all we have to operate with are different regimes of truth, how can we proceed? We have, then, two competing positions: On the one hand, a view whereby power distorts the truth through ideologies in favor of certain groups; on the other hand, a position whereby we only have access to competing accounts of the truth. Certainly, discourse analysis from a poststructuralist perspective doesn't solve all the dilemmas of standard CDA/S outlined above. To make it useful, we need to resolve a number of difficulties: The need for forms of textual analysis that enable more fine-grained analysis; the need to rethink the locus of enunciation; and the need to be able to speak of truth, reality, or materiality without worrying that this undermines poststructuralist purity. Poststructuralist claims that everything is discursive are all very well, but as Luke (2002, p. 103) makes clear, the real work comes when we try to "trace, politically, which discourses have which material and discursive effects and consequences for communities, cultures, and human subjects."

Postlinguistic Challenges

One concern suggested earlier is that mainstream CDA/S tends to operate with a limited version of language/discourse that is not well suited to understanding how politics or subjectivity are connected to language. As Poynton

(1993a) argues, "no linguistics that does not and cannot engage with central issues of feminist and poststructuralist theory concerning questions of subject production through discursive positioning can be taken seriously as a theory of language" (p. 2). Poststructuralism presents some very interesting challenges for applied linguistics. On one level, it asks how different constructs are produced and maintained. What are the discourses that produce binaries such as native speaker–non-native speaker, first language–second language, qualitative–quantitative, integrative–instrumental, acquisition–learning? On another, it opens up many received categories for questioning. If gender or ethnicity are not so much pregiven but constructed in and performed through discourse (see Chapter 4), how do we start to understand the ongoing production of such identities in and through language? Language is always already political.

McNamara (2019, p. 20) explains poststructuralism as showing how "discourses circulate in social spaces, constructing possibilities for the way in which we see others and are seen by them." These processes of "everyday mutual surveillance, of recognizing and being recognized in terms made available within discourses" allow us to see that everyday racism, constructs of gender, homophobia, and heteronormative assumptions are part of broad social forms of power and knowledge, as well as realized and repeated in everyday conversations and interactions. It is this relation between the micro-actions of conversations and the macro-concerns of discrimination and subjectivity that McNamara (2019) focuses on in particular. As García, Flores, and Spotti (2017, p. 4) suggest, *critical poststructuralist sociolinguistics* builds on Foucault's insight that "power is not concentrated in a single place, but is ubiquitous and exercised in social encounters." It allows for analysis of political and economic inequalities, while also questioning many of the givens (such as languages) of sociolinguistics. It is this emphasis on both challenging broad assumptions about language and providing a framework for close analytic work of the micro-actions of language and power that make a poststructuralist account potentially more useful than structuralist and neo-Marxist orientations.

Poststructuralism, therefore, opens up a space for a view of language and discourse that goes beyond some of the limitations of a combination of linguistics and ideology critique. As Mills (1997) explains, the turn away from ideology toward discourse reflects a desire to "develop an intellectual practice concerned to analyze the determinants of thinking and behavior in a more complex way than is possible when using terms like ideology" (p. 29). The benefits of the move away from a more Marxian framework toward a more Foucauldian one is that it allows for more complex and subtle analyses. The Marxist model of ideology "implied a simplistic and negative process whereby individuals were duped into using conceptual systems which were not in their own interests" (Mills, 1997, p. 30). A poststructuralist approach to critical discourse analysis allows for a move away from the frequent clumsiness of a model that works with ideologies produced by dominant groups. It sees discourses as having multiple and complex origins rather than a basis in one form of economic relations. It avoids the problems of claiming to reveal the truth by unmasking the obfuscatory workings of ideology. It gets away from a view that meaning resides in texts and can be extracted from them. As Patterson (1997) points out, "the idea that something resides in texts awaiting extraction, or revelation, by the application of the correct means of interpretation is precisely the assumption that poststructuralism set out to problematise" (p. 427).

Nevertheless, a poststructuralist position on discourse has a number of gaps that need filling if it is to be usable for critical applied linguistic projects: A limited set of tools to do the linguistic work that is needed to show *how* texts are related to larger broader formations; a need to broaden its scope from Northern contexts; and a means to get beyond assumed relativism and to be able to speak of truth, reality, and material conditions. Fairclough (1992b) criticizes Foucault's discourse analysis because it "does not include discursive and linguistic analysis of real texts" (p. 56). This challenge has been taken up by Lee (1996), Poynton (1993a, 1996), and Threadgold (1997), who have argued for the possibilities of doing feminist poststructuralist work while using linguistic tools. According to Poynton (1993a, p. 2), there is "a need for the recuperation within poststructuralist theory of certain kinds of linguistic knowledge" in order to shed light on the ways "discourses are actually constructed and the linguistic means by which subjects come to be constituted in terms of specific power/knowledge relations". Similarly, Lee (1996, p. 5) argues for the use of linguistic analysis as a way of "engaging with the density and specificity of texts."

For Threadgold (1997, p. 14), linguistic analysis and the metalinguistic tools of discourse analysis make it possible to analyze the "relations between the micro-processes of texts and the macro-processes of cultural and social difference" that other feminist and poststructuralist discourses cannot address. Poynton's (1996) and Lee's (1996) proposal for a "feminist (post)linguistics" (Lee, 1996, p. 5) that combines feminism, poststructuralism, and text analysis presents us with a useful way forward. It overcomes the concern that poststructuralism does not in itself suggest a political position: It may give us useful ways of analyzing "hegemony—people's compliance in their own oppression— without assuming that individuals are necessarily simply passive victims of thought" (Mills, 1997, p. 30), but it is that very flexibility that needs grounding within a clearer political agenda. While it is clearly the case that Foucault's "arguments about knowledge and truth were not so much relativist, as highly politicised" (Barrett, 1991, p161), poststructuralist analysis gains strength when it is combined with both forms of textual analysis and particular forms of politics (feminist, anti-racist and so on).

McNamara's (2019) combination of conversation analysis (CA) and Butler's (1997) idea of performativity is a good example of this: If we want to see how subjectivities are called into being, we have to look at the micropolitics of language use. Qin (2020) likewise combines an analysis of curriculum materials (suggested sentence openings), performativity, and critical race theory to show how learners' subjectivities were constituted and reformulated in classroom activities. In order to understand the wider workings of the world, it is important to focus on local language practices, but we should not get too caught up in the micro-workings of language lest we lose sight of the bigger picture. This is a more complex argument than one that just insists that the micro is in the macro and the macro in the micro. It shows rather how iterability – the importance of repetition and its failure always to be the same – and interaction are connected, suggesting that "the notion of turn-by-turn building of interaction corresponds in an important way to the notion of *iterability* in poststructuralism, that is, that nothing is given a priori, as it were, but has to be achieved in each iteration" (McNamara, 2019, p. 138).

The open, questioning stance that poststructuralism takes, as well as its insistence on critical analysis both of the material world and of the tools by which we conduct such analysis (critical resistance; Hoy, 2004), also makes it a more flexible framework for addressing different kinds of questions in different parts of the world. It nonetheless will always run the danger of being seen as a Northern framing of the world, and one that can look esoteric, elitist, and distanced from the material conditions of the Global South. Like more traditional approaches to CDA/S, therefore – Shi-Xu's (2015) critique of CDA/S applies equally across these different strands – poststructuralist discourse analysis needs to be able to show its relevance and its adaptability to the concerns of the majority world. Like the Brazilian adoption of Pêcheux-influenced discourse analysis, poststructuralism needs to be grounded in local conditions of inequality, thought, and analysis. A grounding in textual and political analysis – a focus on situated practices – can make this possible but only if this is located within a wider decolonial politics.

Poststructural analysis also needs to develop a clearer position on truth and reality. Pointing to problems in critical literacy and discourse analysis, Luke (2013) argues that we need "an acknowledgement of the existence of 'truth' and 'reality' outside of the particular texts in question" (p. 146). Is it useful, Luke asks, to suggest that "texts about the Holocaust or slavery, or about global warming constitute yet further or more textual representations of the world?" (p. 146). The problem, Luke (2013) suggests, is that since the linguistic or discursive turn in the social sciences, the "conventional wisdom" has been that "realities are socially constructed by human beings through discourse" (p. 136). But what about "truths, facts about history, social and material reality that they purport to represent?" (p. 146). Luke goes on to argue that critical literacy or critical discourse analysis need "a commitment to the existence and accessibility of 'truth', 'facts' and 'realities' outside of the texts in question." (p. 146). As discussed in Chapter 4, the idea that things are socially constructed is often misconstrued to suggest that things are not real. Social constructions such as language, race, and gender are very real, but are as they are because of social practices. The problem from a poststructuralist point of view has been that an interest in how discourses construct reality has become too much of a central focus without also making it clear that realities are real, regimes of truth are truths, and that discourses have material consequences.

In a similar vein, Latour (2004) argues that "a certain form of critical spirit has sent us down the wrong path, encouraging us to fight the wrong enemies and, worst of all, to be considered as friends by the wrong sort of allies because of a little mistake in the definition of its main target" (p. 231). This error, Latour argues, was that in critiquing empiricism or positivism or particular claims to truth, critical work came to focus on the ways in which truth or reality were constructed – it moved away from reality – rather than trying to get closer to the facts. What we need, Latour argues, is to change the focus of critique, to cultivate "a stubbornly realist attitude" through a realism that deals not so much with "matters of fact," but rather with "matters of concern" (p. 231). This is important: We need to be able to make connections between discourses and materiality, discourse and reality. This does not mean we need to accept neo-Marxist claims to have the last word on material relations – far from it – nor that reality is represented in discourse – there are nonrepresentational ways forward here (Thrift, 2007) – but rather that we need to try to bring elements of these traditions together, "historical materialist critique of the state and political economy, on the one hand, and poststructuralist and postmodern theories of discourse, on the other" (Luke, 2013, p. 139). Understanding the complementarity of these traditions is more important than getting lost in their differences.

Critical Literacies

While CDA/S has been a widely adopted approach to text analysis, particularly as a methodological framework for research, critical literacy has been a significant domain of what we might call applied CDA. Simply put, critical literacy can be understood in terms of enabling students to read the world critically, putting the tools of critical discourse analysis in the hands of our students. There are a number of different strands in critical literacy. In this section, I will give an account of different ways of doing critical literacy, as well as some key debates within the field. Of particular importance will be the discussion as to whether literacy education – and this applies to education more broadly and will also be discussed in Chapter 6 – should be centrally about providing access to powerful forms of literacy or providing a space for diverse forms of literacy.

There are a number of different ways of approaching critical literacy (Luke & Walton, 1994), that can be understood as a "coalition of educational interests" that use "the technologies of writing and other modes of inscription" as part of broader projects "for social change, cultural diversity, economic equity, and political enfranchisement" (Luke & Freebody, 1997, p. 1). As Luke (1997a) suggests, although critical approaches to literacy share an orientation toward understanding literacy (or literacies) as social practices related to broader social and political concerns, there are a number of different orientations including text analytic approaches, Freirean-based critical pedagogy, and feminist and poststructuralist orientations. Chun (2015) proposes a set of common themes

Table 5.3 Critical Literacies

Critical Literacies	Features	Concerns
Social practices	Understanding literacies in social rather than cognitive terms	Literacy practices as social practices; potentially lacking political or pedagogical frames
Genres of power	Overt instruction in powerful linguistic forms	Focus on access and critique of liberal egalitarianism; potentially transmissive model based around text analysis that lacks a social dimension
Freirean pedagogy	Relating the word to the world and the lives of students	Focus on literacy as political and involving the inclusion of students' worlds; possibly fails to engage with how voice brings about change

in approaches to critical literacy, including: Drawing on the lived experience of students and teachers, forming shared and common goals, using an approach to language that focuses broadly on social semiotics, making questions of power at both local and global levels central to an understanding of language and education, engaging with students' and teachers' understanding of the everyday, incorporating a form of critical self-reflexive practice, and creating and renewing a sense of community. Combining various accounts of critical literacy (Chun, 2015; Lankshear, 1997; Lee, 1997; Luke 1997a), we can distinguish various ways of doing critical literacy (see Table 5.3).

Literacies as Social Practices

This starting position is one that notes that literacies are social practices. This is not in itself a particularly critical orientation but it is a first step in recognizing that literacy needs to be understood in social rather than cognitive terms, as something we do as part of our social lives rather than as isolated skills to do with reading and writing, decoding, and encoding texts. Rather than two of the so-called 'four skills' of language education (listening, speaking, reading, and writing), literacy is viewed from this perspective as a practice. It is worth recalling, as the discussion in Chapter 2 reminds us, that practices are understood as embedded and repeated social actions, things we do every day with social ramifications. Rather than a view that literacy is beneficial in and of itself – what has been termed the 'literacy myth' or the 'autonomous view' of literacy (Gee, 1996; Street, 1995) – the understanding of literacies as social practices pluralizes *literacies,* questions the divide between oracy and literacy (which, amongst other things divided the world on questionable grounds into the literate and non-literate), and insists literacies have to be seen for how they operate in social domains.

Building on the ethnographic studies particularly of Heath (1983) – and note here again the importance, as discussed above, of understanding texts ethnographically – and her demonstration of the ways different communities do different things with words, studies of literacy became social, hence *literacy practices* (Baynham,1995), *social literacies* (Street, 1995), or *multiliteracies* (Cope & Kalantzis, 2000; 2013). Heath showed the importance of this understanding for schooling, since middle-class homes tended to mirror the literacy practices of school more closely than did the literacy events of the different working-class homes she studied. This links to the discussion in Chapter 6 of Bourdieu's understanding of cultural capital. Heath's argument was not that homes should change to match school literacy practices but that schools should learn to accommodate different orientations toward texts. Work in this tradition has looked critically at workplace literacies and numeracies (Lankshear, 1997; Yasukawa & Black, 2016), the role of early school and home reading materials in the socialization of children (Davies, 1989; Luke, 1988), the reading practices of teenage and adult women (Radway, 1984; Talbot, 1995; Walkerdine, 1990), or access and denial of access to literacy for women.

Rockhill's (1994, pp. 247–8) study of Hispanic immigrant women in California points to a central dilemma that literacy "is caught up in the material, racial and sexual oppression of women, *and* it embodies their hope for escape." Literacy, learning English, going to school can be both "a threat and a desire," enabling change, yet threatening the lives they know. While literacy is often "women's work but not women's right" (p. 248), their desire to "be somebody" by gaining literacy in English and the threat that such desires pose to the patriarchal structures of many family lives leaves many immigrant women in a conflictual and ambiguous situation. Viewing literacies as social practices is therefore a crucial step toward any understanding of literacy and power. Literacy studies have developed extensively from these early insights, impelled both by the need to engage with new literacy practices, such as digital literacies, and with a range of developments in thinking about literacy in terms of spatial and material practices (Mills, 2016), for example. These trends have come together in recent work that looks at digital literacies in tertiary education (Gourlay, 2021), arguing that notions of disembodied, 'virtual' interactions overlook the material entanglements of people, knowledge practices, texts, and artifacts, thus bringing non-human actors into view and downplaying the insistence on the individual human subject.

Viewing literacies as social practices does not in itself suggest a critical stance (aside from the critique of cognitivist approaches to literacy) but can nevertheless be mapped against critical applied linguistic themes (as can be seen very clearly in Rockhill's, 1994, study): The domination of particular forms of literacy in many contexts, especially educational; disparate forms of access to literacy, particularly in terms of gender; discriminatory forms of exclusion around different kinds of literacy, for example, in terms of academic writing; different ways that control over forms of literacy is perceived in positive and negative terms, most evidently in terms such as 'illiterate'; and in terms of the desires people have for and through their engagement in literacy practices. Studies of literacy practices are generally sociological or anthropological in nature – trying to understand literacies in society – rather than the more applied (pedagogical) interventions to which I now turn.

Powerful Genres or Powerful Voices?

The spread of so-called student-centered pedagogies in the 1970s and 1980s in many parts of the world – with their move away from explicit instruction of grammar, and evolution toward whole language approaches in first language education and communicative language teaching in second language educa- tion – came under critical scrutiny from a number of directions. While the conservative critique bewailed what it claimed to be falling standards, poor grammar, inability to spell, and poor reading and writing skills, a more criti- cal orientation sought to divert this discussion away from a reactionary back- to-basics discourse in favor of the development of critical literacy materials. Liberal approaches to teaching, particularly as they evolved in student-centered or process pedagogies, it was argued, eschewed explicit instruction and instead relied on an idealistic and romantic view (traceable back to the educational ideas of Rousseau) of the natural evolution of the child. Encouraging students to express themselves – a process that would lead, it was claimed, to individ- ual development (and possibly, even, empowerment) – was all very well but it favors those children that already have access to the skills (linguistic and cultural capital) needed to succeed.

Access and Explicit Pedagogy

Delpit (1995) takes issue with so-called student-centered expressive pedago- gies, with their claims that a democratic approach to learning will empower learners as autonomous individuals. She suggests that this approach to edu- cation fails to give children from outside the mainstream culture of school- ing (White, middle-class culture) access to the culture of power. Liberals, she suggests, "seem to act under the assumption that to make any rules or expectations explicit is to act against liberal principles, to limit the freedom and autonomy of those subjected to the explicitness" (p. 26). For Delpit (1988, 1995), minority children need explicit instruction in the "culture of power": "If you are not already a participant in the culture of power, being told explicitly the rules of that culture makes acquiring power easier" (1995, p. 25). This is not, she makes clear, to denigrate Black language or culture but it is to make explicit to students that "there is a political power game" being played and "if they want to be in on that game there are certain games that they too must play" (pp. 39–40). Students must therefore "be *taught* the codes needed to par- ticipate fully in the mainstream of American life" (p. 45).

Also in opposition to progressivist pedagogies, Fairclough (1992) and his colleagues (Ivanič, 1990, Janks and Ivanič, 1992) developed the notion of Critical Language Awareness (CLA) explicitly in reaction to what they saw as the inadequate approach to questions of language and power in general language awareness materials. CLA aims to "empower learners by providing them with a critical analytical framework to help them reflect on their own language experiences and practices and on the language practices of others in the institutions of which they are a part and in the wider society within which they live" (Clark & Ivanič, 1997, p. 217). The need for critical language awareness has been taken up by Alim (2005), arguing that students of color need to understand how White ways of speaking and seeing the word and the world dominate (White) public space and denigrate other ways of speaking and using languages. CLA has also been important in understanding academic language use: Clark (1992) explains the goals of CLA to provide students with "the opportunities to discover and critically examine the conventions of the academic discourse community and to enable them to emancipate themselves by developing alternatives to the dominant conventions" (p. 137). This work is the precursor to long line of work in critical approaches to academic literacy and languages for specific purposes (Benesch, 2001; Chun 2015; Wallace, 1992)

A similar dissatisfaction with whole language and other student-centered approaches led to the development of the genre-based literacy movement, based on the argument that the liberal progressivist approaches to instruction disadvantaged children from minority backgrounds; in its place was proposed a form of critical literacy based on overt instruction of genres (Cope, Kalantzis, Kress, Martin, & Murphy, 1993), or an "explicit pedagogy for inclusion and access" (Cope & Kalantzis, 1993, p. 64). If teaching "is to provide students with equitable social access" (p. 67), it needs to link the social purposes of language to predictable patterns of language (genres). On the face of it, this can look a little like Honey's (1997. p. 240) argument for teaching standard English: One of the "most powerful factors contributing to the disadvantage of America's underclass—Blacks and other ethnic groups, and lower-class Whites—is in reality capable of being changed: I refer to their ability to handle standard English."

From Honey's way of thinking, we can alleviate social inequality by teaching powerful forms of language, a position that has been widely critiqued for its unexamined notion of an inherently powerful standard version of the language, the learning of which can act as a panacea for all sorts of other social ills: Poverty, racism, class bigotry, and so on. This overlooks the problem that many forms of prejudice will not be overcome by using language in a particular way: As Wiley and Lukes (1996) point out, "for all too many African Americans, the fact that mastery of the language does not ensure economic mobility or political access makes manifest the fallacy of standard English as the language of equal opportunity" (p. 530). Flores and Rosa (2015, p. 150) similarly argue that raciolinguistic ideologies "produce racialized speaking subjects who are constructed as linguistically deviant even when engaging in linguistic practices positioned as normative or innovative when produced by privileged white subjects." Or as Alim and Smitherman (2012, p. 55) put it, the "somber reality for many African Americans is that, still, no matter how 'articulate' yo ass is, upon visiting in person, can't nuthin fool the landlord now, baby – you Black, Jack!"

Delpit's (1995) or Cope and Kalantzis' (1993) cases for explicit pedagogy and access to dominant forms of language and literacy, however, are based not on a belief about the inherent superiority of one particular language variety (standard English, for example), but rather on a pragmatic orientation to the contingencies of power (an understanding of the workings of power rather than an assumption of what is powerful), critical awareness (helping students understand that in an unequal world, this is what they may need to know), arguments around access (unless students have access to certain language forms, they will never be able to do certain things), and careful analysis of language forms deemed important (the identification of genres of power was the result of extensive research) (Cope & Kalantzis, 1993; Kress, 1993).

There are nonetheless various problems here. First, it is not clear that genre analysis (using systemic functional linguistics) actually reveals the operation of powerful language. The concern, similar to some of the problems with CDA/S discussed above, is the assumption that technical descriptions of language (even when they claim to be 'functional' descriptions) do not in fact provide sociological analyses of the social functioning of texts. The apparent revelations yielded by text analysis are mistakenly assumed to show "sociological 'truths' about how schools and social structures work to structure and produce unequal outcomes" (Luke 1996, p. 316). Various cognitive effects, pedagogical processes, and political imperatives are then supposed to flow from such analyses. This takes us back to a central concern for critical applied linguistics: While textual and linguistic analysis needs to be a significant part of what we do, we need at the same time to be wary of the danger of believing that technical skills in textual analysis reveal sociological truths about social inequality. This becomes particularly insidious when one particular model of grammatical analysis – with its "fetishization of technicism and a celebration of a masculinist mode of knowledge production" (Lee, 1996, p. 198) – is allowed to stand in for more careful social analysis. Once "such a singular view of the world" forms the central part of the analysis, it all too easily allows its "unwitting conservatism" to promote "politically reactionary" solutions (Corson, 1997, p. 175).

Although the argument for access to powerful language may make political sense, we need much more careful analyses of what actually *is* powerful. And such an argument can never come from an internal analysis of texts; rather, it must be a sensitive sociological analysis of texts in context. As suggested with respect to CDA/S, unless we have ethnographies of text production and reception, we should be very wary of making assumptions about the meanings and effects of texts. The access argument itself also needs critical scrutiny, since it is based on a "liberal-democratic politics of equality" (Lee, 1997, p. 411). While access to literacy remains a basic sociological issue—women around the world, for example, continue to have lower rates of literacy than men—an argument for critical literacy based on access to genres of power remains questionable in terms both of its politics and its assumptions about language. Although this tradition of critical literacy broadened its scope in later iterations, particularly through the idea of *multiliteracies* (Cope & Kalantzis, 2000; New London

Group, 1996), it still needs to be able to demonstrate that explicit instruction can bring about social change (Prain, 1997). The danger here, which signals a warning to all domains of critical applied linguistics, is that if we attempt critical work through one methodological or analytic lens, we can end up all too quickly with a reactionary politics. Critical work must always be on the move.

The Word and the World

An alternative approach to critical literacies emerged through developments of the work of Paulo Freire. Whereas the version of critical literacy discussed above focused predominantly on questions of access to powerful forms of language, this version of critical literacy focuses on the opposite side of access, namely the possibility for participation, the possibility for different languages and cultures, and forms of knowledge to be allowed a pedagogical role. Genre literacy, Lee (1997) observes, is something of a "pedagogy of deferral" (students are not literate until they have mastered key genres). Freirean forms of critical literacy, by contrast, might be seen as a pedagogy of *inclusion* (it is the students' own languages and lives that form the stuff of critical literacy). For Freire "Reading the world always precedes reading the word, and reading the word implies continually reading the world" (Freire & Macedo, 1987, p. 35). As he developed literacy programs among the poor in Brazil – and later elsewhere – Freire's literacy pedagogy always started with the real-world concerns of the people, who helped generate the world lists used for literacy instruction (such as *tijolo*, brick; *favela*, slum).

Literacy education was always political, either domesticating or liberating. Freire argued that standard literacy programs with their meaningless exercises served only as a form of *banking* education, a *transmission* of received knowledge from teachers to students. What was needed, by contrast, was a liberatory education – a *pedagogy for the oppressed* as his best-known book (Freire, 1970) was called – that started with the local conditions and concerns of people. Freire saw literacy education as a form of *conscientização* – conscientization – that would bring people to understand that the conditions they lived in were not natural but were rather something against which they could take action. Freirean-based approaches to critical literacy have been developed in many parts of the world. Bee's (1993, p. 106) program for immigrant women in Australia saw literacy as a "means for enabling women who have been conditioned to accept second-class status to affirm their aspirations as valid and their knowledge and views of life as genuine contributions to the net stock of human understanding."

Reading and writing would not be empowering unless they were tied to an understanding of the structural impediments these women faced, a form of critical literacy intended to help women both read the word (gain in literacy) and the world (understand the nature of gendered oppression). Working with migrant farm workers in Colorado, Graman (1988) developed a Freirean ESL pedagogy (generative words included *bonus* and *short-hoe* – two issues of great significance to these farm workers), that sought to address "the existential, political, and axiological questions touching the lives of both students and teachers" (p. 441). Various forms of *participatory* education (Auerbach, 2000) have also drawn on these traditions, seeking to involve learners and their communities in the educational process: "The classroom becomes a context in which students analyze their reality for the purpose of participating in its transformation" (Auerbach, 1995, p. 12). Walsh's (1991, pp. 126–7) *critical bilingualism* – not just speaking two languages but "becoming conscious of the sociocultural, political, and ideological contexts in which the languages (and therefore the speakers) are positioned" – also draws on Freirean pedagogy.

There are, nonetheless, various problems with Freirean pedagogies. Freire's work has been criticized over the years on many grounds, including a reductive view of oppressed and oppressors, an inability to see women's literacy as more than an addition to economic oppression, and a tendency to be overoptimistic about the effects of conscientization. Weiler (1992, p. 325) takes Freirean pedagogy to task for dealing with abstracted notions of liberatory teachers and oppressed students, without engaging with the "lived subjectivities of teachers and students located in a particular society and defined by existing meanings of race, gender, sexual orientation, class, and other social identities." None of these is of course a necessary characteristic of Freirean pedagogy. As we have seen, contextualized accounts of feminist, antiracist, and other pedagogies overcome these issues quite quickly. Perhaps more interesting has been the way that Freire has been taken up particularly in North American contexts, where "Freire's generative themes" become "incentives for open project pedagogy, in which the students freely investigate what matters most in their lives" (Tochon, 2019, p. 272). The injunction to start with what matters to the students then elides into a more individualized pedagogy of self-exploration and self-expression.

This version of critical literacy is most centrally concerned with the *voices* of marginalized students, arguing that the dominant curricula and teaching practices of mainstream schools silence the ideas, cultures, languages, and voices of students from other backgrounds. The focus of this approach is on opening up a space for the marginalized to speak, write, or read (*voice* does not refer necessarily to oral language) so that the voicing of their lives may transform both their lives and the social system that excludes them. As Giroux (1988) argues, voice "constitutes the focal point" for a critical theory of education: "The concept of voice represents the unique instances of self-expression through which students affirm their own class, cultural, racial, and gender identities" (p. 199). It refers to our own articulation of agency against the exclusions of structure and thus is supposed to be not so much a liberal humanist celebration of free will but a struggle for the power to express oneself when those forms of expression are discounted by mainstream forms of culture and knowledge.

Although this sense of voice is intended to be a critical and political version of language use, a view that acknowledges the struggle to make oneself heard (akin in some ways to Kramsch's, 2021, *symbolic capital*), it has been critiqued for failing to avoid North American individualistic idealism (Cope & Kalantzis, 1993; Luke, 1996). This touches on another important point raised at various junctures in this book: The ways in which ideas are taken up and reworked in the Anglosphere. Not only did Freire's literacy work in Recife in the 1960s very obviously predate its influence in North America (which is generally seen to start with the 1970 publication of the translated *Pedagogy of the Oppressed* (*Pedagogia do Oprimido*), but it also developed in dialogue with other traditions (the work of Césaire, Fanon, and others from the French Caribbean, for example), and has continued as an educational and literacy movement both in Brazil and in other places influenced by this work (literacy movements from Cuba to Timor Leste), operating both independently and in dialogue with its English-language off-springs (Boughton, 2011; 2012).

Conclusion: Toward A Politics of Text

I have dwelt in this chapter on two particular areas of contention in critical discourse analysis and critical literacies: First, the division between discourse and Discourse, or structuralist and poststructuralist accounts of discourse and power; second, the distinction between access and inclusive focuses in literacy. While it might be tempting to connect these two debates, suggesting that poststructuralist orientations may be generally inclined to inclusivity or recognition rather than access, the connection is a tenuous one. If there are similarities, these may have more to do with the lives that these ideas take on in different contexts: An inclusive focus on voice and a poststructuralist focus on identity are more a result of the particular cultural take up of these ideas in parts of the Global North, than with the way these ideas were originally framed. Rather than positing two irreconcilable camps – Discourse/inclusivity versus discourse/access – it is more fruitful to see how aspects of each can be brought together.

The problem with the access versus inclusion argument is that *neither* of these two models of critical literacy has an adequate account of how power relates to language and literacy. As Delpit (1988) – who is often invoked as a supporter of the 'access' version of literacy – has suggested, we need to work on both sides of this argument: The skills versus process distinction is a false dichotomy and an unproductive debate (Delpit, 1988). We need to provide access while challenging forms of power, a position taken up in Paris and Alim's (2017) *culturally sustaining pedagogy* (see Chapter 6). The difficulty for genre versions of critical literacy is that "without a sociological theory of power, conflict and difference, such models fail to provide an account for why and how some discourses, knowledges and texts 'count' more than others" (Luke, 1996, p. 312). Meanwhile, interpretations of Freirean-style critical literacy that emphasize voice as the writing/speaking of marginalized people – though we should remind ourselves that this has been a very particular way of framing Freirean pedagogy that many would not adhere to – fail to account for how this speaking invokes power. Each model, Luke (1996, p. 315) argues, is "based on broad assumptions about the sociological effects and consequences of literacy." Genre pedagogies operate from the "logocentric assumption that mastery of powerful text types can lead to intellectual and cognitive development, educational achievement and credentials, and enhanced social access and mobility," while the Freirean model sees power vested "phonocentrically in the 'dangerous memories' of individual and collective voice" (p. 315).

Both seem to suggest that their "preferred literate practices directly inculcate 'power'." Neither genre-based literacy pedagogy nor inclusionary forms of critical literacy come to grips "with their assumptions about the relationship between literacy and social power" (Luke 1996, p. 309). What we need instead are close understandings of how power operates in relation to language, and this takes us back to the need for detailed sociological and ethnographic studies of the local workings of power (see the discussion of the global spread of English in Chapter 3, for example). Rather than relying on prior sociological assumptions about power on which we can base an analysis of language and ideology, we need to keep the question of power open, as *that which is to be explained*. If we assume power to be already sociologically defined (in the hands of dominant groups), and we see our task as using linguistic analysis of texts to show how that power is used, our work is never one of exploration, only of revelation. If, on the other hand, we are prepared to see power as in need of explanation, then our analyses of discourse aim to explore how power may operate, rather than to demonstrate its existence.

This also allows us to keep questions of *voice* on the table: The notion was caricatured and critiqued from an access-oriented position, linking it always to process-oriented pedagogies that seemingly just wanted people to express themselves. Voice, for Blommaert (2005, p. 4), by contrast, refers ways in which "people manage to make themselves understood or fail to do so." This is a question of access to and deployment of discourses in specific contexts, and can only be understood through close attention to questions of power. It is akin to Kramsch's (2021, p. 11) focus on *symbolic power*, which she explains as concerned "not just with the capacity to make yourself understood but with the capacity to make yourself listened to, taken seriously, respected and valued." *Symbolic power* (*le pouvoir symbolique*) – drawing in particular on the work of Bourdieu (1991) – is "the power to construct social reality by creating and using symbols" (2021, p. 5). It is our capacity to act symbolically on the world. It seems unwise to dismiss this interest in voice and symbolic power on the grounds that it focuses on self-expression. As Giroux (1988), Blommaert (2005), and Kramsch (2021) all make clear, it is about the possibility of those who are not being heard – people of color, women, minorities, Indigenous people, Deaf communities, scholars from the Global South – being taken seriously.

We have also seen across these different approaches, particularly access literacies and CDA/S, common problems that stem in part from a belief that linguistic frameworks such as systemic functional linguistics or discourse analysis can provide a technical solution to social problems. This puts too much emphasis on analytic frameworks rather than looking at the social life of texts.

Table 5.4 Critical Approaches to Text

Textual Relations	Features
Pretextual history	Sociohistorical associations of the text
Intratextual relations	Discourse analysis of textual aspects
Contextual materialities	Physical location, participants, and indexicalities
Intertextual interactions	Overt and covert references to other voices and texts
Subtextual implications	Ideological, discursive, or cultural meanings invoked by texts
Post-textual interpretations	Meanings and affective and material relations derived from texts

In order to deal with the politics of texts, we need at the very least to consider not just *intratextual* relations (linguistic analysis) but also *pretextual*[3] history (sociohistorical associations of the text and its production), *contextual* materialities (physical location and participants), *intertextual* interactions (overt and covert references to other voices and texts), *subtextual* implications (broader ideologies, cultural frames, or discourses invoked by texts), and *post-textual* interpretations (the meanings people derive from those texts, and the material consequences) (Pennycook, 2007, pp. 53–4) (Table 5.4).

This last point refers again to the reception of texts but also emphasizes that not only do texts suggest the likelihood of certain readings, but the readers themselves are embedded in particular discourses and come to any text with a history of interpretation. Rather than texts, in some liberal approaches to textual analysis (Widdowson, 1998), being open to any interpretation, there are as Hall (1994, p. 207) suggests, "preferred meanings" of texts—within any society or culture, there are dominant or preferred meanings or interpretations—and readers, listeners, or viewers may interpret texts in line with, in negotiation with, or in opposition to such preferred readings. This suggests an understanding of texts that avoids both an overdetermination by social structure (of which some critical approaches can be guilty) and an underdetermination that suggests that texts are simply open to all interpretations (a pitfall of liberal approaches to text).

Whatever concerns there may be about various approaches to CDA/S or critical literacies, it is clear we need ways of dealing critically with texts. CDA/S has of course moved on considerably since its early days and some of the particular concerns discussed here (Fairclough may be seen as the 'father' of the field, but his interests no longer determine the way it is done or the focus of the analyses). It has been reworked to take on more feminist concerns in *feminist critical discourse analysis* (Lazar, 2007), and has now become a framework to look at any number of issues, from green discourse (Horsbøl, 2020) to discourses around marriage equality (Ku, 2020) or non-heteronormative discourses among online gamers (Potts, 2015). This diversity means that on the one hand, the critical focus with which it once started has been inevitably watered down and dispersed, but on the other hand, it is no longer so tied to modernist visions of power and ideology. While Jones (2007) and Widdowson (1998) – from very different perspectives – question whether there can ever be such a thing as critical discourse analysis (for Jones the normative tools of discourse analysis cannot provide a purchase on critical social issues, while for Widdowson 'critical' and 'analysis' are contradictory), we need something that enables us to do forms of social analysis through texts.

Whether we follow van Leeuwen's (2008) view that discourses are social practices that have become texts, or Luke's (2013, p137) argument that the "key philosophical and political issue in this millennium" concerns the relation between "cultural systems of representation" (from traditional print to text messages) and "social and economic reality," the need is clear for socially and politically engaged analysis. This is not a search for linguistic manifestations of social reality so much as the search for the production of social reality itself: This is social analysis, "situated political practice: a machine for generating interpretations and for constructing readings, none of which is neutral or unsituated" (Luke, 1997b, p. 349). In a time of fragmented media, open and flagrant mistruths by newspapers and politicians (or as Jacquemet, 2020 suggests, just 'bullshit'), people need to be able to engage with texts critically. We might see the current state of fragmented discourse, conspiracy theories, targeted misinformation campaigns, blatant lies, as in part a failure of critical literacy (but also education more broadly), but it also suggests the urgent need to regroup and refocus.

This does not necessarily entail a choice between discourse as productive or reflective of reality: We need to be able to grasp the realities of social life, of economic disparity, of forms of discrimination. It may in the end be unproductive to continue to worry about whether we are in the discourse or ideology camp – many big-D Discourse analysts have realized that the idea of ideology may still be useful, even if only because of its popular usage. Perhaps more important is the need to partially "provincialize" language in this account, "to recognize its limits…to open ourselves up to a world of communicating and knowing beyond – or beside/s – words" (Thurlow, 2016, p. 19). This is not just to do multimodal analysis, but to take on board questions of the body, of affect, of the senses. And this work will need forms of pedagogical action – whether we call this critical language awareness, critical literacy, or critical pedagogy – that develops ways in which students can move to resist and change the discourses that construct their lives. This will of necessity include questions of access: "If students are to learn how to read the world critically, they must be given access to discourses that can allow them to analyse that world" (McCormick, 1994, p. 49), but also to forms of critical reading that enable them to see better, and act on, the ways the world is constructed discursively, and the very real forms of material inequality that are part of this.

This is the task of mapping the material and discursive effects of discourses on different people and communities, and working through the pedagogical implications. As Hernandez-Zamora (2010, p. 191) reminds us, "intellectual and symbolic work remains the realm of white minds equipped with sophisticated knowledge, language, and literacy tools, whereas most enslaving labor work remains assigned (or enforced) to brown hands." The issue ultimately is not then to enforce the same white languages and literacies on people of color but to *decolonize* literacy and develop critical literacies as tools of decolonization. The difference between official, standard, and access-based approaches to education and grassroots, community, resistant education is that while the first "aims to educate people to acquire skills and habits to fit and function in society *as it is* (unjust, organized in castes, individualistic, market-driven, etc.), the aim of alternative forms of education has always been the *decolonization of minds*" (Hernandez-Zamora, 2010, p. 200). Many of these issues will be the focus of the next chapter that looks at critical pedagogy.

Notes

1. Fairclough (1995) concedes this in the introduction to his book *Critical Discourse Analysis*: "The principle that textual analysis should be combined with analysis of practices of production and consumption has not been adequately operationalized in the papers collected here" (p. 9).
2. This, by the way, is more or less what Foucault meant by the order of discourse (*l'ordre du discours*) which may be better translated as domains or the field of discourse, rather than the 'order/disorder' taken up by Wodak and Fairclough. A similar point could be made about *pouvoir-savoir* and many other terms that have not travelled well across languages and philosophical frameworks.
3. Widdowson (2004) also uses the ideas of *pretext* and *context*, though in his linguistic-cognitive framing, pretext refers to something akin to presuppositions and context to schemas, whereas in my view both the pretextual and contextual put much more emphasis on the social and material conditions of the text.

6   The Politics of Language Pedagogy

Language Education: Political from Top to Bottom

Education, like language, is political from top to bottom. And language education, the central focus of this chapter, is doubly so. Issues raised in previous chapters already suggest many concerns for language education: Struggles over which languages and which versions of language are to be taught in schools, over the role of minority and first languages in education, over the roles forms of difference – race, gender, sexuality, and disability – have in classrooms, over the issues discussed in the previous chapter concerning access and inclusion. Whereas classrooms from a liberal perspective are construed as fairly neutral sites of pedagogical transaction – where teachers are engaged in imparting knowledge of language to students or setting up the conditions for students to learn – Auerbach (1995) suggests that we must understand the social and ideological relations within the classroom and their relation to a larger world outside: "Pedagogical choices about curriculum development, content, materials, classroom processes, and language use, although appearing to be informed by apolitical professional considerations, are, in fact, inherently ideological in nature, with significant implications for learners' socioeconomic roles" (p. 9).

We may be tempted to think of the politics of language education in terms only of broad concerns about language planning, educational policy, and, particularly in recent times, the effects of neoliberal political economy (a decline in state-provided education; an increase in inequality, competition, accountability, and casualization) (Flubacher & Del Percio, 2017). We should be careful at the same time, however, not to neglect "the political content of everyday language and language learning practices" and an understanding of "the societal context in which learning takes place, roles and relationships in the classroom and outside, kinds of learning tasks, and the content of the language that is learned" (Benson, 1997, p. 32). From this point of view, "the classroom functions as a kind of microcosm of the broader social order" (Auerbach, 1995, p. 9). Once we start to look at language classrooms through a critical lens, "dynamics of power and inequality show up in every aspect of classroom life, from physical setting to needs assessment, participant structures, curriculum development, lesson content, materials, instructional processes, discourse patterns, language use, and evaluation" (Auerbach, 1995, p. 12). It is this political understanding of the language classroom that is the primary focus of this chapter.

There are a number of concerns that need to be thought through, however, if we view the classroom as a "microcosm of the social order." Does this mean that social relations in classrooms merely reflect those of the broader social world (a position akin to the language-reflects-reality argument critiqued in Chapter 3)? Or, if we acknowledge that classrooms also operate in a more dynamic way than this, how can we conceptualize ways in which what happens in classrooms may be related to broader social and political domains? These are concerns that Suresh Canagarajah (1993, p. 612) raised in his critical ethnography of his own English classroom during renewed hostilities between the Sinhala government and Tamil nationalists in northern Sri Lanka. Given the extreme conditions under which this English class was taught – with students mainly from rural communities and the poorest economic groups and government planes bombing the vicinity of the university during placement tests – we might expect Canagarajah to suggest that everything inside the classroom is determined by what is going on outside. He is interested in a more complex story, however: Despite such loud and urgent claims to see what happens in this classroom as a reflection of the outside world, he goes on to argue for an understanding of the *relative autonomy* of classrooms, suggesting both that they are social and cultural domains unto themselves and that they are interlinked with the world outside.

Canagarajah (1993) shows how anything from student annotations in textbooks (they were using *American Kernel Lessons: Intermediate*) to favored learning styles and resistance to his own preferred teaching approaches are connected in compound ways to the social and cultural worlds both inside and outside the classroom. Looking at these many dimensions—teaching style, textbooks, language, and cultural background—he shows how we need to steer a careful path between an overdetermined notion of the classroom as a mere reflection of the outside world and an underdetermined vision of classrooms as autonomous islands unto themselves. So the task is not merely to try to map the micro-activities of classrooms against the macro-dimensions of society, but to try to gain detailed understandings of the contextual workings of power. This argument echoes points I have made in previous chapters about understanding language and texts from a situated perspective. Our classrooms have permeable walls (Pennycook, 2000): They are affected by and have effects on the wider social, cultural, economic, and political world. Classrooms are dynamic spaces that are interlinked in multiple directions with the world outside. As educators, we have to believe this: Otherwise our only role is to reproduce the social world as it is. I turn in the next sections to questions of reproduction and resistance in education.

Reproduction, Structure, and Agency

To understand language classrooms within a wider context, I shall turn first of all to questions of reproduction and resistance in education. In contrast to an optimistic (neo)liberal view of education that it provides opportunity for all (anyone can go to school, receive equal treatment, and come out at the end as whatever they want), more critical analyses have pointed out that schools are far greater agents of social reproduction than of social change. Schools operate within the larger field of social economic and political relations, and as key social institutions, they ultimately serve to maintain the social, economic, cultural, and political status quo rather than upset it. From Althusser's (1971) observation that schools were the most significant part of the *ideological state apparatus* (as opposed to the *repressive state apparatus* of police, army, courts, and prisons) and were crucial for the ideological subjugation of the workforce, to Bowles and Gintis' (1976) illustration of how schools operate to reproduce the labor relations necessary for the functioning of capitalism, this focus on the roles of schools in the reproduction of social inequality has been a key insight from critical sociology of education.

This applies as much to second language education as it does to education more broadly, both in relation to educational roles and to languages themselves. English language education for refugees, for example, has been critiqued for emphasizing language competencies and functions appropriate for minimum-wage work: "following orders, asking questions, confirming understanding, and apologizing for mistakes" (Tollefson, 1991, p. 108). Auerbach (1995, p. 17) makes a similar point, suggesting that work-oriented language education is either aimed at "specific job-related vocabulary and literacy tasks (reading time cards or pay stubs)" or at attitudes and behaviors deemed appropriate in the workplace "learning how to call in sick, request clarification of job instructions, make small talk, follow safety regulations." While it can be argued that providing English language education does provide social and economic opportunities, it is nonetheless the case that refugees are typically offered forms of education (if there is any education on offer) that prepare them for work "as janitors, waiters in restaurants, assemblers in electronic plants, and other low-paying jobs offering little opportunity for advancement" regardless of whether they have skills that might qualify them for other forms of work (Tollefson, 1991, p. 108).

This is a consistent problem with functional of appropriacy-oriented pedagogical approaches to language education. While they can appear much better suited to learners than other curricular frameworks – they focus on student needs and appropriate language use – they run the danger of assuming certain roles for those students and their language practices that may be as restrictive as they are redemptive. "Teaching students that the ability to 'switch' between 'home languages' and 'appropriate languages' can lead to academic success" de los Rios, Martinez, Musser, Canady, Camangian, and Quijada (2019, p. 360) argue, following Flores and Rosa (2015), "disregards the material realities of white supremacy." Suggesting that the use of what is considered standard language in the public sphere (while maintaining other language styles elsewhere) will lead to social and economic benefits overlooks the broader forces of discrimination at operation in society (Alim & Smitherman, 2012). Rosa and Flores (2017b, p. 186) therefore insist on a *critical raciolinguistic perspective* to examine how "discourses of appropriateness, which permeate asset-based approaches to language education, are complicit in normalizing the reproduction of the White gaze by marginalizing the linguistic practices of language-minoritized populations." Functional and appropriacy-based language education runs the danger of maintaining rather than challenging current conditions of inequality.

When languages such as English are involved, it is clear that education plays an important role in reproducing the use and status of language. As Benson (1997, p. 27) observes, the "acceptance of English as a second language very often implies the acceptance of the global economic and political order for which English serves as the 'international language'" (p. 27). ELT, or education in other major languages, becomes part of a cycle of reinforcement: The more it is emphasized, the more it is in demand, and the more other languages are excluded from the educational domain. Indeed, one might suggest that Teaching English to Speakers of Other*ed* Languages might more accurately describe the implications of TESOL. In the international context, English language teaching can be viewed as a major player in the reproduction of an international class of English speakers. Once English has become tied to certain economic and social forces and institutions, education in the language will always tend toward the reproduction of those conditions (O'Regan, 2021). And to promote English over other languages in school on the basis that this is about providing 'access' to English for all is to reproduce linguistic inequalities and racial hierarchies (Macedo, 2019).

As Giroux (1983) points out, however, arguments about social reproduction through schooling leave us with large-scale social analysis rather than an understanding of either how such reproduction takes place or how it may be resisted. This takes us back to one of the key concerns in this book – how to balance largescale critical analysis of inequality with local understandings of its operations – and one of the central elements that informs that discussion: Structure and agency. While this itself a very structuralist distinction (there are other ways to think about this), it can help us see what is at stake here. In establishing his position on the relative autonomy of classrooms, Canagarajah (1993) critiques two earlier articles on critical approaches to TESOL by myself (Pennycook, 1989) and Peirce (1989). My article on methods in language teaching suggested in part that the concept of *method* was a product of Western academic thinking and was exported to periphery classrooms around the world as part of a global export of Western knowledge and culture. Peirce's article focused on the emergence of "People's English" in South Africa, suggesting that this use of English represented a new form of possibility for Black South Africans. Canagarajah chides my "delineation of ideological domination through TESOL" for being "overdetermined and pessimistic," while Peirce's "characterization of the possibilities of pedagogical resistance" is criticized for being "too volitionist and romantic" (p. 602).

Arguing that both of us need to attend to the complexities of classrooms themselves rather than the "politics of TESOL-related macro-structures" (p. 603), Canagarajah argues that Peirce needs to focus more on the adjective (*relative*) while I needed to focus more on the noun (*autonomy*): My view was too much of a top-down structural imposition of methods that overlooks the partial autonomy of classrooms (how teachers and students take up, appropriate and change teaching methods), while Peirce's view was too much of an agentive position that overlooks structural constraints (how language use is always subject to wider social forces). Canagarajah (1993, p. 603) himself goes on to "interrogate the range of behaviors students display in the face of domination." Here, then, we have a basic debate within critical theory: The same issues can be seen, for example, in discussions of linguistic imperialism (top-down structure) and English as a lingua franca (bottom-up agency).

A great deal of macro critical work seeks to identify the social and ideological structures that limit our possibilities as humans. In Marxist, structuralist, and poststructuralist analyses of social and political power, the individual almost disappears from view. Various strands of critical theory take aim at the individualistic, humanist version of the free-willed subject, an understanding of humans that is a product of a very particular social, cultural, and historical era (Pennycook, 2018a). To be sure, this version of human autonomy has been very important in pushing back against views of people in eternal obeisance to God, or cogs within a given social order. Yet when coupled with liberal and neoliberal ideologies, this vision of humans as free individuals, the center of their own universes, subjects giving meaning to the word and the world through their own thought, lacks an understanding of how society, culture, and ideology make us anything but free.

Instead of free-willed subjects deciding what they want to do, we have classes of people, relations of power, and means by which such relations are expressed (ideologies and discourses) that leave the individual somewhat devoid of the potential to act. The issue, then, is not how free-thinking individuals act in relation to social structure but rather how that social structure may also profoundly affect how people think. Giddens (1979) uses the term *structuration* to capture the relation and the mutual interdependence of structure and agency. In this view, there is a constant reciprocal structuring, with social structures both the medium and the product of social action. Thus, what we do, think, or say is always affected by larger questions of social power, and – at least to some extent – continually reproduces those same relations, which in turn affect what we do, think, or say. This position also sheds light on why even the smallest words and deeds may have major implications, why a classroom utterance, textbook illustration, favoring of a particular version of a translation, arrangement of seats, or choice of language are part of a much larger whole. As with the discussion in Chapter 5 of relations between conversational moves, sentence openings, and wider racial constructions (McNamara, 2019; Qin, 2020), this helps us see how social relations are both reproduced and changed.

The macro-structure versus micro-agency distinction is not the only, or even the best, way to consider the functioning of society. Bourdieu (1977) – to whom we will return shortly – viewed *practice* as a way to steer a course between the grand and seemingly deterministic theories of critical social science, where human action is a by-product of larger social structures, and a voluntaristic humanistic conception of individuals operating in a social vacuum. The way forward here for Bourdieu was to think in terms of practice – how people do things – and then to develop ways of thinking about how such practices became sedimented and regulated. His notion of habitus, therefore, became a bridge between large social forces and the doing of the everyday, a way to describe how wider social forces become inscribed onto the body. Practice theory more broadly (Pennycook, 2010; Schatzki, 2001; 2002) provides a different way of thinking about this by focusing on how social actions are clustered into social practices. Social life, Schatzki (2002, p. 70) suggests, is "policed by a range of such practices as negotiation practices, political practices, cooking practices, banking practices, recreation practices, religious practices, and educational practices."

However we try to get at these issues, it is clear that on overemphasis on broad forms of constraint may miss the ways people nonetheless manage to act, while an overemphasis on the capacity to act will miss the constraints on action. It is better, as Ahearn (2012, p. 278) suggests, to think of agency as "the socioculturally mediated capacity to act." There are many other questions, about agency (nonhuman agency, for example) that I shall not develop further here (Bennett, 2010; Rosiek Snyder, & Pratt, 2020). The challenge for critical applied linguistics is to find ways to understand how we think, act, and behave that on the one hand acknowledge our locations within social, cultural, economic, ideological, discursive frameworks but on the other hand allow us at least some possibility of freedom of action and change.

The difficulty, simply put, is getting the balance right. We need to be able to talk about and identify structural racism – ways in which racism is embedded in institutional structures rather than being an individual act of discrimination – and we need to be able to see how individual acts of racism (sexism or homophobic discrimination) are never just that: They are always part of a wider circulation of discourses and discriminations that in turn reinforce the wider institutional forms of discrimination. To pursue this challenge, we need ways of thinking about social class, gender, ideology, power, resistance, and human agency. It is not adequate to talk in terms of people as either ideological dupes or autonomous subjects; it is not sufficient to assume on the one hand that reading a text will lead us to believe the ideological messages in that text or on the other hand that anyone can read a text as they choose; it will not help us understand classrooms if we assume they are just a reflection of the broader social reality, but neither will it be enough just to aim for student autonomy or to assume that "learner-centered" pedagogy is an adequate response to social

Table 6.1 Alternative Conceptions of School and Society

	Liberal Standpoint	Reproductive Standpoint	Resistance Standpoint
Knowledge and curriculum	Knowledge as neutral	Knowledge reflects dominant interests	All knowledge is political
Social role of schools	Equal opportunities for everyone	Indoctrination of young people	Conflicting forms of culture and knowledge
Social relations in schools	Classroom as site of educational transaction	Classroom reflects external social roles	Classroom as site of struggle

power (Benson, 1997; Pennycook, 1997a). Liberal, reproductive, and resistance (see below) approaches to education are outlined in Table 6.1.

Social and Cultural Reproduction

Bernstein's Elaborated and Restricted Codes

Returning to questions of social reproduction – the ways that educational and other institutions, reproduce rather than change forms of social inequality – we also need accounts of *how* such processes happen. It is one thing to note, from a structural perspective, that poor kids go to poor schools, get a poor education, and end up poor, but we also need to understand what processes account for this (beyond just a lack of quality education). Theories of cultural reproduction take up where theories of social reproduction leave off: They focus much more closely on the actual means by which schooling reproduces social relations. One version of cultural reproduction can be found in the work of Basil Bernstein (1972), for whom a central concern was the relation between social class, language, education, and knowledge. Bernstein set out to investigate how "the class system has affected the distribution of knowledge" so that "only a tiny percentage of the population has been socialized into knowledge at the level of the meta-languages of control and innovation, whereas the mass of the population has been socialized into knowledge at the level of context-tied operations" (Bernstein, 1972, p. 163). What Bernstein was claiming, therefore, was that social classes were tied to forms of language-based socialization perpetuated through schools that gave only a very limited social class access to forms of knowledge.

Bernstein's views have been quite influential in some circles, particularly for genre-based versions of critical literacy (see Chapter 5), where the questions he raises of differential access to powerful forms of language and meta-language, and his arguments in favor of explicit pedagogies, have led to the strong orientation toward overt pedagogy in this form of critical literacy (Christie, 1998; Williams, 1998). Certainly his views suggest the need for a critical understanding of several key concerns: The liberal democratic vision that all language is equal is highly questionable; language and knowledge are socially distributed rather than available to all; and the hope that progressivist pedagogies based on self-expression can be emancipatory overlooks questions of access to and control over language. As Williams (1992) suggests, "whatever its limitations, the work of Bernstein and his associates ... has served to demonstrate the role of the education system in producing and reproducing the written standard" (p. 143). Yet Bernstein's views have been critiqued from many directions. In sociolinguistics, it was not only the inadequate descriptions of these codes, but the ways they were linked to social class (a view, it must be said, influenced by a failure to grasp questions of class by many commentators) that have led his views to be categorized as "influential socially regressive deficit arguments" (Aveneri, Graham, Johnson, Riner, & Rosa, 2019, p. 2), that is to say views that explain inequality in terms of a linguistic gap between working class or Black children and their White and middle class counterparts.

Ultimately, as Jones (2013) makes clear, there is insufficient evidence to support the existence of Bernstein's codes, while the assumptions about *elaborated* and *restricted* codes arguably do amount to a deficit theory. Bernstein's "language deficit position" obscures the powerful role of the education system itself as the "engine of social reproduction" by shifting the focus onto working class children and their communicative styles (Jones, 2013, p. 176). For Giroux (1983), Bernstein's view remains a deterministic view of reproduction, while for Bourdieu (1991, p. 53), his "fetishizing of the legitimate language" fails to relate "this social product to the social conditions of its production and reproduction." And to the extent that they have been taken up by *access-oriented* (see Chapter 5) approaches to education – focused centrally on giving students access to dominant codes – they are open to the same critique: For too long "scholarship on 'access' and 'equity' has centered implicitly or explicitly around the question of how to get working-class students of color to speak like middle class White ones" (Paris & Alim, 2014, p. 87). The answer of course is not to deny access to dominant linguistic forms but to build pedagogical approaches around the cultures and practices of the students, an issue to which we return later.

Bourdieu and Cultural Capital

Pierre Bourdieu offers a more credible version of cultural reproduction. Notions such as *cultural capital*, which point to the means by which inequality is sustained, have become part of the applied linguistic vocabulary. Exploring different ways of understanding language and power, Luke (1996) suggests that Bourdieu provides a more useful way of looking at how power operates in particular contexts than, for example, Foucault. A Foucauldian model of power, he argues, leaves us with a version of power that is everywhere, yet always differently realized, and thus never very amenable to empirical analysis. Although Foucault's concept of power takes us usefully beyond modernist visions of the powerful versus the non-powerful, it may not lend itself readily to contextual analysis of power. Bourdieu, by contrast, describes power in terms of the forms of capital people have access to, use and produce in different cultural fields. As Thompson (1991) explains, Bourdieu "views the world as a multi-dimensional space, differentiated into relatively autonomous fields; and within each of these fields, individuals occupy positions determined by the quantities of different types of capital they possess" (p. 29). Such capital is by no means only economic, nor simply something one owns, but rather something that has different value in different contexts, mediated by the relations of power and knowledge in different social fields.

Bourdieu (1986) discusses four main forms of capital (economic, social, cultural, and symbolic), with symbolic capital – the recognition of value – being crucial for any of the others to be effective. Unlike standard views of political economy, Bourdieu sees economic capital as only one among the different forms of capital. Understanding power is always contextual: It depends on the symbolic capital it is given in any field. The notion of cultural capital, Bourdieu (1986, p. 243) explains, was first developed to "explain the unequal scholastic achievement of children originating from the different social classes." What interested Bourdieu – particularly in his work with Passeron (Bourdieu & Passeron, 1970), translated into English as *Reproduction in Education, Society and Culture* (1977) – were the ways that different forms of cultural capital that children brought to school (their ways of talking and doing) were valued differently. This notion of cultural capital as the differential value given to different cultural (and linguistic; Bourdieu, 1982) forms in education can be related to other work such as Shirley Brice Heath's (1983) ethnography of how different communities in the Carolinas in the United States socialize their children into different ways of *taking from books*—different types of *literacy events*—and how the language and literacy skills of these children are differently valued in school (see also Chapter 5).

Cultural capital takes three forms: Embodied cultural capital is the part of the *habitus* we internalize through socialization and education (see the discussion above of practices). Bourdieu's notion of *habitus*, an important precursor to more recent understandings of embodiment (Bucholtz & Hall, 2016), can be seen as a bridge between structure and agency (Jenkins, 1992), a notion of embodied habits, dispositions, attitudes, and behaviors that become written onto our bodies. What we learn at home and at school are not merely cognitive skills but rather are embodied practices. Objectified cultural capital takes the form of material cultural goods that can be transferred from one person to another. Institutionalized cultural capital takes the form of various credentials or certificates. It is often the case that whatever one may have gained in terms of embodied capital is of little significance without the sanctification of institutionalized capital. Cultural capital, furthermore, is of little value unless it can be used in specific social contexts, access to which is provided by one's social capital. Social capital, then, has to do with group membership, one's ability to participate in different social contexts, and thus to use and gain other forms of capital. One might, for example, have the embodied and objectified cultural capital to enter certain domains (business, academic communities, etc.), yet one may still be excluded on social terms (through issues of gender, ethnicity, race, sexual orientation, etc.). Finally, in Bourdieu's account, none of these forms of capital matter unless they are accorded symbolic capital; that is to say, unless what they represent is acknowledged as having legitimacy, they will not be usable as capital.

Such a framework provides quite productive means for analyzing the repro- duction of social inequality though the global symbolic capital of English, or the effects of the embodied linguistic/cultural capital of the native speaker, or the power of the institutional linguistic/cultural capital of language exam- inations such as TOEFL. Native speakers of English have linguistic capital that can be turned into economic capital (access to jobs), particularly because of the symbolic capital accorded to English (Brutt-Griffler & Samimy, 1999). Lin's (1999) analysis, using Bourdieu, of four classrooms in Hong Kong, takes as a starting point a "concern with exploring ways of doing TESOL that do not participate in the reproduction of student disadvantage" (p. 394). As she observes, the cultural and linguistic capital or habitus middle-class students brought to school was compatible with the forms of schooling they were exposed to, while the incompatibility between schooling and the habitus of working-class students in other classrooms led to student opposition and fur- ther reproduction of disadvantage. In one classroom, however, she saw the possibility of breaking away from these forms of social and cultural production as the incompatible habitus of the students was "being transformed through the creative, discursive agency and efforts of their teacher" (p. 409). Kramsch (2021) similarly draws on the work of Bourdieu for her understanding of *sym- bolic power*, arguing that we should pay greater attention in language educa- tion to *social symbolic aspects of language* that would enable a focus on being respected, valued and taken seriously rather than just being heard.

Bourdieu therefore provides a number of useful tools for thinking about power, context, and language, and how schooling may reproduce inequality. His work has also been subject to considerable critique. Three main concerns are relevant here (Table 6.2): First, although his sociology avoids the large top- down views of others, it is often still seen as deterministic. As Jenkins (1992, p. 175) observes, Bourdieu fails to show how actors can actually intervene

Table 6.2 Strengths and Weaknesses of Bourdieu in Relation to Language Education

Strengths	Potential Weaknesses
Contextualized sociologies of power: How ways of using language are recognized	Reproductive model of social relations
Relational view of power: How fields such as ELT favor or disfavor ways of speaking and doing	Economic and rational model of accumulation
Habitus as embodied forms of socialized power; how language practices become ingrained	Power as outside language rather than potentially within

to change how things happen. Bourdieu "vociferously rejects determinism while persistently producing deterministic models of social process." Second, although his use of different versions of capital (social, cultural, symbolic) is supposed to take us beyond the economic domain, the capital, trade, and marketplace metaphors he uses still suggest a rational model of capital accumulation: Bourdieu appears to "maintain a rationalist perspective on practice whereby it is ultimately reducible to the accumulation of cultural capital, i.e., of power," a position that "fails to take into account the non-rational constitution of desire" (Friedman, 1990, p. 313). And third, as Butler (1997) argues, Bourdieu's view of language and power is premised on the prior existence of forms of power that underlie uses of language: "If one argues that language itself can only act to the extent that it is 'backed' by existing social power, then one needs to supply a theory of how it is that social power 'backs' language in this way" (p. 158). As discussed in previous chapters, it is important from an applied linguistic perspective that we have modes of analysis that do not assume that language merely reflects prior relations of social power.

Resistance, Change, and Critical Language Pedagogies

These critical understandings of social and cultural reproduction in education take us usefully beyond a view of education as either a domain separate from society or a place of equal opportunity (Table 6.1). Instead, they locate schooling in the context of social class, race, gender, and inequality. Schools are precisely part of society, indeed a key social institution, and as such are part of the inequitable operations of society. Despite various critiques of ways of thinking about cultural reproduction, it remains a fundamental concern for understanding why education does not realize the promises for social change it sometimes claims, and why economic inequalities, racial discrimination, gendered disparities, and more are constantly replayed in our schools. As Giroux (1983) and Canagarajah (1993, 1999b) warn, however, there is a danger here that this view of reproduction allows no understanding of opposition and resistance, of the complex ways in which students and teachers act within the context of schooling. As argued at various points in this book, for critical applied linguistics to be of any use – and for us to have any role as educators or as agents for change rather than mere commentators on injustice – it needs to be able to do far more than just critique the reproduction of inequality.

What is needed, then, is a way of understanding resistance and change. This is important not only because we need better understandings of what actually goes on in classrooms but also because as educators we need a sense that we can actually do something. A problem with broad critical analysis is that it is often fundamentally pessimistic: We live in a patriarchal, homophobic, racist world increasingly governed by the interests of neoliberal politics and economics. This is not an inaccurate understanding of the world as far as it goes, but we also need to be able to believe in some alternative, a prospect for change: Faced by harsh realities, as educators we still need a sense of radical hope (hooks, 2003) (see Introduction and Chapter 1). We need alternative visions of how things can be, as well as potential ways of getting there. So we turn in this next section to questions of student resistance, before exploring forms of critical language pedagogy. This is one of the central issues in developing a usable critical applied linguistics. As I already argued in the context of critical theories of language and text (Chapters 3 and 5), we need to escape deterministic critical analyses to be able to show how critical applied linguistics may make a difference.

Resistance and Cultural Politics

It is for these reasons that Giroux (1988) talks of the need to develop a language of both critique and hope in critical educational theory and why Roger Simon (1992) talks of a pedagogy of possibility. Neither is a position advocating hope or possibility without acknowledging all that they are up against. From this perspective, we are now able to look at how different possibilities are struggled over in educational (or other) contexts. And we are able to argue that all such struggles are part of, but not completely determined by, larger social and cultural forces. Such a vision of the struggle between alternative worlds is the domain of cultural politics. This not culture in the reified sense of difference critiqued in Chapter 4, but rather culture as the way we make sense of the world. The notion of cultural politics gives us a way of getting at questions to do with the politics of classrooms. Cultural politics have to do with whose versions of reality gain legitimacy, whose representations of the world gain sway over others (Jordan & Weedon, 1995; Pennycook, 1994b). From this perspective, classrooms become sites of cultural struggle, contexts in which different versions of the world, preferred modes of learning and teaching, are under dispute.

Students resist teachers' pedagogies, and teachers resist students' practices. What may appear to be lack of ability or lack of preparation may in fact be resistance, as Kumaravadivelu (1999) observed when students' "unwillingness to prepare for the class and to participate in class discussions appeared to me to be a form of passive resistance" (p. 454). These forms of resistance may occur at multiple levels but are always connected both to the classroom and to the world beyond (Winn & Jackson, 2011). In schools in the US, "students in urban schools often resist American schooling ideologies because its 'official' curricula silence the voices, sensibilities, and lived experiences of dispossessed youth of color throughout the country" (Camangian, 2015, p. 424). We should be cautious not to assume that such resistance necessarily holds out hope for positive social change. To the extent that it may take the form of anything from absenteeism and unruly behavior to plagiarism (Pennycook, 1996a) or refusing to write (Kinloch, 2017), it may hold the potential for change but also for keeping things as they are (social reproduction).

As Canagarajah (1999b) suggests, we should not exaggerate the potential for resistance to bring about political and material empowerment; not only are forms of resistance often disorganized and disruptive acts that may change little, but we also need to remind ourselves that changes in schools may or may not lead to wider social change. Canagarajah (1993, p. 617) describes how the students in his class opposed "the alien discourses behind the language and textbook" but also opted for a product- rather than a process-oriented pedagogy, which he felt was ultimately to their disadvantage. They resisted his more Westernized teaching approach and opted instead for an approach to learning with which they were more familiar. They annotated the textbooks with anything from "Tamilization" of the characters or the addition of phrases to dialogues (in English) such as "I love you darling," to the inclusion of references to the struggle for Tamil independence. We need to understand student resistance to what we do, but if we want to make productive use of it, we need consider how it can be channeled in effective ways (Haque, 2007).

Textbooks themselves are of course a topic for a much wider critical analysis, bringing together the critical textual studies (critical discourse studies and critical literacies) discussed in the previous chapter, and the pedagogical focus on the classroom. According to Dendrinos (1992, p. 152), EFL textbooks are not merely instruments for "constructing learners as subjects of the educational institution" but also "for positioning them as particular social subjects." Gray's (2010; 2012) critical analyses of global ELT textbooks show how they inscribe a set of values in English associated with "individualism, egalitarianism, cosmopolitanism, mobility and affluence" (Gray, 2010, p. 3), that is to say, the very cultural and ideological formations with which English is connected in international contexts. Many EFL textbooks, Dendrinos suggests, "portray a reality of the will and freedom of individuals who are alone in shaping their life in any way they choose" (p. 159), a view very much in accord with the (neo-)liberal humanist account of social action. They also portray a very "specific social reality concerning the family institution, concerning gender, ethnicity, race and class" (p. 177).

As the discussion in the previous chapter made clear, texts do not simply convey meanings that are absorbed by readers: Textbooks are talked about, resisted, or ignored (Sunderland, Rahim, Cowley, Leontzakou & Shattuck, 2000) and to understand how they operate, we need critical classroom ethnographies. They nonetheless derive from dominant cultural contexts and are often interpreted through related discourses. All teaching materials carry cultural and ideological messages. The pictures, the lifestyles, the stories, the dialogues are all full of cultural content, and all may potentially be in disaccord with the cultural worlds of the students. Everything we use in class is laden with meanings from outside and interpretations from inside. Once we open up this perspective of the cultural politics of classrooms, we can start to see how everything that goes on in classrooms is both locally important and globally significant.

This is not a relation where the classroom is determined by the outside world, a mere reflection of what happens elsewhere; it is one where the classroom is part of the world, both affected by what happens outside its walls and affecting what happens there. Classrooms, from this perspective, are also sites where identities are produced and changed. The language we teach, the materials we use, the way we run our classrooms, the things students do and say, all can be seen in social and cultural terms, and thus, from a critical perspective as social political and cultural political questions. Assumptions about "active" and "passive" students, about the use of groupwork and pairwork, about self-interest as a key to motivation ("tell us about yourself"), about memorization being an outmoded learning strategy, about oral communication as the goal and means of instruction, about an informal atmosphere in the class being most conducive to language learning, about learning activities being fun, about games being an appropriate way of teaching and learning—all these, despite the claims by some researchers that they are empirically preferable, are *cultural and ideological preferences.*

Critical Pedagogies

If classroom resistance by students may take many forms and lead in multiple directions, it is also one element that can be taken up as part of a critical pedagogy. We need forms of critical praxis to counter the reproductive forces of education. There are a range of different critical approaches to education, many drawing on Freirean forms of pedagogy (see Chapter 5). Critical pedagogy itself can be seen as part of a North American tradition in the writings of Giroux (1988), McLaren (1989), Kanpol (1994, 1997), and others. This approach to critical pedagogy has been particularly strong in its critique of formal education, suggesting that it "always represents an introduction to, preparation for, and legitimation of particular forms of social life" (McLaren, 1989, p. 160). Once one acknowledges the cultural politics of schooling, the fact that curricula represent not so much timeless truths and knowledge but rather very particular ways of understanding the world, then one can start to develop a critical form of pedagogy that addresses the marginalization and exclusion of students in schools by encouraging them to develop their own voice (and see Chapter 5). Voice in this context is understood as far more than just speaking; rather, it is a broader understanding of developing the possibilities to articulate alternative realities. It is less about the medium of voice (speaking and writing) and more about finding possibilities of articulation. The ultimate goal of critical pedagogy, as Kanpol (1994, 1997) describes it, remains tied to a vision of more inclusive social democracy: It is a pedagogy of inclusion.

This version of critical pedagogy has come in for considerable critique. From the more reactionary ends of education, it has been condemned for imposing its political agenda on students at the expense of actually teaching students what they want or need. As the discussion above suggests, however, it is clear that educational institutions are already imposing a particular set of ideologies on students. At the same time, it is also evident that imposition is not such an easy task anyway: Students will resist critical pedagogy if they don't see its values. More plausible critiques have pointed to the tendency to remain at the level of grand theorizing rather than pedagogical practice (Gore, 1993; Usher & Edwards, 1994); employing a simplistic version of empowerment and dialogue that obscures power relationships between students and teachers; failing to develop an adequate understanding of how giving people voice can bring about their empowerment; and working with too simple an understanding of the multiplicities of oppression so that it is too easily assumed that students will side with the "oppressed" and against the "oppressors" (Ellsworth, 1989). Critical pedagogy, from many of these critics' point of view, is too firmly ensconced in a form of emancipatory modernism that operates with a universal narrative of change, and fails to deal with situated complexities (Usher & Edwards, 1994). The inclusionary focus, with its emphasis on voice, has also been critiqued (Luke, 1996), as has the concept of 'dialogue' which rests, according to Simon (1992, p. 96), on a simplistic distinction between a transmission pedagogy (what Freire called banking education, where students are simply taught what is deemed important) and a process whereby "student 'voice' is 'taken seriously'" which is "both a vague and trivial statement."

These critiques of what we might call mainstream critical pedagogy point in several useful directions. They remind us that critical work will always be critiqued not only from those who oppose such forms of criticality, but also from a wide range of other critical thinkers. The moment we start to accept unquestioningly the work of critical pedagogy, critical literacy, critical discourse analysis, or critical language awareness, we are no longer engaged in a critical project. It also points to a need reiterated throughout this book to ensure that critical work stays grounded both in terms of being aware of its own locus of enunciation – critical pedagogy has been critiqued as a Northern, White male endeavor (Echeverri-Sucerquia, 2020; Lather, 1995) – and engaged with educational contexts at a more local level. It is also worth reminding ourselves that critical pedagogy, as Gore (1993) relates, was nonetheless a means by which she was able to understand and enunciate her frustrations at mainstream education.[1] Critical pedagogies, furthermore, like critical literacies, refer to a wide range of diverse practices: The Freirean-inspired, feminist, and antiracist work of bell hooks, for example, with its focus on *talking back* (hooks, 1989) *engaged pedagogy* and *teaching to transgress* (hooks, 1994) presents a very different strand of critical pedagogical work. It is to an array of critical language pedagogies that I now turn.

Critical Language Pedagogies

It is worth reminding ourselves that, as with critical literacies or critical discourse studies (Chapter 5), whatever critiques we might make of certain ways of doing critical work, it is clear that we desperately need critical language pedagogies in our schools and classrooms. Critical pedagogies of many sorts are an ongoing and urgent part of many educational landscapes, and as Crookes (2013) notes, have been going on for a long time. Critical language pedagogy can be seen as "teaching for social justice, in ways that support the development of active, engaged citizens" (Crookes, 2013, p. 8). As discussed in Chapter 2, however, common discourses of diversity, equity, and social justice in teacher education may fail to provide a sufficient grounding for critical educational projects (Dominguez, 2017). Critical language pedagogies can be seen as open to the same challenges and critiques of critical pedagogy in other domains. Johnston (1999, p. 564) suggests that the abstractions and political posturing of critical pedagogy can be alienating, and that while critical pedagogy gave him useful insights into educational contexts in which he worked, it failed to "capture the complex essence of teaching, especially of ESL/EFL teaching in the postmodern world."

Many that come to critical language education, however, come already grounded in a strong focus on the community, popular education, and participation in various critical educational projects (Chun, 2015; Morgan, 1998; Rivera, 1999; Frye, 1999) that help ground critical language pedagogies in local concerns, such as community policing, linguistic resources, migrant status, legal services, housing, and so on. For many educators who come to language education through an adult, popular, or community education lens – seeing themselves as already involved in political action for change – critical language pedagogy is the linguistic and educational arm of ongoing political activism. It is important that our critical educational projects are indeed grounded in local political concerns, seeking out *critical moments* in our educational endeavors rather than making overblown claims about our critical projects, which are inevitably small, local, and circumscribed (Pennycook, 2004c).

A common mainstream suspicion that critical language educators focus on politics at the expense of language can be refuted on two grounds: First, as suggested at the beginning of this chapter, since language is inevitably political and language education doubly so, a focus on language and politics is inescapable. Freirean pedagogy has always insisted on the dual focus on the *word* and the *world* (Freire & Macedo, 1987). As noted in Chapter 4, language classrooms are all too often "a place where cultural stereotypes and problematic ideas about self and others are reproduced." (Echeverri-Sucerquia 2020, p. 28). Language pedagogy cannot ignore this: It needs to "confront liberal-democratic notions of equality with rigorous questions of difference" (Lee, 1997, p. 429) and to explore ways in which views of the Other are embedded in language education (Umbarila-Gómez, 2011). Second, as accounts of critical language education make clear, the focus is always on both critical education and language education: Morgan's (2004) discussion of his classes on the Quebec referendum for independence shows how he connects grammar to wider social concerns, while Chun's (2015) work on English for academic purposes in the context of the Occupy movement similarly shows how a focus on social movements can ground good language pedagogy while engaging students in key contemporary concerns.

Similarly, *culturally relevant pedagogy* (Ladson-Billings, 1995) – subsequently developed into *culturally sustaining pedagogies* by Paris (2012) – rests on the proposition that a critical pedagogical approach to language education needs to focus on academic success (challenging students to think and succeed in schools), cultural competence (helping students understand their own and others' backgrounds, including mainstream culture) and developing a critical consciousness to challenge the current social order. These forms of *resource, asset,* or *culturally sustaining pedagogies* (CSP) (Paris, 2012; Paris & Alim, 2014; 2017) argue that educational practices need to be more than merely relevant to the cultural practices of young people; rather they need to "support young people in sustaining the cultural and linguistic competence of their communities while simultaneously offering access to dominant cultural competence" (Paris, 2012, p. 95). In the terms discussed in Chapter 5, this is a statement of both inclusion and access.

Paris and Alim (2014) suggest that while students need access to Dominant American English (DAE) and associated interactive and schooling practices, the role of DAE is changing, and a multiracial and multilingual society requires a different approach to educational outcomes: "equity and access can best be achieved by centering pedagogies on the heritage and contemporary practices of students and communities of color" (Paris & Alim, 2014, p. 87). CSP critiques schools for assimilating minorities and eradicating their languages and cultures and insists on the need to sustain the linguistic and cultural practices of students of color. Such a position is by no means blind to the White middle-class norms that have long been the gatekeepers to social opportunities but neither do they therefore opt to teach these norms uncritically. This is a call for a pluralist (multilingual, multiethnic) pedagogy but one that confronts the racist contexts of education (Paris & Alim, 2017).

This work has also been developed in relation to linguistic and cultural revitalization in Indigenous communities, as "critical culturally sustaining/ revitalizing pedagogy (CSRP)" (Lee & McCArty 2017, p. 62) which focuses particularly on transforming the legacies of colonialism that have done so much damage to the languages, cultures, and knowledges of Indigenous people (McCarty & Lee, 2014; Coulter & Jimenez-Silva, 2017). This decolonizing theme can be found in related strands of critical education, such as de los Ríos, Martinez, Musser, Canady, Camangian, and Quijada's (2019) approach to challenging the colonial roots of English education in the US. The contemporary sociopolitical landscape, they argue, is marked by "fervent white nationalism, religious and linguistic intolerance, and anti-immigrant and racist discourses" that have their origins in colonial relations and a have a major influence on English language teaching (de los Ríos, Martinez, Musser, Canady, Camangian, & Quijada, 2019, p. 364). They take up Winn's (2013; 2018) framework of *restorative justice* – focusing on the interconnectedness of history, race, justice, and language – to propose a *critical translingual approach* to English language education that draws, amongst other influences, on the antiracist work of Flores and Rosa (2015), the critical language pedagogy of Alim (2005), and the translanguaging practices emphasized by García and her colleagues (García, Johnson, & Seltzer, 2017; and see Chapter 3, and Pennycook, 2019).

Decolonizing education could be taken as an overarching current theme not only of education more broadly (Battiste, 2013; hooks, 2013; Prah, 2018) but also of contemporary critical concerns in language education (Makalela, 2018). A project to decolonize English language education at the primary school level in Mexico focused both on shifting the discourses that constructed English as the necessary language of 'progress,' and finding ways to engage Indigenous students in much deeper ways in the educational process (López-Gopar, 2016). Culturally sustaining/revitalizing pedagogy Dominguez (2017) insists, requires a "*decolonized* mindset that must be developed, cultivated, lived, and deeply felt" (p. 224) "How can the field of foreign language education decolonize itself?" asks Macedo (2019, p. 14) How can it "justify its vast whiteness as reflected in classrooms, teacher preparation programs, and national and international language teacher organizations?" (Macedo, 2019, p. 14). Although the CSRP agenda deals with Black, minority, and Indigenous concerns (Coulter & Jimenez-Silva, 2017), all of which could be considered concerns of the Global South (the South is not just a geographic orientation, it is also a geopolitical one), this also points to the need to look elsewhere, to be aware that the struggles faced in North America (from which much of the above discussion is drawn) should by no means define the scope of critical pedagogies, that the vast majority of language educators around the world, while largely excluded from major applied linguistic and educational organizations (Anya, 2020; Bhattacharya, Jiang, & Canagarajah, 2019) are people of color.

Language educators and teacher educators "need to build our own theories of language learning and build a theoretical TESOL and L2 knowledge base starting with southern epistemologies that have historically countered economic, political, and cultural hegemony: We need to be active producers of knowledge" (Echeverri-Sucerquia, 2020, p. 29). Teaching languages from a critical perspective, therefore, has to have a decolonizing perspective, one that focuses both on the colonizing roles of language pedagogy in historical and contemporary terms (Macedo, 2019), and a focus on alternative knowledges form the Global South. Critical pedagogy needs to be understood in terms of North-South relations and different forms of knowledge and ways of doing education, that is to say, not just different cultural orientations but different ways of thinking about language, culture and pedagogy (Guilherme, 2012; 2015). It has to involve elements of critical language awareness of how standardized versions of language operate in relation to White public spaces and normative values. It needs elements of critical intercultural understanding, to be able to look at one's own and other cultures, and the ways they are constructed, maintained, and viewed by others (see Chapter 4). And it needs a vision of social transformation, or an alternative world worth striving for as well as means to develop activist students (Camangian, 2015 (Table 6.3). This is a critical pedagogy "that names, interrupts, challenges, critiques" and offers different possibilities for "language classrooms, curricula, schools, and communities that in turn affect societies and human life as a whole" (Gounari, 2020, p. 5)

Table 6.3 Key Aspects of Critical Language Education

Five Elements	Focus
Language learning for social change	Critical language pedagogies aimed at social transformation in students' lives
Support for student cultures and voices	Culturally relevant/sustaining pedagogies that support the voices of people who too often go unheard
Critical language awareness	Critical awareness of how standardized versions of the language operate in relation to White public spaces and normative values
Critical approach to multilingualism	Critical translingual approaches that open space for alternative language uses
Decolonizing perspective	Focus both on the colonizing roles of language pedagogy and the need for southern epistemologies

Toward An Ethics of Language Pedagogy

I have tried to present in this chapter a number of ways in which critical applied linguistics may help inform various forms of critical language pedagogy. I argue in this chapter for a view of the classroom as both connected to the wider social world and partly a domain unto itself. Everything outside the classroom, from community and national language policies to social and cultural contexts of schooling, may have an impact on what happens in the classroom. But the classroom itself is a social domain, not merely a reflection of the larger society beyond the classroom walls but also a place in which social relations are played out, and therefore a context in which we need to directly address questions of social power. Everything in the classroom, from how we teach, what we teach, how we respond to students, to the materials we use and the way we assess the students, need to be seen as social and cultural practices that have broader implications than just pieces of classroom interaction.

For Auerbach (1995), these concerns point in two directions: On the one hand, classrooms need to "include explicit analysis of the social context" outside the classroom; on the other hand, "students must be involved in making pedagogical choices inside the classroom" (p. 28). In any educational domain, therefore, we need to focus on the cultural politics of what we do, and understand the implications of our own and our students' pedagogical choices as both particular to the context and related to broader domains. The challenge is to understand this relation and to find ways of always focusing on the local while at the same time keeping an eye on the broader horizons. This view that our classroom walls are permeable means that what we do in our classrooms is about changing the worlds we live in. Thus, we also need to have ways of thinking about and beyond the relations between structure and agency, how micro-actions on one level may be part of macro forces on another, and how within the macro forces of society we are still able to change, resist, and act with some degree of autonomy.

Doing critical work is dangerous work. The memories and narratives we may seek to introduce into our classes or research may indeed be perilous. The effects of what we do may be profound. Graman (1988, p. 447), for example, lists some of the changes that came about in the lives of some of his students as a result of his teaching: One of them "became ostracized from his religious group because of his new perspective on Nicaragua," leading him to ask hard questions with lasting intellectual and ethical implications. Another spoke of the "willpower she gained in the dialogic class which enabled her to seek a divorce she had wanted for years" (p. 447). Once our critical projects are grounded in the real lives of others, we need to think very carefully where things may lead and whether we can justify ethically what we are engaged in. But for those who say we are just language teachers or just applied linguists and should not involve ourselves with such concerns, I say that we already are involved. We cannot bury our heads in the sand and claim these are not our concerns. We cannot sit on the fence and say we cannot make choices.

The discussion of critical pedagogy pointed once again to the need to be suspicious about modernist narratives of education, empowerment, and emancipation and to engage with the challenges presented by situated action, knowledge, and pedagogies. It also points in the direction of *ethics*. Just as van Leewen (2018) argues that CDA/S ultimately had to rest on moral forms of evaluation (see Chapter 5), so critical education needs to be grounded in an ethical or moral vision, a point "where each one of us is obliged to make an ethical decision, to say: *here I stand*. (Or, at the level of collective responsibility, *here we stand*)...,here and now I face an *other* who demands of me an ethical response" (Kearney, 1988, p. 361). Gee (1993) arrives at a similar point when he suggests we have to consider the *effects* on other people of what we do and say. At the end of our questioning and discussions, we come against "two conceptual principles that serve as the basis of *ethical human discourse* (talk and interaction)" (p. 292): "That something would *harm* someone else...is *always* a good reason (though perhaps not a sufficient reason) *not* to do it" (p. 292), and "One always has the ethical obligation to explicate ... any social practice that there is reason to believe advantages oneself or one's group over other people or groups" (p. 293).

Corson (1997) notes that very little attention has been paid to questions of ethics in applied linguistics, apart from a rather superficial view of ethics in research. Indeed, discussions of ethics in applied linguistics have failed to go beyond issues of "professional conduct," whether in discussions of research or of "ethicality" in language testing. Corson goes on to argue that it must ultimately be on ethical grounds that we make epistemological choices. He suggests three basic ethical principles drawn from moral philosophy: The principle of equal treatment (compare Gee's second principle), the principle of respect for persons (compare Gee's first principle), and the principle of benefit maximization (a more utilitarian concern with the consequences of actions). Taking issue with the tendencies toward foundational or hegemonic theory construction, Corson argues that "only an inclusive epistemology" is consistent with all three of these ethical principles, so applied linguistics needs to "open its windows to other disciplines and to other points of view, especially to the points of view of its informants, clientele, and potential victims" (Corson, 1997, p. 183) This takes us back once again to the insistent demands of Southern Theory that critical projects have to be open to a greater diversity of forms of knowledge (de Sousa Santos, 2018; Pennycook and Makoni, 2020).

No longer can applied linguistics continue to believe arrogantly in its methods, canon of knowledge, or research. At this point we have to deal with key ethical decisions. This is not a normative morality, a fixed body of codes to follow; there are no religious or objective morals to speak of, only confrontation with the real ethics of hard decisions. And these ethical decisions do not occur outside social and power relations: "ethics are not acted out in the spirit of human isolation but rather mirror the responsibilities of relationship rather than the obligations encumbered within an autonomous self-sufficient moral reason" (Simon, 1992, p. 26). This is an argument for ethics not as part of a fixed moral code that guides the behavior of the individual but rather as part of a contingent way of thinking and acting that is always in relation to social, cultural, and political concerns. Simon (1992) confronts these questions when he speaks of his "project of possibility" as "the situated refusal of the present as definitive of that which is possible." Such an educational vision that is "capable of narrating stories of possibility" is "constrained within an ethical imagination that privileges diversity, compassionate justice, and securing of the conditions for the renewal of human life" (p. 30).

Diversity, justice, and renewal are themes that have reoccurred throughout this chapter, and also this book. While these may be ethical principles, they are nor normative positions, but rather as Kearney (1988) puts it "the ethical demand to imagine *otherwise*" (p. 364). Such a vision demands a major rethinking of what applied linguistics might be about. Instead of being a canon of normative knowledge about language acquisition, teaching methods, translation, and so on, it becomes a project to address the ethical demands of language education, of the global spread of English, of the available choices in translation, of language in the workplace, of the complexities of literacy. This chapter has sought to develop a critical view of language education that attempts to deal with the challenges of domination (contextual effects of power in classrooms), disparity (inequitable educational access), discrimination (sexist, racist and other forms of exclusion), difference (diverse cultures and ways of being that students bring to the classroom), and desire (hopes for alternative futures). In the final chapter, we shall turn to some of these concerns in a discussion of what it means to *do* applied linguistics as an educator, researcher, or activist.

Note

1. My own pathway to critical applied linguistics was similar. It would certainly include reading Marx, Marcuse, and critical pedagogy, as well as Foucault, Butler, and Fanon. Even if I now distance myself from some of these perspectives, they were the stepping-stones I used on the way. Just as the end goal of critical applied linguistics is a shifting space, so too are the possible pathways.

7 Doing Critical Applied Linguistics

This concluding chapter does several things: It pulls together some of the main themes that have cut across the book; it looks at ways in which doing critical applied linguistic can be an educational, research, or activist project; and it suggests various broad principles that underpin critical applied linguistic work. I remake the argument here for why critical applied linguistics matters – possibly more now than it did before – and suggest how many of the new directions that inform the field can take us toward important domains of political and intellectual inquiry. Toward the end of the chapter, I return to one of the recurring themes of this book: How to steer a path between an open-ended critical applied linguistics that needs to avoid incorporation into a school of thought or a set of fixed principles, and a critical applied linguistics that also of necessity has to adopt certain moral and political standpoints?

Critical Themes

Throughout this book, I have compared different constellations of knowledge, language, and politics. I have tried to show how different ways of thinking about politics and knowledge have different implications for critical applied linguistics projects. Mainstream approaches to sociolinguistics and language planning have inadequate theories of the social, suggesting that language simply reflects rather vague social categories. Liberal egalitarian approaches to language, with their insistence on linguistic equality, have given us an understanding that no one way of using language is better than another, that different varieties of World Englishes or English as a Lingua Franca should be acknowledged alongside their cousins in the center, that ownership of English no longer rests in the hands of its so-called native speakers, and that minority languages and bilingual education should be supported. Social justice perspectives bring a further moral and political aspect to these arguments, particularly through frameworks of language rights.

These are important insights, but they lack a more incisive understanding and critique of the power structures within which languages operate. They suggest that texts are always open to interpretation and that critical analysis is therefore an imposition of an ideological standpoint. They maintain hope in the liberal dream of educational opportunity, viewing education as an impartial context of knowledge transaction in which everyone has a chance to succeed. Liberal egalitarian approaches to difference maintain a humanist stance that suggests diversity is a superficial covering that can divert attention from essential human similarities. By so doing, this view tends to erase the importance of difference. As Williams (1992) puts it, these frameworks may aim to support the disenfranchised, yet they do so with perspectives that reflect the ideologies of the dominant. To make sense of language in an inequitable world, applied linguistics can no longer justify forms of optimistic egalitarianism that are of no help in framing questions of *domination* (contingent and contextual effects of power), *disparity* (inequitable access to material and cultural goods), *discrimination* (ideological and discursive frames of exclusion), *difference* (constructions and realities of social and cultural distinction), and *desire* (operations of ideology, agency, identity, and transformation).

Modernist critical approaches to applied linguistics, by contrast, focus more specifically on the relations between language and politics. While this emancipatory modernist framework provides an important basis for critical applied linguistic work, the use of neo-Marxist analyses of power, ideology, and awareness has various limitations: It tends to operate with a clumsy version of power located in dominant groups; it views ideology in a way that is opposed in too simple terms to a knowable reality; in unreflective fashion, it suggests that scientific knowledge of reality can help us escape from the falsity of ideology; and it can be much stronger in its analysis of structural inequalities than of possibilities for change. It raises important concerns such as linguistic imperialism or educational indoctrination, locating language in inequitable but static social conditions. In terms of textual analysis, it provides us with forms of critical literacy and critical discourse analysis that relate textual meanings to broader social, economic, and political concerns, but tend toward the social determination of meaning, the focus on texts rather than reactions to texts, and the suggestion that awareness of textually encoded ideologies can lead to emancipation. Critical approaches to education emphasize the ways in which schooling reproduces inequality, while offering pedagogies of social inclusion and voice to overcome the discriminatory processes of schooling.

An alternative position can also be sketched out that similarly views language as fundamentally political, but is less certain about the possibility of an emancipatory position outside ideology. This view of situated practice conceives of power more in terms of its micro operations in relation to questions of class, race, gender, ethnicity, sexuality, and so on, and argues that we must also account for the politics of knowledge and the locus of enunciation. In terms of the politics of language, it suggests that language is productive of social relations and points to the need to understand how people resist and appropriate forms of language oppression. A performative view sees language both as a set of repeated acts that produce the appearance of substance, and as a site of resistance to and appropriation of norms and forms of standardized discourse. The spaces opened up by Queer theory and raciolinguistics render

Table 7.1 Frameworks of Politics, Epistemology, and Applied Linguistics

Framework	Politics and Epistemology	Forms of Analysis	Flaws and Limitations
Liberal egalitarianism	Liberal pluralism, structuralism egalitarianism, and the separation of politics from academic work	Emphasis on individual differences, openness of textual meaning, equality of languages, and possibilities of schooling	Inadequate social theory; weak approaches to social difference, inequality, and conflict; language reflects reality
Emancipatory modernism	Neo-Marxist politics and ideological analysis; macro structures of domination	Linguistic domination, ideologies in texts, schooling as social reproduction, inclusionary approach to difference	Top-down critiques of structural inequality; limited by deterministic social vision, ideology, and emancipation
Situated practice	Grounded local politics, poststructuralist focus on situated analysis	Language as performative, focus on resistance, analysis of the social through language, engagement with history and difference	Skepticism toward technical solutions, micro relations of power; emergent politics; lack of overarching framework

race, gender, and sexuality not fixed categories of difference but rather inter-secting spaces of discrimination and engagement with desire and the body. In terms of the politics of texts, situated approaches seek to understand ethno-graphically how texts come to take on meaning. A problematizing stance on schooling takes up questions of resistance and is skeptical about the notion that awareness can lead to emancipation, leading us in the end toward an ethically engaged pedagogy (Table 7.1).

At the same time, we should not overplay these differences, or become too caught up in internal debates about how we do critical applied linguistics. My point in drawing attention to these different ways of going about criti-cal work is not so much to discredit one in favor of the other, but rather to argue that different critical approaches operate with different assumptions and may have different outcomes. There is no one way of doing critical work. All critical approaches share common concerns about the deep-seated inequali-ties and discriminations in schools, media texts, workplaces, institutions, and conversations. They share an interest in getting beyond methodological indi-vidualism to focus instead on institutions, social formations, ideologies, and discourses. They may get at deep-seated forms of discrimination and inequality in different ways, but all critical standpoints view such concerns in systemic terms, whether we look at practices (as sedimented social action), discourses (as formations of power and knowledge), ideologies (as ideas formulated in the interests of the powerful), institutions (as social formations that structure society), or northern epistemologies (as ways the Global North systematically excludes the Global South). These different perspectives all seek to get beyond individualistic and liberal accounts of choice, freedom, and the individual.

Guidelines for A Critical Praxis

An understanding of language as central to human life, and as fundamentally tied up with the cultural politics of the everyday, demands that applied linguistics is informed by more than a liberal egalitarian vision of the world. Critical applied linguistics deals with many domains of significant language use, from education for children from minority backgrounds to interpreting between Deaf and hearing communities, from inequitable practices in legal proceedings to discriminatory images in the media. We stand therefore at the heart of crucial educational, cultural, and political issues of our time. These are questions of sexual identities, raciolinguistic differences, and silenced voices, and this is one additional meaning of *critical*: Critical applied linguistics is concerned with some of the most critical contemporary issues. It therefore needs social, political, and economic analyses that locate language within a critical exploration of inequality, working both with and against critical concepts such as class, patriarchy, or imperialism. Such analyses need to take us beyond visions that leave little space for change: Critical applied linguistics needs forms of enquiry that can lead to forms of action. We need not only large-scale theories of society but also ways of thinking about change, resistance, and alternatives, and a vision of language that not only reflects but also produces and therefore can alter social relations.

It is vital that we do not allow critical applied linguistics to become a fixed canon of ideas, methods, or techniques, a canon of knowledge and texts with its gurus and gatekeepers. This has been a problem with some areas of work - critical pedagogy, critical discourse analysis, and critical literacy, for example – where various rigidities and dogmas have become attached to the field. Critical applied linguistics is better seen as a way of thinking, a way of going about applied linguistics that constantly seeks to push our thinking in new and provocative ways. Above all, critical applied linguistics should not be seen as a separate domain, something carried out by a small group of like-minded educators; it needs instead to be part of *every* discussion about language learning, translation, language in the workplace; it needs to foster debate, discussion, argument, dissent. There are a number of different ways critical applied linguistics can operate: It can be part of what we teach in applied linguistics, an approach to research, and an activist practice. I explore each of these briefly below.

Critical Applied Linguistics in the Curriculum

At least two problems emerge in the tertiary teaching context. Aside from all those applied linguistics courses that ignore more critical perspectives – and are as a result ethically and politically compromised – others either do the critical work as an add-on (the 'final week' focus on critical perspectives) or put all their eggs in one critical basket. In the first case, a course in discourse analysis may include a week or two on critical discourse analysis; a subject on literacy might include work in critical literacy; and courses on methodology, curriculum, or teacher education may look at the work done in critical pedagogy. While the inclusion of critical perspectives is to be welcomed, there are problems with this approach: The underlying assumption is generally that it is important to include critical perspectives (this is, thus, a liberal, inclusive framework) but these are not central to the field; the 'critical week' is shuffled off toward the end of the semester so that its position remains peripheral; and it only dips into critical work in desultory fashion, thus failing to explore basic questions to do with ideology, power, racism, gender, sexual identity, and so forth.

A more serious approach may attempt a more sustained engagement with critical applied linguistics by making it part of the curriculum through a course in critical applied linguistics. In some ways, this is a bit like taking all the 'critical weeks' and sticking them together. So now we have a course that deals with critical discourse analysis, critical literacy, critical language awareness, gender, sexuality, raciolinguistics, critical approaches to ELT, critical language testing, and so on. This can be an attractive course that finally allows sustained semester-long engagement with critical work. Yet such a course also has its drawbacks: It runs the danger of isolating critical applied linguistics as a particular and separate approach to language-related domains, and thus it can help sustain the isolation of critical approaches in relation to other subjects. It also runs the danger of solidifying critical applied linguistics into a fixed subject matter. Critical applied linguistics runs the danger of becoming a subdiscipline of applied linguistics that draws on applied linguistics and critical theory.

While both of these approaches are much better than nothing, it is important to consider ways in which critical applied linguistics can become more diffuse, an approach infusing the domain more broadly. There are a number of advantages to this: It allows greater possibilities of coverage and of approaches, and it means that critical applied linguistics is no longer an option among others. The imperative to develop broader, more ethically accountable, and more transformative frameworks of knowledge in applied linguistics suggests the possibility not of *peripheral* critical work but of *pervasive* critical work. From this point of view, we can start to envision critical applied linguistics less in terms of models or methodologies and more in terms of an ethical, epistemological, and political attitude toward all questions in language education, literacy, translation, or language use in the workplace. Following Green's (1997) discussion of the notion of the 'critical' in critical literacy, we can start to reclaim applied linguistics as always already political from the outset. This means we can start with a politicized understanding of applied linguistics, with the view that any applied linguistics worth the name is political and an instrument and a resource for *change*, for challenging and changing the wor(l)d. From this standpoint, critical applied linguistics might be seen not so much as an alternative approach to applied linguistics but rather as *applied linguistics with a conscience.*

Critical applied linguistics is a way of doing applied linguistics that helps refresh the conceptual repertoires of applied linguistics. We can think of (critical) applied linguistics less in disciplinary or inter- or transdisciplinary terms, and more as temporary assemblages of thought and action that come together at particular moments when language-related concerns need to be addressed (Pennycook, 2019). This flexible account of applied linguistic practice takes us not only beyond concerns about its disciplinary status but also beyond the idea of an inter/transdisciplinary applied linguistics (de Moita Lopes, 1998). It also helps us see how applied linguistic practices, which may appear diverse, confused, or undisciplined, are instead the conjoining of different language-oriented projects, epistemes, and matters of concern (Latour, 2004). This opens up applied linguistics to an ethical engagement with alternative ways of thinking about language and context from the Global South, so that renewal of applied linguistics comes not via other disciplines but rather through alternative forms of knowledge.

Disciplines are held in place by a range of factors, such as conferences, handbooks, departments, courses, textbooks and so on, that seek to frame the area and its work. Disciplines, like standard languages, have always been exclusionary: On the upside, they help consolidate ideas, enhance collaboration, bring solidity to a field; on the downside, they narrow the area of interest, its ideas and methods, and they exclude so much that does not fit. One role of critical applied linguistics is to challenge these hegemonic knowledge structures. While this may bring a downside of insecurity, instability, and incoherence, it also brings many benefits of flexibility, innovation, and breadth. Like language standardization, while there may be gains to be made by such processes or normalization, this history of consolidation and exclusion has also rendered applied linguistics unhelpfully narrow in its epistemologies, politics, and methods. There are a number of reasons to reject claims to disciplinary status for applied linguistics, including a more persuasive argument that a field of applied study is ordered not so much by a core disciplinary focus but rather by the questions it asks and the fields it engages with – language policy, language in the professions, language in education, and so on – and that the understandings of language, the matters of concern, and the research tools to engage with them change accordingly.

Questioning the notions of language and languages within applied linguistics has several effects. It opens up applied linguistics to a wider set of possibilities about what matters: As Toohey (2019, p. 953) suggests, for example, ideas born of new forms of materialism, such as assemblages or entanglements, have major implications for applied linguistic pedagogy and research, encouraging us "to ask new questions, and be alert to innovate, experiment, and learn new ways of teaching, researching, and being." The dynamic potential of critical applied linguistics and the importance in the world of areas that it deals with should make this area not some secondary compendium of other areas but rather a constellation of key ideas and themes that others should be looking to for inspiration. Applied linguistics has for too long gone about trying to solve its own problems without creating sufficiently interesting theory, research, or praxis to be of much interest to other domains. A dynamic critical applied linguistics, by contrast, becomes a field of inquiry that people in cultural studies, literary theorists, educationalists, sociologists, anthropologists, psychologists, political scientists, and many others can look toward for leading ideas in critical domains. With changes to the ways linguistics and socio- and applied linguistics fit together – linguistics is losing its status as the intellectual center to which social and applied effects are added – these shifts in the ways we think about applied linguistics open up possibilities of starting the long overdue process of reassembling applied linguistics as a constellation of shifting interests around language matters in the world.

Critical Applied Linguistic Research

Similar points can be made about research from a critical applied linguistic perspective: All applied linguistic research could helpfully learn from critical perspectives Heller, ietikäinen, and Pujolar, 2018. Current social conditions are "fraught with real threats to human difference, and many language learners and multilinguals are under siege" (Ortega, 2019, p. 23). Research in second language acquisition, Ortega suggests, needs to see "multilingualism as central to both the human experience of language and the research goals of SLA, simultaneously bringing into center stage social justice as it relates to language learning." Research in critical applied linguistics therefore needs to respond to the same broad concerns of any critical applied linguist project: Difference, desire, domination, discrimination, and disparity. It requires a mode of working that engages seriously with difference; the inclusion of participants' interests, desires, and lives; a focus on the workings of power and inequality; an engagement with alternative forms of knowledge, particularly from the Global South; and an orientation toward transformative goals (see Table 7.2).

Research from a critical applied linguistic perspective that seeks to engage seriously with difference takes as a starting point the concern that the categories with which we may operate – according to cultural or gender differences, for example – must always be open to critical investigation. Rampton's (1995b) work on "language crossing" – the use of language varieties from groups to which one does not normally "belong" is a good example of this. Drawing on Gilroy's (1987) critique of ethnic absolutism, Rampton talks of crossing as

Table 7.2 Five Elements of Critical Applied Linguistic Research

Questioning difference	Asking how difference is constructed and why it matters
Participants' worldviews	Situated knowledge and taking participants seriously
Issues of power	Questions of knowledge, power, and research topics
Diverse perspectives	Openness to alternative (Southern) perspectives
Transformative agendas	Catalytic validity and transformative goals

involving "the active ongoing construction of a new inheritance from within multiracial interaction itself" (Rampton, 1995b, p. 297). Any notion of identity from this point of view is seen as both provisional and political, as firmly located within social, cultural, and historical relations. Drawing on Inoue's (2006) emphasis on the *listening subject* and Lo and Reyes' (2009) work on 'yellow English' and what they call the "distinctiveness paradigm" – the view that a group speaks a language variety distinguishable from another – Rosa (2019, p. 6) insists on the importance of focusing away from the preidentified racialized body toward the "interpretive practices of racially hegemonic perceiving subjects." That is to say our focus has to be not so much on the practices of the racialized subject but on the "White perceiving subjects" (p. 6). This is to turn the tables on assumed categories of identification and to focus instead on processes of *"raciolinguistic enregisterment"* (Rosa and Flores, 2017a, p. 631) whereby language and race, or other forms of co-naturalization of people and language, are mapped onto each other.

At the same time that critical research questions the way difference is categorized as different, it also needs to engage deeply with the ways in which people understand their own different ways of being. In line with the arguments in this book for *situated* forms of knowledge and action, this focus makes participants' lives and concerns central. Auerbach's 2000) *participatory action research* promotes research by students on the matters that concern them as a means to bring the outside world into the classroom and to take the classroom into the outside world (Rivera, 1999). Drawing on Heath's (1983) suggestions for involving students and teachers in researching the literacy practices of their communities, Norton Peirce (1995) similarly argues for "classroom based social research" to "engage the social identities of students in ways that will improve their language learning outside the classroom and help them claim the right to speak" (p. 26). Following Corson's (1997) argument for critical realism in applied linguistics, a position that takes the perspectives of participants as real, Jewell's (1998, p. 5) study of transgender identity in an ESL class, insists on the importance of "students' writings or speakings of their lived experiences in relation to ESL" to bring about a "clearer picture of the array of actual actors who use English."

Linking these first two perspectives – questioning the categories of people and language with which we operate, and seeking to understand how people themselves construct their own views – Albury (2017, p. 47) makes a case, drawing on Preston (2011), for *folk linguistic* approaches to research: "Postmodernism and critical theory call on us, as researchers, to reflect on the fundamental world-views and biases we bring to our work, and folk linguistics allows us to actively investigate how different cultures and world-views perceive the nature of language." By drawing on participants' views on language and identity, "critical sociolinguistic research methods" can both question "socially-constructed beliefs" about languages and people (Albury, 2017, p. 38) and investigate how local language ideologies and ontologies operate (Pennycook & Makoni, 2020). Coupled with forms of research such as *critical ethnography* (Anderson, 2009; Canagarajah, 1993; Mills, 2007), or indeed *critical linguistic ethnography* – as a means to understand language disabilities in multilingual families (Martin, 2012) or more broadly as a way to understand both the local contingencies of multilingual discourse and the broader social and historical frames within which they occur (Martin-Jones & Gardner, 2012) – critical applied linguistic research approaches seek to shed light on the ways language use occurs amid inequitable social relations.

These approaches to research all make questions of power central to their investigation. Power operates at multiple levels across any such field of endeavor. It has to do with questions of knowledge and power within different research paradigms – opposing "the noncommittal objectivity and scientism encouraged by the positivistic empirical attitude behind descriptive ethnography" (Canagarajah, 1993, p. 605) – and making a case for politically committed research. It also has to do with the domains and topics of research, the ways in which a particular set of concerns over language use (translation, access to services, social interactions, medium of instruction in schools) intersect with institutional (education, legal, medical) and social (class, race, gender, sexuality, disability) forms of power. Across a broad sweep of matters of concern involving language, critical applied linguistic research is always involved with questions of power, from questions of minority language speakers, or classed and raced language variety speakers seeking more equitable schooling conditions (Flores & Chaparro, 2018; Lin, 1999), to gender and sexual identity in language classrooms (Nelson, 2009; Sunderland, 1994), from discrimination within the legal system faced by Indigenous and minority peoples (Eades, 2010; Lippi-Green, 1997), to the struggle for recognition through forms of popular culture (Ibrahim, 1999; Williams, 2017). Of course, as discussed throughout this book, how power is understood may vary considerably – from modernist versions of those that have power dominating those who do not, to more diffused versions of the social operations of power – but critical applied linguistic research is always engaged with questions of power.

In the wider field of social scientific research, it has been acknowledged that research "needs emancipation from hearing only the voices of Western Europe, emancipation from generations of silence, and emancipation from seeing the world in one colour" (Guba & Lincoln, 2005, p. 212). As Chilisa (2011, p. 1) puts it, "current academic research traditions are founded on the culture, history, and philosophies of Euro-Western thought" and "exclude from knowledge production the knowledge systems of formerly colonized, historically marginalized, and oppressed groups." Central to many of these approaches is the idea of *decolonization* of research methodologies (Smith, 2012) and the development of alternative approaches to research. As Albury (2016, p. 30) remarks, if current theories "continue to define language vitality in western ontological terms, then they will enjoy less applicability in the revitalisation of te reo Māori in Aotearoa" (p. 30). Albury's (2017, p. 37) focus is the "decolonisation of sociolinguistic theory and method by understanding, voicing, legitimising, and indeed ultimately applying more ontologies and epistemologies of language than those that generally premise current scholarship." Drawing on different ways of thinking and researching from Indigenous perspectives (Mika, 2016; Martin/Mirraboopa, 2003; Ober 2017), we can not only work with ideas about language compatible with Indigenous thought, but equally importantly, renew current ideas in the field in ways that are surely important for a more resilient applied linguistics. We should of course be cautious of not throwing out the baby with the bathwater and dismissing wholesale Western/Northern approaches to research (Grosfoguel, 2011), but the significant emphasis here is on developing an epistemic perspective from the subaltern side of colonial difference (Pennycook & Makoni, 2020).

Finally, such research needs to have transformative goals, aiming not just to describe but also to change. As a number of critical researchers point out, the critical agenda and the openness to a diversity of research approaches should not render research less rigorous. In this context, Lather (1991) discusses the notion of *catalytic validity*, or "the degree to which the research process re-orients, focuses and energizes participants toward knowing reality in order to transform it" (p. 68). Whereas Guba and Lincoln's (1989) notion of *catalytic authenticity* "refers to the degree to which something is actually done" as a result of research (Lynch, 1996, p. 65), catalytic validity requires that research be judged not merely in terms of whether something is done or not but according to the degree to which such action may be seen as socially transformative, as part of an ethical and political vision of change. Critical applied linguistic research needs to be both rigorous and transformative, to engage with questions of difference and how participants understand their lives, to keep questions of power on the table at all times while also ensuring that this is part of a wider conversation between the Global North and South.

Critical Applied Linguistic Activism

Whatever kind of work we may be engaged in as critical applied linguists, our work needs to be activist, that is, like transformative research, working actively toward social change. Hale (2006, p. 97) draws a distinction between *cultural critique* and *activist research*. Cultural critique, he argues, embraces "familiar progressive desires to champion subaltern peoples and to deconstruct the powerful" but does not require "substantive transformation in conventional research methods to achieve these goals" (Hale, 2006, p. 98). *Activist research*, by contrast, centers on "political alignment with an organized group of people in struggle" and on collaboration at all levels of the research process (Budach, 2019), thus demanding both political and research coalitions that challenge other norms. As suggested in the previous section, changing the way we do research cannot be done on the same old terrain of qualitative versus quantitative research (though post-qualitative approaches are worth exploring; St. Pierre, 2019) or the apparent resolution in 'mixed methods' research. The challenges posed by a critical activist dimension suggest different epistemological foundations, different kinds of collaboration, different types of goals.

The contrast between activism and advocacy sheds some light on some of these assumptions. The distinction rests largely on the idea of working within the system (advocacy) or outside the system (activism). This also suggests another distinction between acting on the behalf of others or acting in collaboration with others. This is often the case with support for minority languages within academic circles: While community members may be activists, working toward support for their languages through whatever channels may be available, academics can be seen more often as advocates, supporting those languages as an institutional insider (with the various advantages and disadvantages this may entail). Flores and Chaparro (2018, p. 368) distinguish between "an advocacy paradigm" where scholars "work *for* language-minoritized communities" and "an empowerment paradigm where scholars are doing work *with* language-minoritized communities in ways that simultaneously challenge power relations between scholars and participants and broader social inequalities" (p. 368). Combined with Hales' (2006) distinction, this insists on working with communities and with their understandings of language and politics.

A further contrast is often made between academic work and activism. This rests by and large on a notion of disinterested scholarship that should guide our work. For Widdowson (2004, p. 173) for example, discussing what he sees as the problems with critical discourse analysis (CDA), "the proponents of CDA can be regarded as activists in that they are critical, but as discourse analysts they are academics." That is to say, the discourse analytic part of CDA needs to be subject to standard academic norms even if the critical part of the equation sets them apart as activists. It is this activism, from this point of view, that is the problem for CDA, clouding their judgements and rendering CDA contradictory: You cannot be both critical (working with a priori assumptions about social inequality) and analytic. This view has made it possible over a long period for mainstream applied linguistics to reject critical approaches (critical discourse analysis, critical pedagogy, and so on) on the grounds that the overt political stance invalidates the intellectual project. As the discussions throughout this book have made clear, this kind of distinction between academic and activist work is at best unhelpful and at worst reactionary.

While the advocacy/activism distinction is one academics need to work with in terms of institutional positioning and political engagement, an assumed division between critical and academic work is one that should be roundly rejected. We would also do well not to accept too easily the common split between activist and intellectual work, as if academic endeavor can only ever be advocacy, and activist work happens elsewhere. "Philosophical activism," Newcomb argues, can be understood as "an effort to gain deeper insight into what it means to be called 'Indigenous' (i.e., dominated)" (2019, p. 156). This is an attempt to "increase our knowledge and deepen our understanding of all the heartache, hardship, and devastation that Western European thought and behavior has put our nations and peoples through" (p. 156). He therefore calls for a "philosophical activism capable of challenging the claim of a right" of domination exercised by colonizing people (p. 168). Some forms of intellectual work that endeavor to change the ways we think about language and politics can also be thought of as forms of language activism, and it is therefore possible to see the intellectual work of critical applied linguistics as one wing of a broader activist engagement.

As discussions above and earlier that call for decolonizing, and seeking alternative ways of thinking about language make clear, a political stance accompanied by normative versions of language will fail to address the decolonial imperative to question the coloniality of linguistic knowledge. This is of particular importance for any language activist project. As discussed at numerous points in this book, unless we question the terms in which we conduct our critical analysis, unless our critical project has sufficient reflexivity as a form of critical resistance (Hoy, 2004), we will fail to engage adequately with the communities with whom we are working. Alternative language frameworks, such as translanguaging (see Chapter 3), are not incompatible with language activism, and indeed in many ways can help people to move forward collectively in their understandings of language diversity. At the same time, such frameworks are not sufficient in themselves. We need to be wary of both linguistic technologies (as discussed in Chapter 5, they cannot themselves do the work of social change) and linguistic innovations that in themselves cannot carry the burden of political action.

It is on these grounds that I have elsewhere emphasized the importance of *translingual activism* rather than just translanguaging itself, as a project that aims to decolonize and provincialize metropolitan languages such as English and to develop a critical pedagogy of the commons that seeks ways of redressing the repressive institutionalization of inequality in contemporary life (Pennycook, 2019). So what versions of language might serve us in this endeavor? Flores and Chaparro (2018, p. 367) argue for "a new paradigm of language activism that connects the implementation of language education policy with other movements that seek to address societal inequities caused by a myriad of factors including poverty, racism, and xenophobia." From this perspective, "a materialist anti-racist approach to language activism" (Flores & Chaparro, 2018, p. 380) links a focus on materialism – though not necessarily one based only in socioeconomic definitions of material circumstances – to questions of class, gender, and race. The point therefore is not whether translanguaging, or some other recent framing of language, is suited for language activism but rather whether the model of language employed can successfully connect people, place, and inequality.

Language activism can be understood broadly. Embracing all forms of activism that use language (including therefore almost any activist work) would be to cast our net too wide, but to make central domains typically seen as activist, such as language revival, would be to view the field too narrowly. From a critical applied linguistic perspective, many kinds of work may be understood in activist terms, from critical language awareness (Alim, 2005) to language education (Schweiter and Chamness Iida, 2020). Language activist work needs to be collaborative, political, and linguistic (McIvor, 2020); it involves struggles over forms of social inequality that directly involve language and therefore needs a version of language open to decolonial critiques and capable of engaging with gendered, racial, and other material disparities. It involves collaborative political and linguistic endeavors aiming to redress social inequalities by decolonizing language while linking it to material concerns around race, gender, place, and disparity.

Critical Principles

This discussion provides us with various useful principles that can inform approaches to critical applied linguistics. In this final section, I shall sketch out various themes that are arguably necessary for any critical applied linguistic project. This will not fit with everyone's ideas of the field, but to me these are necessary aspects of how we can proceed. Such notions cannot be reduced to techniques; neither should they be seen as prescriptions. We should also always be wary of trying to reduce them to technical solutions: The moment we start to believe that our linguistic technologies can solve our social concerns, we have lost sight of the bigger picture. At the same time, this is by no means to suggest that good research – technical, sophisticated, thorough – should not be part of the critical applied linguistic toolkit. Quite the contrary: Our research has to be as good as possible if we are to understand the key concerns with which we want to engage. Indeed, it is tempting to suggest theoretical and research *rigor* – even if this appears a rather outdated term – as central to what we do.

These are then a set of guiding principles (Table 7.3) that should be worth considering when we embark on critical applied linguistic – or as I have argued, any applied linguistic – endeavor. First, is power in all its complexities.

Table 7.3 Critical Applied Linguistic Principles

Themes	Principles
Power	The contingent and contextual effects of power in relation to access, exclusion, reproduction, and resistance
Decolonizing	An applied linguistics that challenges its colonial and racist heritage
Praxis	Critical praxis as a continuous reflexive integration of thought, desire, and action
Ethics	Alternative imaginaries that refuse the present as definitive of what is possible and seek alternative visions
Situatedness	Making apparent the locus of enunciation and understanding the locatedness of knowledge and action
Problematizing practice	A restive problematization of the given, a constant questioning of our applied linguistic and other assumptions
Open and collaborative	Grounded, collaborative practice that engages with and emerges from local ways of knowing and doing

As I have suggested throughout the book, power is central to what concerns us here but it should not be assumed we know what it is or how it operates: Critical applied linguistics needs to help us understand better how power operates in and through language, rather than be satisfied with mapping pregiven explanations of power against forms of language. While it is important to grasp the major forms of power and inequality in the world – neoliberal economics and ideologies that constantly work against common ownership and action; forms of discrimination that constantly reproduce social inequalities along lines of gender, race, and sexuality among others – it is also imperative to grasp the importance of the situatedness of knowledge, action, and power. Power needs to remain as that which must be explained. We need to understand how language is involved in contingent and contextual effects of power (forms of situated domination), inequitable access to material and cultural goods (disparities in who can do what), ideological and discursive frames of exclusion (discriminatory practices of marginalization), constructions of social and cultural distinction (forms of difference), and hopes, actions, and longing for transformation (desire for social change).

This leads us to one of the most urgent aspect of the contemporary critical applied linguistic project: Challenging epistemic racism and decolonizing knowledge. As Kubota (2019) has urged, we need to confront the privilege accorded to white Euro-American knowledge to the detriment of the knowledges of other peoples of the Global South (Pennycook and Makoni, 2020). We have to be able to grapple with Motha's (2020, p. 132) question whether we can "truly be effective applied linguists if we are not willing to consider the ways in which our work is complicit with White supremacy and colonization?" This has to be both an oppositional project – questioning forms of knowledge embedded in the academy – and an expansive project – listening to and taking on board alternative forms of knowledge about language and being that have been ignored. As Nascimento dos Santos and Windle (2020, p. 17) propose for English language education, "classrooms all around the world need to challenge established interaction orders and orders of being to open space for both students and teachers to construct a more democratic and anti-racist pedagogical relationship."

A third concern is how theory, practice, and a critical orientation to work can be allied in a notion of critical praxis. Critical applied linguistics needs a sense of *critical* that is part of a definitive form of politics. The critical here is a political critique and not merely a way of thinking. This is about considering language, difference, texts, and education as political from top to bottom. The political and indeed the ethical should be seen less in terms of a dogmatic claiming of moral and political certitude, however, and more in terms of an ability to politicize anew (Foucault, 1980b). It has also been important to go beyond a practice/theory dichotomy and to think in terms of critical praxis, a continuous reflexive integration of thought, desire, and action (Simon, 1992). This book is not about some sort of critical applied linguistic theory that can now be applied or translated into practice. This unhelpful divide that runs throughout much of applied linguistics (Clarke, 1994) suggests that applied linguists develop theories or do research that can then be applied in classrooms or other settings. We need instead to take the idea of practice far more seriously (Pennycook, 2010), and think in terms of applied linguistics as a theory of the practice (Kramsch, 2015), or as critical praxis (Kubota & Miller, 2017).

In order to ground our visions of change, we cannot simply offer an alternative reality. The engagement with *ethics* and the need for the possibility of an alternative imaginary brings us back to Roger Simon's (1992) notion of "the situated refusal of the present as definitive of that which is possible" (p. 30). Such an educational vision that is "capable of narrating stories of possibility" is "constrained within an ethical imagination that privileges diversity, compassionate justice, and securing of the conditions for the renewal of human life." In the same way that Foucault presents us with the need to seek new schemas of politicization, this is not about establishing a fixed and normative moral position but rather of seeking new frames of ethical thought and conduct, or as Kearney (1988) puts it, "the ethical demand to imagine *otherwise*" (p. 364). Such a vision, of course, demands a major rethinking of what applied linguistics is about. Instead of being a canon of normative knowledge about language learning, workplace communication, or discourse analysis, it needs to address the ethical demands of language education, the ethical implications of the violence of texts, or the ethical concerns of inequalities in the workplace.

These concerns all require a *situatedness* of thought and action. This is about understanding locality and acknowledging the locus of enunciation of our own ideas. As has been stressed repeatedly throughout this book, we have to question claims to universal and transcendent knowledge. Unless we understand the situatedness of different Englishes, of the production and reception of texts, or of pedagogical actions, we miss both the ways power operates and the significance of lived experiences. This implies an understanding of our own locations, our bodies, and the histories that are written onto them. It also suggests hermeneutic, genealogical/historical, and narrative understandings of knowledge that can develop a sense of what we do in critical applied linguistics as both located and in motion. The locus of enunciation, which is more than just a question of who or where the speaker is, but rather refers to the complex of geopolitical and ideological positioning from which ideas are enunciated (Grosfoguel, 2007), insists that we question from where anyone speaks or writes. There are no positions that transcend bodies, politics, and discourse.

One of the paradoxes of critical work emerges from the question of what happens when critical work goes mainstream. I have been suggesting that there is no good reason why all applied linguistics shouldn't adopt critical principles. But would it still be critical? We can already see these tendencies in domains such as critical discourse analysis: Where once there was a strongly-grounded critique of language and society, now there is all too often a research methodology that sounds a bit more interesting than plain old discourse analysis. Here we confront the apparently inevitable tendencies toward orthodoxy and normativity of disciplines and institutions (Pennycook, 2016).

The way forward here – one way of at least providing some hope – is to insist on critical applied linguistics not as fixed body of knowledge and practice but as a set of principles that are always open to change and negotiation. From this point of view, critical applied linguistics can be understood as a problematizing practice; as a restive problematization of the given (Dean, 1994), a constant questioning of our assumptions both within and beyond applied linguistics.

This is also why critical applied linguistics needs to be open and collaborative. It needs to be able to listen. As with the discussion of language reclamation projects, where processes of decolonizing linguistics need to go hand-in-hand with close cooperation between communities and people with varieties of linguistic expertise, so critical applied linguistics has to be a grounded, collaborative practice that engages with, indeed emerges from, local ways of knowing and doing (Sarkar, 2018; McIvor, 2020). Many people around the world have been doing critical applied linguistics for far longer than I have been writing about it. They have no choice: When dominant frames of applied linguistics are exported to the majority world, local projects need to resist the language and methods of mainstream orthodoxies. Critical applied linguistics therefore has to be understood as "an open-ended construction that is contested, incessantly perspectival and multiply-sited" (Lather, 1995, p. 177). It is a way of thinking that is always reflexive about itself, aware of the limits of knowing (Spivak, 1993). It is on these grounds that Echeverri-Sucerquia (2020, p. 30) insists on the importance of "collaborative – not subordinate – North-South relations, where scholars in the South recognize the value of knowledge produced locally." This is why this book is a *critical* introduction to critical applied linguistics, for while part of that critical focus is on inequitable social relations around language as commonly understood, it is also about a reworking of global relations of knowledge production.

Conclusions

In this revised version of critical applied linguistics, I have sought – impossibly – to do justice to at least some of the work that has been done in the two decades since I first tried to pull these different strands of work together. The very impossibility of providing decent coverage of all this work provides grounds for some forms of optimism in what in many other ways seem very dark days. At least it is clear that many people, in many different ways, in many parts of the world, are engaged in critical applied linguistic projects. They may not call it that, or may not wish to affiliate with this kind of label. But teachers, researchers, academics, linguists, activists, and many others are trying to intervene in inequitable linguistic relations, to change the ways language education can be disenfranchising, texts can be discriminatory, policies exclusionary, and much more. We have to continue to do this work since these issues matter deeply. My hope is that a book such as this can help people build tools for such work, think through what is at stake, read like-minded positions, and work toward change.

References

Ahearn, L. (2012). *Living language: An introduction to linguistic anthropology.* Malden, MA: Wiley-Blackwell.

Albury, N. J. (2016). Defining Māori language revitalisation: A project in folk linguistics. *Journal of Sociolinguistics, 20*: 287–311. doi:10.1111/josl.12183

Albury, N. J. (2017). How folk linguistic methods can support critical sociolinguistics. *Lingua, 199,* 36–49.

Alim, H. S. (2005). Critical language awareness in the United States: Revisiting issues and revising pedagogies in a resegregated society. *Educational Researcher, 34,* 24–31.

Alim, H. S., & Paris, D. (2017). What ls culturally sustaining pedagogy and why does it matter? In Paris, D., & H. S. Alim (Eds). *Culturally sustaining pedagogies: Teaching and learning for justice in a changing world.* NY: Teachers College Press. 1–24.

Alim, S., Ibrahim A., & A Pennycook, A. (2009) (Eds). *Global linguistic flows: Global hip hop culture, youth identities, and the politics of language.* New York: Routledge.

Alim, H. S., & Smitherman, G. (2012). *Articulate while Black: Barack Obama, language and race in the US.* Oxford: Oxford University Press.

Alim, H. S., & Smitherman, G. (2020). "Perfect English" and White supremacy. In J. McIntosh, and N. Mendoza-Denton, (Eds). *Language in the Trump era: Scandals and emergencies,* (pp. 226–236). Cambridge: Cambridge University Press.

Althusser, L. (1971). *Lenin and philosophy and other essays.* London: New Left Books.

Anderson, K. (2009). *War or common cause? A critical ethnography of language education policy, race and cultural citizenship.* Charlotte, NC: Information Age Publishing.

Anya, U. (2020). African americans in world language study: The forged path and future directions. *Annual Review of Applied Linguistics, 40,* 97–112.

Appadurai, A. (1990). Disjuncture and difference in the global cultural economy. In M. Featherstone (Ed). *Global culture: Nationalism, globalization and modernity* (pp. 295–310). London: Sage.

Appiah, K. A. (1993). *In my father's house: Africa in the philosophy of culture.* Oxford: Oxford University Press.

Appleby, R. (2013). Desire in translation: White masculinity and TESOL', *TESOL Quarterly, 47*(1), 122–147.

Appleby, R. (2014). *Men and masculinities in global English language teaching.* London: Palgrave.

Appleby, R. (2018). Academic English and elite masculinities, *Journal of English for Academic Purposes,* vol. *32,* pp. 42–52.

Appleby, R. (2019). *Sexing the animal in a post-humanist world: A critical feminist approach.* London: Routledge.

Arrighi, B. (Ed). (2007). *Understanding inequality: The intersection of race/ethnicity, class, and gender*. Lanham, MD: Rowman & Littlefield.

Arruzza, C., Bhattacharya, T., & Fraser, N. (2019). *Feminism for the 99%: A manifesto*. London: Verso.

Ashcroft, B., Griffiths, G., & Tiffin, H. (1989). *The empire writes back: Theory and practice in post-colonial literatures*. London: Routledge.

Atkinson, D. (1997). A critical approach to critical thinking in TESOL. *TESOL Quarterly, 31*, 71–94.

Auerbach, E. (1993). Reexamining English only in the ESL classroom. *TESOL Quarterly, 27*, 9–32.

Auerbach, E. (1995). The politics of the ESL classroom: Issues of power in pedagogical choices. In J. Tollefson (Ed.), *Power and inequality in language education* (pp. 9–33). New York: Cambridge University Press.

Auerbach, E. (2000). Creating participatory learning communities: Paradoxes and possibilities. In J. K. Hall & W. Eggington (Eds.), *The sociopolitics of English language teaching* (pp. 143–164). Clevedon, UK: Multilingual Matters.

Auerbach, E., & Wallerstein, N. (1987). *ESL for action: Problem-posing at work*. Reading, MA: Addison Wesley.

Austin, J. L. (1962). *How to do things with words*. Cambridge, MA: Harvard University Press.

Aveneri, N., Graham, R., Johnson, E., Riner, R., & Rosa J., (Eds). (2019). Introduction: Reimagining language and social justice. *Language and social justice in practice* (pp. 1–16). New York: Routledge.

Bailey, R. (1991). *Images of English: A cultural history of the language*. Ann Arbor: The University of Michigan Press.

Baker-Bell, A. (2013). I never really knew the history behind African American language: Critical language pedagogy in an advanced placement English language arts class. *Equity & Excellence in Education, 46*, 355–370. doi:10.1080/10665684.2013.806848

Baker-Bell, A., Butler, T., & Johnson, L. (2017). The pain and the wounds: A call for critical race English education in the wake of racial violence. *English Education, 49*, 116–129.

Barad, K. (2007). *Meeting the universe halfway: Quantum physics and the entanglement of matter and meaning*. Durham: Duke University Press.

Barrett, M. (1991). *The politics of truth: From Marx to Foucault*. Stanford, CA: Stanford University Press.

Battiste, M. (2013). *Decolonizing education: Nourishing the learning spirit*. Saskatoon, Canada: UBC Press, Purich Publishing.

Baugh, J. (2018). *Linguistics in pursuit of justice*. Cambridge: Cambridge University Press.

Baynham, M. (1995). *Literacy practices*. London: Longman.

Bee, B. (1993). Critical literacy and the politics of gender. In C. Lankshear & P. McLaren (Eds.), *Critical literacy: Politics, praxis and the postmodern* (pp. 105–132). Albany: State University of New York Press.

Belenky, M., Clinchy, B., Glodberger, N., & Tarule, J. (1986). *Women's ways of knowing: The development of self, voice and mind*. New York: Basic Books.

Bell, A. (2014). *The guidebook to sociolinguistics*. Chichester: Wiley Blackwell.

Benesch, S. (1996). Needs analysis and curriculum development in EAP: An example of a critical approach. *TESOL Quarterly, 30*, 723–738.

Benesch, S. (1999). Thinking critically, thinking dialogically. *TESOL Quarterly*, *33*, 573–580.

Benesch, S. (2001). *Critical English for academic purposes: Theory, politics, and practice*. Mahwah, NJ: Lawrence Erlbaum Associates.

Bennett, J. (2010). *Vibrant matter: A political ecology of things*. Durham, NC: Duke University Press.

Benquet, M. and Bourgeron, T. (2021). *La finance autoritaire: Vers la fin du néolibéralisme*. Paris: Raisons d'Agir.

Benrabah, M. (2013). *Language conflict in Algeria: From colonialism to post-independence*. Bristol: Multilingual Matters.

Benson, P. (1997). The philosophy and politics of learner autonomy. In P. Benson & P. Voller (Eds.), *Autonomy and independence in language learning* (pp. 18–34). London: Longman.

Berlin, I. (2003). *The Crooked timber of humanity: Chapters in the history of ideas*. In H. Hardy (Ed) (second edition [1st ed 1990]), London: Pimlico.

Bernstein, B. (1972). Social class, language and socialization. In P. P. Giglioli (Ed.). *Language and social context: Selected readings* (pp. 157–178). Harmondsworth: Penguin.

Bex, T., & Watts, R. J. (Eds.). (1999). *Standard English: The widening debate*. London: Routledge.

Bhatt, A., & Martin-Jones, M. (1992). Whose resource? Minority languages, bilingual learners and language awareness. In N. Fairclough (Ed.). *Critical language awareness* (pp. 285–302). London: Longman.

Bhattacharya, U, Jiang, L., & Canagarajah S. (2019). Race, representation, and diversity in the American Association for Applied Linguistics. *Applied Linguistics*, doi:10.1093/applin/amz003

Blackledge, A. & Creese, A. (2010). *Multilingualism: A critical perspective*. London: Continuum.

Block, D. (1996). Not so fast: Some thoughts on theory culling, relativism, accepted findings and the heart and soul of SLA. *Applied Linguistics*, *17*, 63–83.

Block, D. (2014). *Social class in applied linguistics*. London: Routledge.

Block, D. (2015). Social class in applied linguistics. *Annual Review of Applied Linguistics*, *35*, 1–19.

Block, D. (2018a). *Political economy and sociolinguistics: Neoliberalism, inequality and social class*. London: Bloomsbury.

Block, D. (2018b). What on earth is language commodification? In S. Breidbach, L. Küster, & B. Schmenk, (Eds). *Sloganizations in language education discourse* (pp. 121–141). Bristol: Multilingual Matters.

Block, D. (2018c). The political economy of language education research (or the lack thereof): Nancy Fraser and the case of translanguaging, *Critical Inquiry in Language Studies*, *15*(4), 237–257

Block, D. (2019). *Post-truth and political discourse*. Cham: Palgrave.

Block, D, Gray, J., & Holborow, M. (2012). *Neoliberalism and applied linguistics*. London: Routledge.

Blommaert, J. (2005). *Discourse: A critical introduction*. Cambridge: Cambridge University Press.

Blommaert, J. (2010). *The sociolinguistics of globalization*. Cambridge: Cambridge University Press.

Borjian, M. (2013). *English in post-revolutionary Iran*. Bristol: Multilingual Matters.

Boughton, B. (2011). Timor-Leste: Building a post-conflict education system. In C. Brock, & L. Pe Symaco (Eds.), *Education in South-East Asia* (pp. 177–196). Oxford: Symposium Books.

Boughton, B. (2012). Adult literacy, political participation and democracy. In M. Leach, N. C. Mendes, A. B. da Silva, B. Boughton, & A. da Costa Ximenes (Eds.). *Peskiza foun kona ba/Novas investigações sobre/New research on/Penelitian baru mengenai Timor-Leste* (pp. 362–368). Hawthorn: Swinburne Press.

Bourdieu, P. (1977). *Outline of a theory of practice.* Cambridge: Cambridge University Press.

Bourdieu, P. (1982). *Ce que parler veut dire: L'économie des échanges linguistiques.* Paris: Fayard.

Bourdieu, P. (1986). The forms of capital. In J. G. Richardson (Ed.). *Handbook of theory and research for the sociology of education* (pp. 241–258). Westport, CT: Greenwood.

Bourdieu, P. (1991). *Language and symbolic power.* Oxford, UK: Polity.

Bourdieu, P., & Passeron, J.-C. (1970). *La reproduction. Éléments pour une théorie du système d'enseignement.* Paris: Les Editions de Minuit.

Bourdieu, P., & Passeron, J.-C. (1977). *Reproduction in education, society and culture.* London: Sage

Bowles, S., & Gintis, H. (1976). *Schooling in capitalist America.* New York: Basic Books.

Braidotti, R. (2013). *The posthuman.* Cambridge: Polity.

Brigstocke, J., Dawney L., & Kirwan S. (Eds). (2016). *Space, power and the commons: The struggle for alternative futures.* London: Routledge.

Britzman, D. (1995). Is there a queer pedagogy? Or, stop reading straight. *Educational Theory, 45,* 151–165.

Brookfield, S. (1987). *Developing critical thinkers.* Milton Keynes: Open University Press.

Bruthiaux, P. (2003). 'Squaring the circles: Issues in modeling English worldwide'. *International Journal of Applied Linguistics, 13*(2), 159–177.

Bruthiaux, P. (2008). 'Dimensions of globalization and applied linguistics', in P. Tan & R Rubdy (Eds). *Language as commodity: Global structures, local marketplaces* (pp. 1–30). London: Continuum.

Brutt-Griffler, J., & Samimy, K. (1999). Revisiting the colonial in the postcolonial: Critical praxis for nonnative English-speaking teachers in a TESOL program. *TESOL Quarterly, 33,* 413–431.

Bucholtz, M., & Hall, K. (2008). All of the above: New coalitions in sociocultural linguistics. *Journal of Sociolinguistics, 12*(4), 401–431.

Bucholtz, M., & Hall, K. (2016). Embodied sociolinguistics. In N. Coupland (Ed.), *Sociolinguistics: Theoretical debates.* Cambridge: Cambridge University Press (pp. 173–197).

Budach, G. (2019). Collaborative ethnography, in: K. Tusting (ed.) *The Routledge handbook of linguistic ethnography,* New York: Routledge. 198–212.

Busch, B. (2012). The linguistic repertoire revisited. *Applied Linguistics, 33:* 503–523.

Busch, B. (2017). Expanding the notion of the linguistic repertoire: On the concept of *Spracherleben*—The lived experience of language. *Applied Linguistics, 38*(3) 340–358.

Burnett, L. (1962). *The treasure of our tongue.* London: Secker & Warburg.

Butler, J. (1990). *Gender trouble: Feminism and the subversion of identity.* New York: Routledge.

Butler, J. (1993). *Bodies that matter: On the discursive limits of "sex."* London: Routledge.

Butler, J. (1997). *Excitable speech: A politics of the performative.* New York: Routledge.

Camangian, P. (2015). Teaching like lives depend on it: Agitate, arouse, inspire. *Urban Education*, 50 (4), 424–453.

Cameron, D. (1990). Demythologizing sociolinguistics: Why language does not reflect society. In J. Joseph & T. Taylor (Eds.), *Ideologies of language* (pp. 79–96). London: Routledge.

Cameron, D. (1995). *Verbal hygiene*. London: Routledge.

Cameron, D. (1997). Performing gender identity: Young men's talk and the construction of heterosexual masculinity. In S. Johnson & U. H. Meinhof (Eds.), *Language and masculinity* (pp. 47–64). Oxford, UK: Blackwell.

Cameron, D. (2007). *The myth of Mars and Venus: Do men and women really speak different languages?* Oxford: Oxford University Press.

Cameron, D., and Kulick D. (2003). *Language and sexuality*. Cambridge: Cambridge University Press.

Canagarajah, A. S. (1993). Critical ethnography of a Sri Lankan classroom: Ambiguities in student opposition to reproduction through ESOL. *TESOL Quarterly, 27*, 601–626.

Canagarajah, S. (1999a). On EFL teachers, awareness, and agency. *ELT Journal, 53*, 207–214.

Canagarajah, S. (1999b). *Resisting linguistic imperialism in English teaching*. Oxford, UK: Oxford University Press.

Canagarajah, S. (2013). *Translingual practice: Global Englishes and cosmopolitan relations*. New York: Routledge.

Canagarajah, S. (2017). *Translingual practices and neoliberal policies: Attitudes and strategies of African skilled migrants in anglophone workplaces*. Cham: Springer.

Chilisa, B. (2011). *Indigenous research methodologies* New York: Sage.

Chomsky, N. (1965). *Aspects of the theory of syntax*. Cambridge, MA: MIT Press.

Chomsky, N. (1971). *Problems of knowledge and freedom*. New York: Pantheon.

Chomsky, N. (1974). Human nature: Justice versus power [dicussion with M. Foucault]. In F. Elder (Ed.), *Reflexive water: The basic concerns of mankind* (pp. 133–198). London: Souvenir Press.

Chomsky, N. (1979). *Language and responsibility*. New York: Pantheon.

Chomsky, N. (2013) *On anarchy*. London: Penguin.

Chrisman, L., & Williams, P. (1994). Colonial discourse and post-colonial theory: An introduction. In P. Williams & L. Chrisman (Eds.), *Colonial discourse and postcolonial theory. A reader* (pp. 1–20). New York: Columbia University Press.

Christie, F. (1998). Learning the literacies of primary and secondary schooling. In F. Christie & R. Misson (Eds.), *Literacy and schooling* (pp. 47–73). London: Routledge.

Chun, C. (2015). *Engaging with the everyday: Power and meaning making in an EAP classroom*. Bristol: Multilingual Matters.

Clark, R. (1992). Principles and practice of CLA in the classroom. In N. Fairclough (Ed.), *Critical language awareness* (pp. 117–140). London: Longman.

Clark, R., & Ivanič, R. (1997). *The politics of writing*. London: Routledge.

Clarke, M. (1994). The dysfunctions of the theory/practice discourse. *TESOL Quarterly, 28*(1), 9–26.

Coates, J. (Ed). (1998). *Language and gender: A reader*. Oxford, UK: Blackwell.

Cohn, B. (1996). *Colonialism and its forms of knowledge: The British in India*. Princeton, NJ: Princeton University Press.

Connell, R. (2019). *The good university: What universities actually do and why it's time for radical change*. London: Zed Books.

Cope, B., & Kalantzis, M. (1993). The power of literacy and the literacy of power. In B. Cope & M. Kalantzis (Eds.), *The powers of literacy: A genre approach to teaching writing* (pp. 63–89). London: The Falmer Press.

Cope. B., & Kalantzis, M. (Eds.). (2000). *Multiliteracies: Literacy learning and the design of social futures*. London: Routledge.

Cope, B., & Kalantzis, M. (2013). 'Multiliteracies': New literacies, new learning. In M. R. Hawkins (Ed.). *Framing language and literacies: Socially situated views and perspectives*. New York: Routledge, 105–135.

Cope, B., Kalantzis, M., Kress, G., Martin, J., & Murphy, L. (1993). Bibliographical essay: Developing the theory and practice of genres based literacy. In B. Cope & M. Kalantzis (Eds.). *The powers of literacy: A genre approach to teaching writing* (pp. 231–247). London: The Falmer Press.

Corson, D. (1997). Critical realism: An emancipatory philosophy for applied linguistics? *Applied Linguistics, 18,* 166–188.

Coulmas, F. (1998). Language rights—Interests of state, language groups and the individual. *Language Sciences, 20,* 63–72.

Coulter, C., and Jimenez-Silva, M. (Eds). (2017). *Culturally sustaining and revitalizing pedagogies: Language, culture and power*. Bingley: Emerald Publishing.

Crawford, A. (1999). "We can't all understand the whites' language": An analysis of monolingual health services in a multilingual society. *International Journal of the Sociology of Language, 136,* 27–45.

Crenshaw K. (1991). Mapping the margins: Intersectionality, identity politics, and violence against women of color. *Stanford Law Review. 43*(6): 1241–1299.

Crookes, G. (2013). *Critical ELT in action: Foundations, promises, praxis*. New York: Routledge

Crystal, D. (1997). *English as a global language*. Cambridge, UK: Cambridge University Press.

Cushman, E. (2016). Translingual and decolonial approaches to meaning making. *College English, 78*(3) 234–242.

Davies, A. (1996). Review article: Ironising the myth of linguicism. *Journal of Multilingual and Multicultural Development. 17*(6): 485–596.

Davies, A. (1999). *An introduction to applied linguistics: From theory to practice*. Edinburgh: Edinburgh University Press.

Davies, A. (2005). *A glossary of applied linguistics*. Edinburgh: Edinburgh University Press.

Davies, B. (1989). *Frogs and snails and feminist tails*. Sydney, Australia: Allen & Unwin.

Day, R. (2005). *Gramsci is dead: Anarchist currents in the newest social movements,* London: Pluto Press.

Dean, M. (1994). *Critical and effective histories: Foucault's methods and historical sociology*. London: Routledge.

Delpit, L. (1988). The silenced dialogue: Power and pedagogy in educating other people's children. *Harvard Educational Review, 58,* 280–298.

Delpit, L. (1995). *Other people's children: Cultural conflict in the classroom*. New York: The New Press.

Dendrinos, B. (1992). *The EFL textbook and ideology*. Athens, Greece: N.C. Grivas.

de los Ríos, C., Martinez, D., Musser, A., Canady, A., Camangian, P., & Quijada, P. (2019). Upending colonial practices: Toward repairing harm in English education, *Theory into Practice, 58*(4), 359–367.

de Moita Lopes, L. P. (1998). A transdisciplinaridade é possível em lingüística apli-
cada? [Is transdisciplinarity possible in applied linguistics?]. In I. Signorini &
M. Cavalcanti (Eds.), *Lingüística aplicada e transdisciplinaridade* (pp. 113–128).
Campinas, Brazil: Mercado de Letras.

de Saussure, F. (1922/1983) *Course in general linguistics*. (trans by R Harris of *cours de
linguistique générale*.) La Salle, Ill: Open Court.

de Schutter, H. (2016). The liberal linguistic turn: Kymlicka's freedom account
revisited. *Dve Duvomini: Two Homelands, 44*, 51–65.

de Sousa Santos, B. (2014). *Epistemologies of the South: Justice against epistemicide*. New
York: Routledge.

de Sousa Santos, B. (2018). *The end of the cognitive empire: The coming of age of
epistemologies of the South*. Durham, NC: Duke University Press.

de Souza, L. M. (1994). Post colonial literature and a pedagogy of revisioning: The
contribution of Wilson Harris. *Claritas, 1*, 55–61.

de Souza, L. M. (2017). Epistemic diversity, lazy reason, and ethical translation in
postcolonial contexts. The case of Indigenous educational policy in Brazil. In C.
Kerfoot & K. Hyltenstam (Eds.), *Entangled discourses: South-north orders of visibility*
(pp. 189–208). New York: Routledge.

de Souza, L. M. (2019). Glocal languages, coloniality and globalization from below' in
M. Guilherme, & L. M. Menezes de Souza (Eds). *Glocal languages and critical intercultural awareness: The South answers Back* (pp. 17–41). New York: Routledge.

Diniz de Figueiredo, E., & Martinez, J. (2019). The locus of enunciation as a way
to confront epistemological racism and decolonize scholarly knowledge. *Applied
Linguistics*. doi:10.1093/applin/amz061

Dominguez, M. (2017). "Se hace puentes al andar:" Decolonial teacher education as
a needed bridge to culturalty sustaining and revitalizing pedagogies. In Paris, D., &
H. S. Alim (Eds). *Culturally sustaining pedagogies: Teaching and learning for justice in a
changing world*. NY: Teachers College Press. 225–246.

Douglas Fir Group. (2016). A transdisciplinary framework for SLA in a multilingual
world. *Modern Language Journal, 100*, 19–47.

Dua, H. (1994). *Hegemony of English*. Mysore, India: Yashoda Publications.

Duchêne, A., & Heller M. (Eds). (2013). *Language in late capitalism: Pride and profit*.
London: Routledge.

Duff, P., & Uchida, Y. (1997). The negotiation of teachers' sociocultural identities and
practices in postsecondary EFL classrooms. *TESOL Quarterly, 31*, 451–486.

Dussel, E. (1977). *Filosofía de liberación*. México: Edicol.

Eades, D. (2010). *Sociolinguistics and the legal process*. Bristol: Multilingual Matters.

Echeverri-Sucerquia, P. A. (2020). Critical pedagogy and L2 education in the Global
South *L2 Journal, 12*(2), 21–33.

Educational Linguist. (2018). #MeToo Comes to Educational Linguistics https://educational
linguist.wordpress.com/2018/04/21/metoo-comes-to-educational-linguistics/

Elegant, N. (2018). Penn removes portrait of former GSE dean with alleged history
of sexual harassment. https://www.thedp.com/article/2018/04/gse-getup-sexual-
harassment-dell-hymes-portrait-removal-upenn-penn-philadelphia

Ellsworth, E. (1989). Why doesn't this feel empowering? Working through the repressive myths of critical pedagogy. *Harvard Educational Review, 59*, 297–324.

Ennser-Kananen, J. (2019). Are we who we cite? On epistemological injustices, citing practices, and #metoo in academia. *Apples – Journal of Applied Language Studies,
13*(2), 65–69.

Errington, J. (2001). Colonial linguistics. *Annual Review of Anthropology, 30*, 19–39.

Errington, J. (2008). *Linguistics in a colonial world: A story of language, meaning and power*. Oxford: Blackwell.

Evans, N., & Levinson, S. (2009). The myth of language universals: Language diversity and its importance for cognitive science. *Behavioral and Brain Sciences, 32*, 429–492.

Evans, V. (2014). *The language myth: Why language is not an instinct*. Cambridge University Press.

Fairclough, N. (1989). *Language and power*. London: Longman.

Fairclough, N. (Ed). (1992). *Critical language awareness*. London: Longman.

Fairclough, N. (1992a). The appropriacy of "appropriateness." In N. Fairclough (Ed.), *Critical language awareness* (pp. 33–56). London: Longman.

Fairclough, N. (1992b). *Discourse and social change*. Oxford, UK: Polity.

Fairclough, N. (1992c). Introduction. In N. Fairclough (Ed.), *Critical language awareness* (pp. 1–29). London: Longman.

Fairclough, N. (1993). Critical discourse analysis and the marketization of public discourse. *Discourse and Society, 4*, 133–168.

Fairclough, N. (1995). *Critical discourse analysis*. London: Longman.

Fairclough, N. (1996). Technologisation of discourse. In C. R. Caldas-Couthard, & M. Coulthard (Eds.), *Texts and practices: Readings in critical discourse analysis* (pp. 71–83). London: Routledge.

Fairclough, N. (2000). Multiliteracies and language: Orders of discourse and intertextuality. In B. Cope & M. Kalantzis (Eds.), *Multiliteracies: Literacy learning and the design of social futures.* (pp. 162–181). London: Routledge.

Fairclough, N., & Wodak, R. (1996). Critical discourse analysis. In T. van Dijk (Ed.), *Discourse analysis* (pp. 258–284). London: Sage.

Fairclough, N., 2001. Critical discourse analysis as a method in social scientific research. In: Wodak, R & Meyer, M. (Eds.), *Methods in critical discourse analysis*, pp. 121–138.

Fanon, F. (1961). *Les damnés de la terre. [The wretched of the earth]* Paris: Gallimard (English translation 1963, C. Farrington: Harmondsworth: Penguin.)

Featherstone, M. (1990). Global culture: An introduction. In M. Featherstone (Ed.), *Global culture: Nationalism, globalization and modernity* (pp. 1–14). London: Sage.

Finnegan, R. (2015). *Where is language? An anthropologist's questions on language, literature and performance*. London: Bloomsbury.

Firth, A., & Wagner, J. (1997). On discourse, communication, and (some) fundamental concepts in SLA research. *Modern Language Journal, 81*, 285–300.

Fish, W. (2016). 'Post-truth' politics and illusory democracy. *Psychotherapy and Politics International, 14*(3), 211–213.

Florence, N. (1998). *bell hooks' engaged pedagogy : A transgressive education for critical consciousness*. New York: Greenwood Publishing Group.

Flores, N. (2013). The unexamined relationship between neoliberalism and plurilingualism: A cautionary tale. *TESOL Quarterly, 47*(3), 500–520.

Flores, N., & Rosa, J. (2015). Undoing appropriateness: Raciolinguistic ideologies and language diversity in education. *Harvard Educational Review, 85*, 149–171

Flores, N., & Chaparro, S. (2018). What counts as language education policy? Developing a materialist anti-racist approach to language activism. *Language Policy*, 17:365–384

Flores, N., & Rosa, J. (2019). Bringing race into second language acquisition. *The Modern Language Journal, 103*, 145–151.

Flubacher, M.-C., and Del Percio, A. (Eds). (2017). *Language, education and neoliberalism: Marketization, dispossession, and subversion.* Bristol: Multilingual Matters.

Forchtner, B. (2011). Critique, the discourse–historical approach, and the Frankfurt School. *Critical Discourse Studies, 8*(1), 1–14. doi:10.1080/17405904.2011.533564

Foucault, M. (1974). Human nature: Justice versus power [discussion with N. Chomsky]. In F. Elder (Ed.), *Reflexive water: The basic concerns of mankind* (pp. 133–198). London: Souvenir Press.

Foucault, M. (1979). *Discipline and punish: The birth of the prison.* New York: Vintage.

Foucault, M. (1980a). *The history of sexuality: Volume 1: An introduction.* New York: Vintage.

Foucault, M. (1980b). *Power/knowledge: Selected interviews and other writings, 1972–1977.* New York: Pantheon.

Foucault, M. (1991). *Remarks on Marx.* New York: Semiotext(e).

Fowler, R. (1996). On critical linguistics. In C. R. Caldas-Coulthard & M. Coulthard (Eds.), *Texts and practices: Readings in critical discourse analysis* (pp. 3–14). London: Routledge.

Fowler, R., Kress, G., Hodge, R., & Trew, T. (Eds.). (1979). *Language and control.* London: Routledge.

Fraser, N. (1995). From redistribution to recognition? Dilemmas of justice in a 'post-socialist' age. *New Left Review, 212*, 68–93.

Fraser, N. (2000). Rethinking recognition. *New left Review, 107–120.*

Fraser, N. (2005). Reframing justice in a globalizing world. *New Left Review, 74*, 41–51.

Freire, P. (1970). *Pedagogy of the oppressed.* New York: Continuum (M. B. Ramos, Trans.).

Freire, P., & Macedo, D. (1987). *Literacy: Reading the word and the world.* South Hadley, MA: Bergin & Garvey.

Friedman, J. (1990). Being in the world: Globalization and localization. In M. Featherstone (Ed.), *Global culture: Nationalism, globalization and modernity* (pp. 311–328). London: Sage.

Friedrich, P., Chaudhuri, A., Figueiredo, E., Fredricks, D., Hammill, M., Johnson, E., Suwannamai Duran, C. & MiJung Y. (2013). Reading Pennycook critically 10 years later: A group's reflections on and questions about critical applied linguistics, *International Multilingual Research Journal, 7:2*, 119–137.

Friginal, E. (2009). Threats to the sustainability of the outsourced call center industry in the Philippines: Implications for language policy. *Language Policy, 8*, 51–68.

Frye, D. (1999). Participatory education as a critical framework for an immigrant women's ESL class. *TESOL Quarterly, 33*, 501–513.

Fuery, P. (1995). *Theories of desire.* Melbourne, Australia: Melbourne University Press.

García, O. (2014). Countering the dual: Transglossia, dynamic bilingualism and translanguaging in education. In R. Rubdy, & L. Alsagoff (Eds.), *The global-local interface and hybridity: Exploring language and identity* (pp. 100–120). Bristol, UK: Multilingual Matters.

García, O., Johnson, S., & Seltzer, K. (2017). *The translanguaging classroom: Leveraging student bilingualism for learning.* Philadelphia, PA: Caslon.

García, O. (2019). Decolonizing foreign, second, heritage, and first languages: Implications for education. In D. Macedo (Ed). *Decolonizing foreign language education. The misteaching of English and other imperial languages* (pp 152–168). London: Routledge Press.

García, O., Flores, N., and Spotti, M. (Eds). (2017). Introduction – Language and society: A critical poststructuralist perspective. *The Oxford handbook of language and society* (pp 1–16). New York: Oxford University Press.

García, O., & Wei, L. (2014) *Translanguaging: Language, bilingualism and education.* Basingstoke: Palgrave Macmillan.

Gebhard, M. (1999). Debates in SLA studies: Redefining SLA as an institutional phenomenon. *TESOL Quarterly*, 33, 544–557.

Gee, J. P. (1993). Postmodernism and literacies. In C. Lankshear & P. McLaren (Eds.), *Critical literacy: Politics, praxis and the postmodern* (pp. 271–296). Albany, NY: State University of New York Press.

Gee, J. P. (1994). Orality and literacy: From *The Savage Mind* to *Ways with Words*. In J. Maybin (Ed.), *Language and literacy in social practice* (pp. 168–192). Clevedon, UK: Multilingual Matters.

Gee, J. P. (1996). *Social linguistics and literacies: Ideologies in discourse.* London: Taylor & Francis.

Gee, J. P.(2000). New people in new worlds: Networks, the new capitalism and schools. In B. Cope, & M. Kalantzis (Eds.), *Multiliteracies: Literacy learning and the design of social futures* (pp. 43–68). London: Routledge.

Gee, J. P. (2018). *Introducing discourse analysis: from grammar to society.* New York: Routledge

Gee, J., Hull, G., & Lankshear, C. (1996). *The new work order: Behind the language of the new capitalism.* Sydney, Australia: Allen & Unwin.

Giddens, A. (1979). *Central problems in social theory: Action, structure and contradiction in social analysis.* Berkeley, CA: University of California Press.

Giddens, A. (1982). *Sociology: A brief but critical introduction.* London: Macmillan.

Gilroy, P. (1987). *There ain't no black in the union jack.* London: Hutchinson.

Giroux, H. (1983). *Theory and resistance in education: A pedagogy for the opposition.* South Hadley, MA: Bergin & Garvey.

Giroux, H. (1988). *Schooling and the struggle for public life: Critical pedagogy in the modern age.* Minneapolis: University of Minnesota Press.

Goldstein, T. (1996). *Two languages at work: Bilingual life on the production floor.* Berlin: Mouton de Gruyter.

Gonçalvez, K., & Kelly-Holmes, H. (Eds). (2021). *Language, global mobilities, blue-collar workers and blue-collar workplaces.* London: Routledge.

Gore, J. (1993). *The struggle for pedagogies: Critical and feminist discourses as regimes of truth.* New York: Routledge.

Gounari, P. (2020). Introduction to the special issue on critical pedagogies. *L2 Journal*, 12(2), 3–20.

Gourlay, L. (2021). *Posthumanism and the digital university: Texts, bodies and materialities.* London: Bloomsbury.

Graman, T. (1988). Education for humanization: Applying Paulo Freire's pedagogy to learning a second language. *Harvard Educational Review*, 58, 433–448.

Gray, J. (1992). *Men are from Mars, women are from Venus: A practical guide for improving communication and getting what you want in your relationships.* New York: Harper Collins.

Gray, J. (2010). *The construction of English: Culture, consumerism and promotion in the ELT global coursebook.* Basingstoke: Palgrave Macmillan.

Gray, J. (2012). Neoliberalism, celebrity and 'aspirational content' in English language teaching textbooks for the global market, in D. Block, J. Gray, & M. Holborow *Neoliberalism and applied linguistics.* London: Routledge. 86–113.

Green, B. (1997). Reading with an attitude; Or deconstructing "Critical literacies." Response to Allan Luke and Peter Freebody. In S. Muspratt, A. Luke, & P. Freebody (Eds.), *Constructing critical literacies: Teaching and learning textual practice* (pp. 227–242). St Leonards, NSW: Allen & Unwin.

Gregg, K. R., Long, M., Jordan, G., & Beretta, A. (1997). Rationality and its discontents in SLA. *Applied Linguistics, 18,* 539–559.

Grosfoguel, R. (2007). The epistemic decolonial turn: Beyond political-economy paradigms. *Cultural Studies 21,* 211–23.

Grosfoguel, R. (2011). Decolonizing, post-colonial studies and paradigms of political economy: Transmodernity, decolonial thinking, and global coloniality. *Transmodernity: Journal of Peripheral Cultural Production of the Luso-Hispanic World, 1* (1)

Guba, E., & Lincoln, Y. (1989). *Fourth generation evaluation.* Newbury Park, CA: Sage.

Guba, E., & Lincoln Y. (2005). Paradigmatic controversies, contradictions, and emerging confluences. In N. K. Denzin, & Y. Lincoln (Eds). *Handbook of qualitative research* (pp. 191–215). Thousand Oaks, CA: Sage.

Guilherme, M. (2012). Critical language and intercultural communication pedagogy. In J. Jackson (Ed.) *The Routledge Handbook of Intercultural Communication* (pp. 357–371). London: Routledge.

Guilherme, M. (2015). Critical pedagogy. In J. M. Bennett (Ed.) *Encyclopaedia of Intercultural Competence* (pp. 138–142). Thousand Oaks, CA: Sage.

Guilherme, M. (2018). 'Glocal languages': The 'glocalness' and the 'localness' of world languages. In S. Coffey & U. Wingate (eds.). *New directions for research in foreign language education* (pp. 79–96). New York: Routledge.

Habermas, J. (1972). *Knowledge and human interests.* London: Heinemann.

Habermas, J. (1984). *The theory of communicative action.* Boston: Beacon.

Habermas, J. (1985). Psychic thermidor and the rebirth of rebellious subjectivity. In R. Bernstein (Ed.), *Habermas and modernity* (pp. 67–77). Cambridge, MA: MIT Press.

Habermas, J. (1998). *On the pragmatics of communication.* Cambridge, MA: MIT Press.

Hacking, I. (2004). Between Michel Foucault and Erving Goffman: Between discourse in the abstract and face-to-face interaction. *Economy and Society, 33*(3) 277–302.

Hale, C. (2006). Activist research v. Cultural critique: Indigenous land rights and the contradictions of politically engaged anthropology. *Cultural Anthropology, 21*(1) 96–120.

Hall, C., Wicaksono, R., Liu, S., Qian, Y., & Xu, X. (2013). *English reconceived: Raising teachers' awareness of English as a 'plurilithic' resource through an online course. ELT Research Papers 13-05:* London: British Council.

Hall, S. (1994). Encoding/decoding. In. D. Graddol, & O. Boyd-Barrett (Eds.), *Media texts: Authors and readers* (pp. 200–211). Clevedon, UK: Multilingual Matters.

Halliday, M. (1978). *Language as social semiotic.* London: Arnold.

Hanson, J. (1997). The mother of all tongues. Review of D. Crystal, *English as a global language,* Cambridge: Cambridge University Press. *Times Higher Education Supplement,* 1288, p. 22.

Haque, E. (2007). Critical pedagogy in English for academic purposes and the possibility for 'tactics' of resistance. *Pedagogy, Culture and Society, 15*(1), 83–106.

Haque, E. (2012). *Multiculturalism within a bilingual framework.* Toronto: University of Toronto Press.

Haraway, D. (1988). Situated knowledges: The science question in feminism and the privilege of partial perspective. *Feminist Studies, 14*(3), 575–599.

Harland, R. (1987). *Superstructuralism: The philosophy of structuralism and post-structuralism.* London: Routledge.

Harris, R. (1981). *The language myth.* London: Duckworth.

Harvey, D. (2005). *A brief history of neoliberalism.* Oxford: Oxford University Press.

Haslanger, S. (2012). *Resisting reality: Social construction and social critique.* Oxford: Oxford University Press.

Haugen, E. (1972). *The ecology of language: Essays by Einar Haugen.* In A.S. Dil (Ed). Stanford, CA: Stanford University Press.

Heath, S. B. (1983). *Ways with words: Language, life and work in communities and class-rooms.* Cambridge, UK: Cambridge University Press.

Heiss, A. (2003). *Dhuuluu-Yala: To talk straight,* Canberra: Aboriginal Studies Press

Heller, M., & McElhinny, B. (2017). *Language, capitalism, colonialism: Toward a critical history.* Toronto: University of Toronto Press.

Heller, M., Pietikäinen, S., & Pujolar, J. (2018). *Critical sociolinguistic research methods: Studying language issues that matter.* New York: Routledge.

Herman, E. S., & Chomsky, N. (1988). *Manufacturing consent: The political economy of the mass media.* New York: Pantheon.

Hernandez-Zamora, G. (2010). *Decolonizing literacy: Mexican lives in the era of global capitalism.* Bristol: Multilingual Matters.

Hickel, J. (2018). *The divide: A brief guide to global inequality and its solutions.* London: Penguin Random House.

Higgins, M., & Coen, T. (2000). *Streets, bedrooms and patios: The ordinariness of diversity in urban Oaxaca: Ethnographic portraits of the urban poor, transvestites, discapacitados, and other popular cultures.* Austin, TX: University of Texas Press.

Hodge, R., & Kress, G. (1988). *Social semiotics.* Cambridge, MA: Polity.

Hogben, L. (1963). *Essential world English.* London: Michael Joseph.

Holborow, M. (1999). *The politics of English: A Marxist view of language.* London: Sage

Holborow, M. (2012). 'What is neoliberalism? Discourse, ideology and the real world', in D. Block, J. Gray, and M. Holborow. *Neoliberalism and applied linguistics.* London: Routledge. 33–55.

Holborow, M. (2015). *Language and neoliberalism.* London: Routledge.

Honey, J. (1983). *The language trap: Race class and the "standard English" issue in British schools.* Kenton, UK: National Council for Educational Standards.

Honey, J. (1997). *Language is power: The story of standard English and its enemies.* London: Faber and Faber.

hooks, b. (1989). *Talking back: Thinking feminist, thinking black,* Toronto: Between the Lines.

hooks, b. (1994). *Teaching to transgress: Education as the practice of freedom.* New York: Routedge

hooks, b. (1996). *Killing rage, ending racism,* London: Penguin.

hooks, b. (2003). *Teaching Community. A pedagogy of hope,* New York: Routledge

hooks, b. (2013). *Writing beyond race: Living theory and practice.* New York: Routledge.

Horsbøl, A. (2020). Green conflicts in environmental discourse. A topos based inte-grative analysis of critical voices. *Critical Discourse Studies, 17*(4), 429–446.

Hoy, D. (2004). *Critical resistance: From poststructuralism to post-critique.* Cambridge, Mass: The MIT Press.

Hovens, D. (2020). Workplace learning through human-machine interaction in a transient multilingual blue-collar work environment. *Journal of Linguistic Anthropology*, 1–20.

Ibrahim, A. (1999). Becoming Black: Rap and hip-hop, race, gender, identity and the politics of ESL learning. *TESOL Quarterly, 33*, 349–369.

Ivanič, R. (1990). Critical language awareness in action. In R. Carter (Ed.), *Knowledge about language and the curriculum: The LINC reader* (pp. 122–132). London: Hodder & Stroughton.

Ives, P. (2015). Global English and the limits of liberalism: Confronting global capitalism and challenges to the nation state. In T. Ricento (Ed). *Language policy and political economy: English in a global context* (pp. 48–71). Oxford: Oxford University Press.

Jacquemet, M. (2020). 45 as a bullshit artist: Straining for charisma. In McIntosh, J and Mendoza-Denton, N (Eds). *Language in the Trump era: Scandals and emergencies* (pp. 124–136). Cambridge: Cambridge University Press.

Jäger, S., & Jäger, M. (1993). *Aus der Mitte der Gesellschaft* [from the middle of society]. Duisburg, Germany: Diss.

Jagose, A. (1996). *Queer theory*. Melbourne: Melbourne University Press.

Janks, H. (1997). Critical discourse analysis as a research tool. *Discourse: Studies in the Cultural Politics of Education, 18*, 329–342.

Janks, H. (2000). Domination, access, diversity and design: A synthesis for critical literacy education. *Educational Review, 52*(2), 175–186.

Janks, H., & Ivanič, R. (1992). Critical language awareness and emancipatory discourse. In N. Fairclough (Ed.), *Critical language awareness* (pp. 305–331). London: Longman.

Jaspers, J. (2018). The transformative limits of translanguaging. *Language and Communication, 58*, 1–10.

Jenkins, J. (2006). 'Current perspectives on teaching world Englishes and English as a lingua franca'. *TESOL Quarterly, 40*(1), 157–181.

Jenkins, R. (1992). *Pierre Bourdieu*. London: Routledge.

Jenks, C. (2017). *Race and ethnicity in English language teaching: Korea in focus*. Bristol: Multilingual Matters.

Jewell, J. (1998). A transgendered ESL learner in relation to her class textbooks, heterosexist hegemony and change. *Melbourne Papers in Applied Linguistics, 10*, 1–21.

Johnson, E. (2015). Debunking the "language gap" *Journal for Multicultural Education, 9*(1), 42–50.

Johnson, M. (2004). *A philosophy of second language acquisition*. New Haven: Yale University Press.

Johnson, S. (1997). Theorizing language and masculinity: A feminist perspective. In S. Johnson & U. H. Meinhof (Eds.), *Language and masculinity* (pp. 8–26). Oxford, UK: Blackwell.

Johnston, B. (1999). Putting critical pedagogy in its place: A personal account. *TESOL Quarterly, 33*, 557–565.

Jones, P. (2007). Why there is no such thing as "critical discourse analysis" *Language & Communication, 27*, 337–368.

Jones, P. (2013). Bernstein's 'codes' and the linguistics of 'deficit' *Language and Education, 27*(2), 161–179.

Jordan, G., & Weedon, C. (1995). *Cultural politics: Class, gender, race and the modern world*. Oxford, UK: Blackwell.

Jordão, C. (1999). Critical pedagogy and the teaching of literature. *Acta Scientarium*, *21*, 9–14.

Joseph, J. (2006). *Language and politics*, Edinburgh: Edinburgh University Press.

Kachru, B. (1990). World Englishes and applied linguistics. *World Englishes*, 9, 3–20.

Kachru, B. (1992). *The other tongue: English across cultures*: Urbana: University of Illinois Press.

Kachru, B. (1996). The paradigms of marginality. *World Englishes*, *15*(1), 241–255.

Kachru, B. (2009). World Englishes and culture wars. In B. Kachru, Y. Kachru, & C. Nelson, (Eds). *The handbook of world englishes* (pp. 446–468). Malden, MA: Wiley.

Kanpol, B. (1990). Political applied linguistics and postmodernism: Towards an engagement of similarity within difference. A reply to Pennycook. *Issues in Applied Linguistics*, *1*, 238–250.

Kanpol, B. (1994). *Critical pedagogy: An introduction*. Westort, CT: Bergin & Garvey.

Kanpol, B. (1997). *Issues and trends in critical pedagogy*. Cresskill, NJ: Hampton Press.

Kaplan, R. (1966). Cultural thought patterns in intercultural education. *Language Learning*, *16*, 1–20.

Kaplan, R. (2002). Preface. In R. Kaplan (Ed). *The Oxford handbook of applied linguistics*. Oxford: Oxford University Press.

Kearney, R. (1988). *The wake of imagination*. Minneapolis: University of Minnesota Press.

Kendon, A. (2004). *Gesture: Visible action as utterance*. Cambridge: Cambridge University Press,

Kinloch, V. (2017). "You ain't making me write" culturally sustaining pedagogies and Black youths' performances of resistance. In D. Paris, & H. S. Alim (Eds). *Culturally sustaining pedagogies: Teaching and learning for justice in a changing world* (pp. 25–42). NY: Teachers College Press.

Knapp, G. A. (2005). Race, class, gender: Reclaiming baggage in fast travelling theories. *European Journal of Women's Studies*, *12*(3) 249–265.

Kothari, R. (2005). *Translating India*. New Delhi: Foundation Books.

Kramsch, K. (1993). *Context and culture in language teaching*. Oxford: Oxford University Press.

Kramsch, C. (2015). Applied linguistics: A theory of the practice. *Applied Linguistics*, *36*(4): 454–465.

Kramsch, C. (2019). Between globalization and decolonization: Foreign languages in the cross-fire. In D. Macedo (Ed). *Decolonizing foreign language education*. New York: Routledge. (pp. 50–72)

Kramsch, C. (2021). *Language as symbolic power*. Cambridge: Cambridge University Press.

Kramsch, C., & Zhang, L. (2018). *The multilingual instructor*. Oxford: Oxford University Press.

Kress, G. (1990). Critical discourse analysis. *Annual review of applied linguistics*. In W. Grabe (Ed), *11*, pp. 84–99.

Kress, G. (1993). Genre as social process. In B. Cope, & M. Kalantzis (Eds.), *The powers of literacy: A genre approach to teaching writing* (pp. 22–37). London: The Falmer Press.

Kress, G. (1996). Representational resources and the production of subjectivity: Questions for the theoretical development of critical discourse analysis in a multicultural society. In C. R. Caldas-Coulthard, M., & Coulthard C. R. (Eds.), *Texts and practices: Readings in critical discourse analysis* (pp. 13–31). London: Routledge.

Kress, G., & Hodge, R. (1979). *Language as ideology*. London: Routledge.

Kress, G., & van Leeuwen, T. (1990). *Reading images*. Geelong, Australia: Deakin University Press.

Ku, E. (2020). 'Waiting for my red envelope': Discourses of sameness in the linguistic landscape of a marriage equality demonstration in Taiwan. *Critical Discourse Studies*, *17*(2), 156–174.

Kubota, R. (1999). Japanese culture constructed by discourses: Implications for applied linguistics research and ELT. *TESOL Quarterly*, *33*, 9–35.

Kubota, R. (2004). Critical multiculturalism and second language education. In B. Norton and K Toohey (Eds), *Critical pedagogies and language learning* (pp. 30–52.). Cambridge: Cambridge University Press.

Kubota, R. (2015). Inequalities of Englishes, English speakers, and languages: A critical perspective on pluralist approaches to English. In R. Tupas (ed.): *Unequal Englishes: The politics of englishes today* (pp. 21–42). London: Palgrave-Macmillan,

Kubota, R. (2016). The Multi/plural turn, postcolonial theory, and neoliberal multiculturalism: Complicities and implications for applied linguistics. *Applied Linguistics*, *37*(4), 474–494. doi:10.1093/applin/amu045

Kubota, R. (2019). Confronting epistemological racism, decolonizing scholarly knowledge: Race and gender in applied linguistics. *Applied Linguistics*, *41*, 712–732.

Kubota, R., & Lin, A. (2009). Race, culture, and identities in second language education. In R Kubota and A Lin (Eds) *Race, culture and identities in second language education: Exploring critically engaged practice* (pp 1–23). New York: Routledge.

Kubota, R & Miller E. (2017): Re-examining and re-envisioning criticality in language studies: Theories and praxis, *Critical Inquiry in Language Studies*,14 (2-3), 129–157 *DOI: 10.1080/15427587.2017.1290500*

Kuhn, G. (2009). Anarchism, postmodernity, and poststructuralism. In R. Amster, A. DeLeon, L. Fernandez, A. Nocella II, & D. Shannon (Eds). *Contemporary anarchist studies: An introductory anthology of anarchy in the academy* (pp 18–25). New York: Routledge.

Kumaravadivelu, B. (1999). Critical classroom discourse analysis. *TESOL Quarterly*, *33*, 453–484.

Kumaravadivelu, B. (2016). The decolonial option in English teaching: Can the subaltern act? *TESOL Quarterly*, *50*(1), 66–85. doi:10.1002/tesq.202

Kusters, A., & Sahasrabudhe, S. (2018). Language ideologies on the difference between gesture and sign. *Language & Communication*, *60*, 44–63.

Kymlicka, W. (1995). *Multicultural citizenship: A liberal theory of minority rights*. Oxford: Clarendon Press.

Kymlicka, W. (2001). *Politics in the vernacular: Nationalism, multiculturalism, and citizenship*. Oxford: Oxford University Press.

Labov, W. (1970). The logic of nonstandard English. In F. Williams (Ed.), *Language and poverty: Perspectives on a theme* (pp. 153–189). Chicago: Markham.

Ladson-Billings, G. (1995). But that's just good teaching! The case for culturally relevant pedagogy. *Theory Into practice*, *34*, 159–165.

Lake, M., & Reynolds, H. (2008). *Drawing the global colour line: White men's countries and the question of racial equality*. Cambridge: Cambridge University Press.

Lakoff, R. (1990). *Talking power: The politics of language*. New York: Basic Books.

Lankshear, C. (with J. P. Gee, M. Knobel, & C. Searle). (1997). *Changing literacies*. Buckingham, UK: Open University Press.

Lantolf, J. (1996). SLA theory building: Letting all the flowers bloom! *Language Learning*, 46, 713–749.

Lantolf, J. (Ed). (2000). *Sociocultural theory and second language learning*. Oxford: Oxford University Press.

Lantolf, J., & Thorne, S. (2006). *Sociocultural theory and the genesis of second language development*. Oxford: Oxford University Press.

Lather, P. (1991). *Getting smart: Feminist research and pedagogy with/in the postmodern*. New York: Routledge.

Lather, P. (1992). Postmodernism and the human sciences. In S. Kvale (Ed). *Psychology and postmodernism* (pp. 88–109). London: Sage.

Lather, P. (1995). Post-critical pedagogies: A feminist reading. In P. McLaren (Ed.). *Postmodernism, postcolonialism and pedagogy* (pp. 167–186). Albert Park, Australia: James Nicholas Publishers.

Latour, B. (2004). Why has critique run out of steam? From matters of fact to matters of concern. *Critical Inquiry*, 30(2): 225–248.

Latour, B. (2015). Telling friends from foes in the time of the anthropocene. In C. Hamilton, F. Gemenne, & C. Bonneuil. (Eds). *The anthropocene and the global environmental crisis* (pp. 145–155). London: Routledge.

Law, J., & Mol, A. (2020). Words to think with: An introduction. *The Sociological Review Monographs*, 68(2) 263–282.

Lazar, M. (2007). Feminist critical discourse analysis: Articulating a feminist discourse praxis. *Critical Discourse Studies*, 4(2), 141–164.

Lear, J. (2006). *Radical Hope: Ethics in the face of cultural devastation*, Cambridge, Mass: Harvard University Press.

Lee, A. (1996). *Gender, literacy, curriculum: Rewriting school geography*. London: Taylor & Francis.

Lee, A. (1997). Questioning the critical: Linguistics, literacy and curriculum. In S. Muspratt, A. Luke, & P. Freebody (Eds.). *Constructing critical literacies: Teaching and learning textual practice* (pp. 409–432). Sydney, Australia: Allen and Unwin.

Lee, T., & McCarty, T. (2017). Upholding Indigenous education sovereignty through critical cultural sustaining/revitalizing pedagogy. In D. Paris, & H. S. Alim (Eds). *Culturally sustaining pedagogies: Teaching and learning for justice in a changing world (pp. 61–82)*. NY: Teachers College Press.

Lent, J. (2018). Steven Pinker's ideas are fatally flawed. These eight graphs show why. https://www.opendemocracy.net/en/transformation/steven-pinker-s-ideas-are-fatally-flawed-these-eight-graphs-show-why/

Leonard, W. (2017). Producing language reclamation by decolonising 'language'. In W. Leonard & H. De Korne (Eds). *Language documentation and description* (Vol. 14, pp. 15–36). London: EL Publishing.

Levon, E., & Beline Mendes, R. (2016). Introduction: Locating sexuality in language. In E. Levon, & R. Beline Mendes (Eds). *Language, sexuality, and power: Studies in intersectional sociolinguistics* (pp. 1–18). Oxford: Oxford University Press.

Lewis, M. (2018). A critique of the principle of error correction as a theory of social change. *Language in Society*, 47 (3), 325 – 346.

Lin, A. (1999). Doing-English-lessons in the reproduction or transformation of social worlds? *TESOL Quarterly*, 33, 393–412.

Lippi-Green, R. (1997). *English with an accent: Language, ideology, and discrimination in the United States*. London: Routledge.

182   *References*

Liu, J. (1999). Non-native-English-speaking professionals in TESOL. *TESOL Quarterly*, 33(1), 85–102.

Lo, A and Reyes, A. (2009). On yellow English and other perilous terms. In A. Reyes, & A. Lo (Eds). *Beyond yellow English: Toward a linguistic anthropology of Asian pacific America* (pp. 3–17) New York: Oxford University Press.

Loomba, A. (1998). *Colonialism/postcolonialism*. London: Routledge.

López-Gopar, M. (2016). *Decolonizing primary English language teaching*. Bristol: Multilingual Matters.

Lorente, B. (2013). The grip of English and Philippine language policy. In L. Wee, R. Goh, & L, Lim (Eds). *The politics of English: South Asia, Southeast Asia, and the Asia pacific* (pp. 187–203), Amsterdam: John Benjamins.

Lorente, B. (2017). *Scripts of servitude: Language, labor migration and transnational domestic work*. Bristol: Multilingual Matters.

Lorente, B., & Tupas, R. (2014). '(Un)emancipatory hybrdity: Selling English in an unequal world', in R. Rubdy & L. Alsagoff (Eds). *The global-local interface and hybridity: Exploring language and identity* (pp. 66–82). Bristol, UK: Multilingual Matters.

Luke, A. (1988). *Literacy, textbooks and ideology: Postwar literacy instruction and the mythology of Dick and Jane*. London: The Falmer Press.

Luke, A. (1996). Genres of power? Literacy education and the production of capital. In R. Hagen & G. Williams (Eds.), *Literacy in society* (pp. 308–338). London: Longman.

Luke, A. (1997a). Critical approaches to literacy. In V. Edwards & D. Corson (Eds.). *Encyclopedia of language and education, vol. 2 literacy* (pp. 143–151). Dordrecht, Netherlands: Kluwer Academic Publishers.

Luke, A. (1997b). The material effects of the word: Apologies, "Stolen children" and public discourse. *Discourse: Studies in the Cultural Politics of Education*, 18, 343–368.

Luke, A. (2002). Beyond science and ideology critique: Developments in critical discourse analysis. *Annual Review of Applied Linguistics*, 22, 96–110.

Luke, A. (2004). Notes on the future of critical discourse studies. *Critical Discourse Studies*, 1(1) 149–152.

Luke, A. (2004). On the material consequences of literacy. *Language and Education*, 18(4), 331–335.

Luke, A. (2013). Regrounding critical literacy: Representation, facts and reality. In M. R. Hawkins (Ed.). *Framing language and literacies: Socially situated views and perspectives*. New York: Routledge, 136–148.

Luke, A., & Freebody, P. (1997). Critical literacy and the question of normativity: An introduction. In S. Muspratt, A. Luke, & P. Freebody (Eds.), *Constructing critical literacies: Teaching and learning textual practice* (pp. 1–18). Sydney, Australia: Allen and Unwin.

Luke, A., McHoul, A., & Mey, J. L. (1990). On the limits of language planning: Class, state and power. In R. B. Baldauf, Jr., & A. Luke (Eds.). *Language planning and education in australasia and the South pacific* (pp. 25–44). Clevedon, UK: Multilingual Matters.

Luke, A., & Walton, C. (1994). Teaching and assessing critical reading. In T. Husen & T. Postlethwaite (Eds.), *International encyclopedia of education* (2nd edition, pp. 1194–1198). Oxford, UK: Pergamon.

Lynch, B. (1996). *Language program evaluation: Theory and practice*. Cambridge: Cambridge University Press.

Lyotard, J.-F. (1984). *The postmodern condition: A report on knowledge*. (Trans by G. Bennington and B Massumi of *La condition postmoderne*, Paris: Minuit, 1979). Minneapolis: University of Minnesota Press.

Macedo, D. (2019). Rupturing the yoke of colonialism in foreign language education. In D. Macedo (Ed). *Decolonzing foreign language education. The misteaching of English and other imperial languages* (pp 1–49). London: Routledge Press

MacSwan, J. (2020). Translanguaging, language ontology, and civil rights. *World Englishes, 39*, 321–333.

Makalela, L. (Ed). (2018). *Shifting lenses: Multilanguaging, decolonisation and education in the Global South*. Cape Town: CASAS.

Makoni, S. (2003). Review of A Davies, *an introduction to applied linguistics: From practice to theory*. and A Pennycook, *critical applied linguistics: A critical introduction. Applied Linguistics, 24*(1), 130–137.

Makoni, S., & Pennycook, A. (2007). Disinventing and reconstituting languages in S. Makoni & A. Pennycook (Eds). *Disinventing and reconstituting languages* (pp. 1–41). Clevedon: Multilingual Matters.

Maldonado-Torres, N. (2007). On the coloniality of being. *Cultural Studies, 21*(2), 240–270.

Marcuse, H. (1964). *One-dimensional man. studies in the ideology of advanced industrial society*. Boston: Beacon Press.

Markee, N. (1990). Applied linguistics: What's that? *System, 18*, 315–324.

Martin, D. (2012). A critical linguistic ethnographic approach to language disabilities in multilingual families. In S. Gardner & M. Martin-Jones (Eds). *Multilingualism, discourse, and ethnography* (pp. 305–318), London: Routledge.

Martin, I. (2014). 'Philippine English revisited'. *World Englishes, 33*(1), 50–59.

Martin, K./Mirraboopa, B. (2003). Ways of knowing, being and doing: A theoretical framework and methods for indigenous and indigenist research, *Journal of Australian Studies, 27*(76), 203–214.

Martin-Jones, M., & Gardner, S. (2012). Introduction: Multilingualism, discourse and ethnography. In S. Gardner & M. Martin-Jones (Eds). *Multilingualism, discourse, and ethnography* (pp. 1–17). London: Routledge,

Martín Rojo, L. (Ed). (2016). *Occupy: The spatial dynamics of discourse in global protest movements* (pp. 1–22). Amsterdam: John Benjamins.

Martín Rojo, L., & del Percio, A. (Eds). (2019). *Language and neoliberal governmentality*. London: Routledge.

Marx, K. (1852). The eighteenth Brumaire of Louis Bonaparte. (Der 18te Brumaire des Louis Napoleon). New York: *Die Revoluion*, 1, http://www.criticalrealism.com/archive/brumaire_intro.html

May, S. (2001). *Language and minority rights: Ethnicity, nationalism and the politics of language*. Harlow: Longman.

May, S. (2011). Language rights: The "Cinderella" human right, *Journal of Human Rights, 10*(3), 265–289.

May, S. (Ed). (2014). *The multilingual turn: Implications for SLA, TESOL and bilingual education*. London: Routledge.

May, S. (2017). Language, imperialism, and the modern nation-state system: Implications for language rights. In O. García, N. Flores, & M. Spotti (Eds) *The Oxford handbook of language and society* (pp. 35–53). New York: Oxford University Press.

Mbembe, A. (2017). *Critique of Black reason* (trans. Laurent Dubois: *critique de la raison nègre)*. Durham. NC: Duke University Press.

McCarthy, T. (1978). *The critical theory of Jürgen Habermas*. London: Hutchinson.

McCarty, T. (2013). *Language planning and policy in Native America: History, theory, praxis*. Bristol: Multilingual Matters.

McCarty, T., & Lee, T. (2014). Critical culturally sustaining/revitalizing pedagogy and indigenous education sovereignty. *Harvard Educational Review*, 84(1), 74–84.

McClintock, A. (1994). The angel of progress: Pitfalls of the term 'postcolonialism.' In P. Williams & L. Chrisman (Eds.), *Colonial discourse and postcolonial theory: A reader* (pp. 291–304). New York: Columbia University Press.

McCormick, K. (1994). *The culture of reading and the teaching of English*. Manchester, UK: Manchester University Press.

McIvor, O. (2020). Indigenous language revitalization and applied linguistics: Parallel histories, shared futures? *Annual Review of Applied Linguistics*, 40, 78–96.

McKay, S. L., & Wong, S. C. (1996). Multiple discourses, multiple identities: Investment and agency in second language learning among Chinese adolescent immigrant students. *Harvard Education Review*, 3, 577–608.

Mclaren, P. (1989). *Life in schools: An introduction to critical pedagogy in the foundations of education*. New York: Longman.

McNamara, T. (2012). Language assessments as shibboleths: A poststructuralist perspective. *Applied Linguistics*, 33(5), 564–581.

McNamara, T. (2015). Applied linguistics: The challenge of theory, *Applied Linguistics*, 36(4): 466–477.

McNamara, T. (2019). *Language and subjectivity*. Cambridge: Cambridge University Press.

Mey, J. (1985). *Whose language? A study in linguistic pragmatics*. Amsterdam: John Benjamins.

Mignolo, W. (2011). *The darker side of western modernity: Global futures, decolonial options* Durham, NC: Duke University Press.

Mignolo, W., & Walsh, C. (2018). *On decoloniality: Concepts, analytics, praxis*. Durham: Duke University Press.

Mika, C. (2016). Worlded object and its presentation: A Māori philosophy of language. *AlterNative: An International Journal of Indigenous Peoples*, 12(2), 165–75.

Milani, T. (2013). Expanding the queer linguistic scene: Multimodality, space and sexuality at a South African university. *Journal of Language and Sexuality*, 2(2), 206–234.

Milani, T. & Lazar, M. (2017). Seeing from the South: Discourse, gender and sexuality from southern perspectives. *Journal of Sociolinguistics*, 21(3), 307–319.

Mills, C. (2014). White time: The chronic injustice of ideal theory. *Du Bois Review*, 11(1), 27–42.

Mills, C. (2017). *Black rights/white wrongs: The critique of racial liberalism*. Oxford: Oxford University Press.

Mills, K. (2007). Access to multiliteracies: A critical ethnography. *Ethnography and Education*, 2 (3), 305–325.

Mills, K. (2016). *Literacy theories for the digital age: Social, critical, multimodal, spatial, material and sensory lenses*. Bristol: Multilingual Matters

Mills, S. (1997). *Discourse*. London: Routledge.

Milroy, J. (1999). The consequences of standardisation in descriptive linguistics. In T. Bex, & R. Watts (Eds). *Standard English: The widening debate* (pp. 16–39). London: Routledge.

Misson, R. (1996). What's in it for me?: Teaching against homophobic discourse. In L. Laskey & C. Beavis (Eds.), *Schooling and sexualities: Teaching for a positive sexuality* (pp. 117–129). Geelong, Australia: Deakin Centre for Education and Change.

Moi, T. (1985). *Sexual/textual politics: Feminist literary theory*. London: Methuen.

Monaghan, P. (2012). Going for wombat - transformations in Wirangu and the Scotdesco community on the far west coast of South Australia. *Oceania*, 82(1), 45–61.

Morgan, B. (1997). Identity and intonation: Linking dynamic processes in an ESL classroom. *TESOL Quarterly*, *31*, 431–450.

Morgan, B. (1998). *The ESL classroom: Teaching, critical practice and community development*. Toronto, Canada: University of Toronto Press.

Morgan, B. (2004). Modals and memories: A grammar lesson on the Quebec referendum on sovereignty. In B. Norton & K. Toohey (Eds.), *Critical pedagogies and language learning* (158–178). New York, NY: Cambridge University Press.

Morgan, B., & Ramanathan, V. (2005). Critical literacies and language education: Global and local perspectives. *Annual Review of Applied Linguistics*, *25*, 151–169.

Motha, S. (2014). *Race and empire in English language teaching*. New York, NY: Teachers College Press, Columbia University.

Motha, S. (2020). Is an antiracist and decolonizing applied linguistics possible? *Annual Review of Applied Linguistics*, *40*, 128–133.

Motha, S., and Lin, A. (2014) 'Non-coercive rearrangements': Theorizing Desire in TESOL. *TESOL Quarterly*, 48/2. 331–359.

Mufwene, S. (2016). A cost-and-benefit approach to language loss. In L. Filipović & M. Pütz (Eds.), *Endangered languages and languages in danger: Issues of documentation, policy, and language rights* (pp. 115–143). Amsterdam: John Benjamins.

Mühlhäusler, P. (1996). *Linguistic ecology: Language change and linguistic imperialism in the Pacific region*. London: Routledge.

Munck, R. (2013). The precariat: A view from the South, *Third World Quarterly*, 34(5), 747–762.

Nakata, M. (2007). *Disciplining the savages: Savaging the disciplines*. Canberra: Aboriginal Studies Press.

Nandy, A. (1983). *The intimate enemy: Loss and recovery of self under colonialism*. Delhi, India: Oxford University Press.

Nascimento Dos Santos, G., & Windle, J. (2020). The nexus of race and class in ELT: From interaction orders to orders of being. *Applied Linguistics*, doi:10.1093/applin/amaa031

Ndhlovu, F. (2018). *Language, vernacular discourse and nationalisms: Uncovering the myths of transnational worlds*. Cham: Palgrave Macmillan.

Nelson, C. (1993). Heterosexism in ESL: Examining our attitudes. *TESOL Quarterly*, *27*, 143–150.

Nelson, C. (1999). Sexual identities in ESL: Queer theory and classroom inquiry. *TESOL Quarterly*, *33*, 371–391.

Nelson, C. (2009). *Sexual identities in English language education: Classroom conversations*. New York: Routledge.

New London Group. (1996). A pedagogy of multiliteracies: Designing social futures. *Harvard Educational Review*, *66*, 60–92.

Newcomb, S. (2019) Original ('Indigenous') nations and philosophical activism. In N. Greymorning (Ed.) *Being indigenous: Perspectives on activism, culture, language and identity* (pp. 156–170). New York: Routledge

Newmeyer, F. (1986). *The politics of linguistics*. Chicago: University of Chicago Press.

Niranjana, T. (1991). Translation, colonialism and the rise of English. In S. Joshi (Ed). *Rethinking English: Essays in literature, language, history* (pp. 124–145). New Delhi, India: Trianka.

Norton, B. (1997). Language, identity, and the ownership of English. *TESOL Quarterly*, *31*, 409–430.

Norton, B. (2000). *Identity and language learning: Gender, ethnicity and educational change*. Harlow: Pearson.

Norton Peirce, B. (1995). Social identity, investment, and language learning. *TESOL Quarterly*, *29*, 9–31.

Norton, B., & Toohey. K. (Eds). (2004). Critical pedagogies and language learning: An introduction. *Critical pedagogies and language learning* (pp. 1–17). Cambridge: Cambridge University Press.

Ober, R. (2017). Kapati time: Storytelling as a data collection method in indigenous research. *Learning Communities: International Journal of Learning in Social Contexts [Special Issue: Decolonising Research Practices]*, *22*, 8–15.

O'Regan, J. (2014). 'English as a lingua Franca: An immanent Critique'. *Applied Linguistics*, *35*(5), 533–552.

O'Regan, J. (2021). *Global English and political economy*. London; Routledge.

Ortega, L. (2014). Ways forward for a bi/multilingual turn in SLA. In S. May (Ed). *The multilingual turn: Implications for SLA, TESOL, and bilingual education* (pp. 32–53). New York: Routledge.

Ortega, L. (2018). Ontologies of language, second language acquisition, and world Englishes. *World Englishes*, *37*, 64–79.

Ortega, L. (2019). SLA and the study of equitable multilingualism. *The Modern Language Journal*, *103*, 23–38.

Parakrama, A. (1995). *De-hegemonizing language standards*. New York: Macmillan.

Paris, D. (2012). Culturally sustaining pedagogy: A needed change in stance, terminology, and practice. *Educational Researcher*, *41*(3), 93–97.

Paris, D., & Alim, H. S. (2014).What are we seeking to sustain through culturally sustaining pedagogy? A loving critique forward. *Harvard Educational Review*, *84*(1), 85–100.

Paris, D., & Alim H. S. (Eds). (2017). *Culturally sustaining pedagogies: Teaching and learning for justice in a changing world*. NY: Teachers College Press.

Park, J. S.-Y. (2013). English, class and neoliberalism in South Korea. In L. Wee, R. Goh, & L. Lim (Eds). *The politics of English: South Asia, Southeast Asia, and the Asia Pacific* (pp. 297–302). Amsterdam: John Benjamins.

Park, J. S.-Y., & Wee, L. (2012). *Markets of English: Linguistic capital and language policy in a globalizing world*. New York: Routledge

Patterson, A. (1997). Critical discourse analysis: A condition of doubt. *Discourse: Studies in the Cultural Politics of Education*, *18*, 425–435.

Paul, R., & Elder, L. (2001). *Critical thinking: tools for taking charge of your learning and your life*. Englewood Cliffs, NJ: Prentice Hall.

Pauwels, A. (1998). *Women changing language*. Harlow: Longman.

Pearson, N. (2011). *Radical hope: Education and equality in Australia*. Collingwood: Black Inc.

Pêcheux, M., Conein, B., Courtine, J-J., Gadet, F., & Marandin, J-M. (Eds). (1981). *Matérialités discursives*. Lille: Presses Universitaires de Lille.

Peirce, B. N. (1989). Toward a pedagogy of possibility in the teaching of English internationally. *TESOL Quarterly*, *23*, 401–420.

Pennycook, A. (1989). The concept of method, interested knowledge and the politics of language teaching. *TESOL Quarterly*, *23*, 589–618.

Pennycook, A. (1990). Towards a critical applied linguistics for the 1990's. *Issues in Applied Linguistics*, *1*, 8–28.

Pennycook, A. (1991). A reply to Kanpol. *Issues in Applied Linguistics, 2,* 305–312.

Pennycook, A. (1994a). Critical pedagogical approaches to research *TESOL Quarterly, 28,* 690–693.

Pennycook, A. (1994b). *The cultural politics of English as an international language.* London: Longman.

Pennycook, A. (1994c). Incommensurable discourses? *Applied Linguistics, 15,* 115–138.

Pennycook, A. (1996a). Borrowing others' words: Text, ownership, memory and plagiarism. *TESOL Quarterly, 30,* 201–230.

Pennycook, A. (1996b). TESOL and critical literacies: Modern, post or neo? *TESOL Quarterly, 30,* 163–171.

Pennycook, A. (1997a). Cultural alternatives and autonomy. In P. Benson & P. Voller (Eds.), *Autonomy and independence in language learning* (pp. 35–53). London: Longman.

Pennycook, A. (1997b). Vulgar pragmatism, critical pragmatism, and EAP. *English for Specific Purposes, 16,* 253–269.

Pennycook, A. (1998a). *English and the discourses of colonialism.* London: Routledge.

Pennycook, A. (1998b). The right to language: Towards a situated ethics of language possibilities. *Language Sciences, 20,* 73–87.

Pennycook, A. (1999a). Introduction: Critical approaches to TESOL. *TESOL Quarterly, 33,* 329–348.

Pennycook, A. (1999b). Pedagogical implications of different frameworks for understanding the global spread of English. In C. Gnutzmann (Ed.), *Teaching and learning English as a global language: Native and non-native perspectives* (pp. 147–156). Tübingen: Stauffenberg Verlag.

Pennycook, A. (2000). The social politics and the cultural politics of language classrooms. In J. K. Hall and W. Eggington (Eds). *The sociopolitics of English language teaching.* Clevedon: Multilingual Matters.

Pennycook, A. (2001) *Critical applied linguistics: A critical introduction* (First edition): Mahwah, NJ: Lawrence Erlbaum

Pennycook, A. (2004a). Language policy and the ecological turn. *Language Policy, 3,* 213–239.

Pennycook, A. (2004b). Performativity and language studies. *Critical Inquiry in Language Studies: An International Journal, 1*(1), 1–19.

Pennycook, A. (2004c). Critical moments in a TESOL praxicum. In B. Norton, & K. Toohey (Eds) *Critical pedagogies and language learning* (pp. 327–346). Cambridge: Cambridge University Press.

Pennycook, A. (2007). *Global Englishes and transcultural flows.* London: Routledge.

Pennycook, A. (2010). *Language as a local practice.* London: Routledge.

Pennycook, A (2016). Mobile times, mobile terms: The trans-super-poly-metro movement. In N Coupland (Ed.) *Sociolinguistics: Theoretical debates* (201–206). Cambridge: Cambridge University Press.

Pennycook, A. (2018a). *Posthumanist applied linguistics.* London: Routledge.

Pennycook, A. (2018b). Applied linguistics as epistemic assemblage. *AILA Review, 31,* 113–134.

Pennycook, A. (2019). From translanguaging to translingual activism. In D. Macedo, (Ed). *Decolonizing foreign language education: The misteaching of English and other colonial languages* (pp. 169–185). Routledge, New York.

Pennycook, A. (2020). Translingual entanglements of English. *World Englishes, 39*(2), 222–235.

Pennycook, A & Makoni, S. (2020) *Innovations and challenges in applied linguistics from the Global South*. New York: Routledge.

Perry, T., & Delpit, L. (Eds). (1998). *The real ebonics debate: Power, language, and the education of African-American children*. Boston, MA: Beacon Press.

Phan, L-H. (2017). *Transnational education crossing 'the West' and 'Asia': Adjusted desire, transformative mediocrity, and neo-colonial disguise*. New York: Routledge.

Phillipson, R. (1992). *Linguistic imperialism*. Oxford: Oxford University Press.

Phillipson, R. (1997). 'Realities and myths of linguistic imperialism'. *Journal of Multilingual and Multicultural Development, 18*(3), 238–248.

Phillipson, R. (1998). Globalizing English: Are linguistic human rights an alternative to linguistic imperialism? *Language Sciences, 20*, 101–112.

Phillipson, R. (1999). Voice in global English: Unheard chords in Crystal loud and clear [review of the book *English as a global language*]. *Applied Linguistics, 20*, 265–276.

Phillipson, R. (2006). Language policy and linguistic imperialism, in T. Ricento (ed.) *An introduction to language policy: Theory and method* (pp. 346–361). Oxford: Blackwell.

Phillipson, R. (2008). 'The linguistic imperialism of neoliberal empire'. *Critical Inquiry in Language Studies, 5*(1), 1–43.

Phillipson. R. (2009). *Linguistic imperialism continued*. London: Routledge.

Phillipson, R., Rannut, M., & Skutnabb-Kangas, T. (1994). Introduction. In T. Skutnabb-Kangas & R. Phillipson (Eds). *Linguistic human rights: Overcoming linguistic discrimination* (pp. 1–22). Berlin, Germany: Mouton de Gruyter.

Phillipson, R., & Skutnabb-Kangas, T. (1995). Linguistic rights and wrongs. *Applied Linguistics, 16*, 483–504.

Phillipson, R., & Skutnabb-Kangas, T. (1996). English only worldwide or language ecology? *TESOL Quarterly, 30*, 429–452.

Phipps, A. (2019). *Decolonising multilingualism: Struggles to decreate*. Bristol: Multilingual Matters.

Piketty, T. (2014). *Capital in the twenty-first century*. (Trans A Goldhammer) Cambridge, Mass: Belknap Press.

Piller, I. (2016). *Linguistic diversity and social justice: An introduction to applied sociolinguistics*. Oxford: Oxford University Press.

Pinker, S. (2018). *Enlightenment now: The case for reason, science, humanism, and progress*. New York: Viking.

Poster, M. (1989). *Critical theory and poststructuralism: In search of a context*. Ithaca, NY: Cornell University Press.

Potts, A. (2015). 'LOVE YOU GUYS (NO HOMO)': How gamers and fans play with sexuality, gender, and minecraft on YouTube *Critical Discourse Studies, 12*(2) 163–186.

Poynton, C. (1993a). Grammar, language and the social: Poststructuralism and systemic-functional linguistics. *Social Semiotics, 3*, 1–21.

Poynton, C. (1993b). Naming women's workplace skills: Linguistics and power. In B. Probert & B. Wilson (Eds.), *Pink collar blues* (pp. 85–100). Melbourne: Melbourne University Press.

Poynton, C. (1996). *Language and difference*. Plenary address to the 21st Annual Conference of the Applied Linguistics Association of Australia, University of Western Sydney, Nepean.

Prah, K. K. (2018). *The challenge of decolonizing education*. Cape Town: Centre for Advanced Studies of African Society

Prain, V. (1997). Multi(national)literacies and globalising discourses. *Discourse: Studies in the Cultural Politics of Education, 18*, 453–467.

Preston, D. (2011). Methods in (applied) folk linguistics: Getting into the minds of the folk. *AILA Review, 24*, 15–39.

Price, S. (1996). Comments on Bonny Norton Peirce's "Social identity, investment, and language learning": A reader reacts. *TESOL Quarterly, 30*, 331–337.

Price, S. (1999). Critical discourse analysis: Discourse acquisition and discourse practices. *TESOL Quarterly, 33*, 581–595.

Pupavac, V. (2012). *Language rights: From free speech to linguistic governance*. New York: Palgrave Macmillan.

Qin, K. J. (2020). Curriculum as a discursive and performative space for subjectivity and learning: Understanding immigrant adolescents' language use in classroom discourse. *The Modern Language Journal*, DOI: 10.1111/modl.12675

Quijano, A. (1991). Colonialidad y modernidad/racionalidad. *Perú Indígena, 29*, 11–20.

Quijano, A. (2007). Coloniality and modernity/rationality. *Cultural Studies 21*(2–3): 168–178.

Radway, J. (1984). *Reading the romance: Women, patriarchy and popular literature*. Chapel Hill: University of North Carolina Press.

Rajagopalan, K. (1999). Of EFL teachers, conscience, and cowardice. *ELT Journal, 53*, 200–206.

Rampton, B. (1995a). *Crossing: Language and ethnicity among adolescents*. London: Longman.

Rampton, B. (1995b). Politics and change in research in applied linguisitics. *Applied Linguistics, 16*, 233–256.

Rampton, B. (1997). Retuning in applied linguistics. *International Journal of Applied Linguistics, 7*(1) 3–25.

Rassool, N. (1998). Postmodernity, cultural pluralism and the nation-state: Problems of language rights, human rights, identity and power. *Language Sciences, 20*, 89–99.

Ratner, C. (2019). *Neoliberal psychology*. Cham: Springer.

Rawls, J. (1971). *A theory of justice*. Cambridge, MA: Harvard University Press

Resende, V de M. (2018). Decolonizing critical discourse studies: For a Latin American perspective, *Critical Discourse Studies*, DOI: 10.1080/17405904.2018.1490654.

Reyes, A. (2017). Inventing postcolonial elites: Race, language, mix, excess. *Journal of Linguistic Anthropology, 27*(2), 210–231.

Ricento, T. (2015). Political economy and English as a 'global' language. In T. Ricento (Ed). *Language policy and political economy: English in a global context (pp. 27–47)*. Oxford: Oxford University Press.

Rivera, K. (1999). Popular research and social transformation: A community based approach to critical pedagogy. *TESOL Quarterly, 33*, 485–500.

Rizvi, F. (1993). Children and the grammar of popular racism. In C. McCarthy & W. Crichlow (Eds). *Race, identity, and representation in education* (pp. 126–139). New York: Routledge.

Roberts, C., Davies, E., & Jupp, T. (1992). *Language and discrimination: A study of communication in multi-ethnic workplaces*. London: Longman.

Robinson, N. (2018). The intellectual we deserve. *Current Affairs*. March 14, 2018. https://www.currentaffairs.org/2018/03/the-intellectual-we-deserve.

Rockhill, K. (1994). Gender, language and the politics of literacy. In J. Maybin (Ed.), *Langauge and literacy in social practice* (pp. 233–251). Clevedon, UK: Multilingual Matters and The Open University.

Roderick, I. (2017). Multimodal critical discourse analysis as ethical praxis, *Critical Discourse Studies*, DOI: 10.1080/17405904.2017.1418401

Rosa, J. (2019). *Looking like a language, sounding like a race: Raciolinguistic ideologies and the learning of Latinidad.* Oxford: Oxford University Press.

Rosa, J., & Flores, N. (2017a). Unsettling race and language: Toward a raciolinguistic perspective. *Language and Society*, 46, 621–647.

Rosa, J., & Flores, N. (2017b) Do you hear what I hear? Raciolinguistic ideologies and culturally sustaining pedagogies. In D. Paris, & H. S. Alim (Eds). *Culturally sustaining pedagogies: Teaching and learning for justice in a changing world.* NY: Teachers College Press, 175–190.

Rosiek, J. L., Snyder, J., & Pratt, S. L. (2020). The new materialisms and indigenous theories of non-human agency: Making the case for respectful anti-colonial engagement. *Qualitative Inquiry*, 26(3–4), 331–346.

Rubdy, R. (2015). Unequal Englishes, the native speaker, and decolonization in TESOL. In R. Tupas (Ed.), *Unequal Englishes* (pp. 42–58). Palgrave: Macmillan.

Said, E. W. (1978). *Orientalism.* London: Routledge & Kegan Paul.

Sanguinetti, J. (1992/3). Women, "empowerment" and ESL: An exploration of critical and feminist pedagogies. *Prospect*, 8(1&2), 9–37.

Sarkar, M. (2018). Ten years of Mi'gmaq language revitalization work: A non-indigenous applied linguist reflects on building research relationships. *The Canadian Modern Language Review/La Revue canadienne des langues vivantes*, 73(4), 488–508.

Schatzki, T. (2001). Introduction: Practice theory. In T. Schatzki, K. K. Cetina, & E. V. Savigny (Eds). *The practice turn in contemporary theory* (pp. 1–14). London: Routledge.

Schatzki, T. (2002). *The site of the social: A philosophical account of the constitution of social life and change.* University Park, Penn: The Pennsylvania State University Press.

Schenke, A. (1991). The "will to reciprocity" And the work of memory: Fictioning speaking out of silence in E.S.L. And feminist pedagogy. *Resources for Feminist Research*, 20, 47–55.

Schenke, A. (1996). Not just a "social issue": Teaching feminist in ESL. *TESOL Quarterly*, 30, 155–159.

Schweiter, J. & Chamness Iida, P. (2020). Intersections of language studies and social/political movements, activism, and participation. *Critical Inquiry in Language Studies.* 17(1) 1–4.

Seidlhofer, B. (Ed). (2003). *Controversies in applied linguistics.* Oxford: Oxford University Press.

Seidlhofer, B. (2011). *Understanding English as a lingua Franca.* Oxford: Oxford University Press.

Shi-xu. (2015). Cultural discourse studies. In. K. Tracy, C. Ilie, & T. Sandel (Eds). *International encyclopedia of language and social interaction*, (1–9). Boston, MA: Wiley-Blackwell.

Shohamy, E. (1997). *Critical language testing and beyond.* Plenary address to the American Association of Applied Linguistics, Orlando, FL.

Shohamy, E. (2001). *The power of tests: A critical perspective on the uses of language tests.* London: Longman.

Shohamy, E. (2005). *Language policy: Hidden agendas and New approaches*. London: Routledge.

Signorini, I., & Cavalcanti, M. (Eds.). (1998). *Lingüística aplicada e transdisciplinaridade* [applied and transdisciplinary linguistics]. Campinas, Brazil: Mercado de Letras.

Simon, R. (1992). *Teaching against the grain: Essays towards a pedagogy of possibility*. London: Bergin & Garvey.

Simpson, W. & O'Regan, J. (2018) Fetishism and the language commodity: a materialist critique. *Language Sciences* 70, 155–166

Singh, J. (1996). *Colonial narratives/cultural dialogues: "Discoveries" of India in the language of colonialism*. London: Routledge.

Skutnabb-Kangas, T. (1988). Multilingualism and the education of minority children. In T. Skutnabb-Kangas & J. Cummins (Eds.), *Minority education: From shame to struggle* (pp. 9–44). Clevedon, UK: Multilingual Matters.

Skutnabb-Kangas, T. (1998). Human rights and language wrongs—a future for diversity? *Language Sciences, 20*, 5–28.

Skutnabb-Kangas, T., & Phillipson, R. (Eds). (1994). *Linguistic human rights: Overcoming linguistic discrimination*. Berlin, Germany: Mouton de Gruyter.

Smith, L. T. (1999). *Decolonizing methodologies: Research and indigenous peoples*. London: Zed Books.

Smith, L. T. (2012). *Decolonizing methodologies: Research and indigenous peoples* (2nd edition). London: Zed Books.

Smith, N. (1999). *Chomsky: Ideas and ideals*. Cambridge, UK: Cambridge University Press.

Sonntag (2003). *The local politics of global English: Case studies in linguistic globalization*. Lanham, Maryland: Lexington Books.

Spack, R. (1997). The rhetorical construction of multilingual students. *TESOL Quarterly, 37*(4), 765–774.

Spivak, G. C. (1993). *Outside in the teaching machine*. New York: Routledge & Kegan Paul.

Sridhar, K. K., & Sridhar, S. N. (1986). Bridging the paradigm gap: Second language acquisition theory and indigenized varieties of English. *World Englishes, 5*(1), 3–14.

St. Pierre, E. (2019). Post qualitative inquiry in an ontology of immanence. *Qualitative Inquiry 25*(1): 3–16.

Standing, G. (2014). *The precariat: The new dangerous class*. London: Bloomsbury.

Stibbe, A. (2015). *Ecolinguistics: Language, ecology and the stories we live by*. London: Routledge.

Street, B. (1984). *Literacy in theory and practice*. Cambridge, UK: Cambridge University Press.

Street, B. (1995). *Social literacies: Critical approaches to literacy in development, ethnography and education*. London: Longman.

Sunderland, J. (Ed.). (1994). *Exploring gender: Questions and implications for English language education*. Englewood Cliffs, NJ: Prentice-Hall.

Sunderland, J., Rahim, A. F., Cowley, M., Leontzakou, C., & Shattuck, J. (2000). From bias "in the text" to "teacher talk around the text": An exploration of teacher discourse and gendered foreign language textbook texts. *Linguistics and Education, 11*(3), 251–286.

Susser, B. (1998). EFL's othering of Japan. *JALT Journal, 20*, 49–82.

Tajima, M. (2018) Gendered constructions of Filipina teachers in Japan's skype English conversation industry. *Journal of Sociolinguistics, 22*(1), 100–117.

Takahashi, K (2013) *Language learning, gender and desire. Japanese women on the move.* Bristol: Multilingual Matters.

Talbot, M. (1992). The construction of gender in a teenage magazine. In N. Fairclough (Ed.), *Critical language awareness* (pp. 174–200). New York: Longman.

Talbot, M. (1995). *Fictions at work: Language and social practice in fiction.* London: Longman.

Tannen, D. (1990). *You just don't understand: Women and men in conversation.* New York: Morrow.

Thesen, L. (1997). Voices, discourse, and transition: In search of new categories in EAP. *TESOL Quarterly, 31,* 543–560.

Thomas, N. (1994). *Colonialism's culture: Anthropology, travel and government.* Oxford, UK: Polity.

Thompson, J. (1991). Editor's introduction. In J. B. Thompson (Ed.), *Language and symbolic power (Pierre bourdieu)* (pp. 1–31). Oxford, UK: Polity.

Threadgold, T. (1997). *Feminist poetics: Poiesis, performance, histories.* London: Routledge.

Threadgold, T., & Kamler, B. (1997). An interview with Terry Threadgold on critical discourse analysis. *Discourse: Studies in the Cultural Politics of Education, 18,* 437–451.

Thrift, N. (2007). *Non-representational theory: Space/politics/affect.* London: Routledge.

Thurlow, C. (2016). Queering critical discourse studies or/and performing 'post-class' ideologies. *Critical Discourse Studies, 13*(5), 485–514.

Tochon, F. (2019). Decolonizing world language education: Toward multilingualism. In D Macedo (ed) (2019) *Decolonzing foreign language education. The misteaching of English and other Imperial languages* (pp. 264–281). New York: Routledge.

Todd, Z. (2016). An indigenous feminist's take on the ontological turn: 'Ontology' is just another word for colonialism. *Journal of Historical Sociology, 29*(1), 4–22. doi:10.1111/johs.12124

Tollefson, J. (1989). *Alien winds: The re-education of America's indochinese refugees.* New York: Praeger.

Tollefson, J. (1991). *Planning language, planning inequality: Language policy in the community.* London: Longman.

Toohey, K. (2019). The onto-epistemologies of new materialism: Implications for applied linguistics pedagogies and research. *Applied Linguistics, 40*(6), 937–956.

Troemel-Ploetz, S. (1991). Selling the apolitical: Review of Deborah Tannen's *You just don't understand. Discourse and Society, 2,* 489–502.

Tsuda, Y. (1994). The diffusion of English: Its impact on culture and communication. *Keio Communication Review, 16,* 49–61.

Tupas, R. (2006). 'Standard Englishes, pedagogical paradigms and conditions of (im)possibility', in R Rubdy & M Saraceni (Eds) *English in the world: Global rules, global roles* (169–185). London: Continuum.

Tupas, R., and Rubdy, R. (2015). Introduction: From world Englishes to unequal Englishes. In R. Tupas (Ed.), *Unequal Englishes* (pp. 1–21). Palgrave: Macmillan.

Tupas, R., & Salonga, A. (2016), 'Unequal Englishes in the Philippines.' *Journal of Sociolinguistics, 20,* 367–381.

Umbarila-Gómez, S. P. (2011). Building students' voices through critical pedagogy: Braiding paths towards the Other. *Colombian Applied Linguistics Journal, 12*(2), 55–71.

UNDP. (2020). *Human development perspectives: tackling social norms: A game changer for gender inequalities.* New York: United Nations Development Program.

UNHCR. (2020). https://www.unhcr.org/en-au/figures-at-a-glance.html.

Usher, R., & Edwards, R. (1994). *Postmodernism and education*. London: Routledge.

van Dijk, T. A. (1993a). *Discourse and elite racism*. London: Sage.

van Dijk, T. A. (1993b). Principles of critical discourse analysis. *Discourse and Society*, 4(2), 249–283.

Van Leeuwen, T. (2008). *Discourse and practice – New tools for critical discourse analysis*. New York: Oxford University Press.

Van Leeuwen, T. (2018). Moral evaluation in critical discourse analysis, *Critical Discourse Studies*, DOI: 10.1080/17405904.2018.1427120

van Splunder, F. (2020). *Language is politics: Exploring an ecological approach to language* London: Routledge.

Vaughan, J. (2020). The ordinariness of translinguistics in indigenous Australia. In J W Lee and S Dovchin (Eds) *Translinguistics: Negotiating innovation and ordinariness* (pp. 90–103). New York: Routledge.

Venuti, L. (1997). *The scandals of translation: Towards an ethics of difference*. London: Routledge.

Walkerdine, V. (1990). *Schoolgirl fictions*. London: Verso.

Wallace, C. (1992). Critical literacy awareness in the EFL classroom. In N. Fairclough (Ed.), *Critical language awareness* (pp. 59–92). London: Longman.

Walsh, C. (1991). *Pedagogy and the struggle for voice: Issues of language, power, and schooling for Puerto ricans*. Toronto, Canada: OISE Press.

Waters, D. (2012). From extended phenotype to extended affordance: Distributed language at the intersection of Gibson and Dawkins. *Language Sciences*, 34, 507–512.

Watkins, M. (1999). Policing the text: Structuralism's stranglehold on Australian language and literacy pedagogy. *Language and Education*, 13(2), 118–132.

Watts, R. (2011) *Language myths and the history of English*. Oxford: Oxford University Press.

Wee, L. (2011). *Language without rights*. Oxford: Oxford University Press.

Weedon, C. (1987). *Feminist practice and poststructuralist theory*. Oxford: Basil Blackwell.

Weedon, C. (1997). *Feminist practice and poststructuralist theory*. (Second edition) Oxford: Basil Blackwell.

Weiler, K. (1992). Teaching, feminism, and social change. In M. Hurlbert & S. Totten (Eds). *Social issues in the English classroom* (pp. 322–337). Urbana, IL: NCTE.

WHO. (2019). https://www.who.int/news-room/fact-sheets/detail/children-reducing-mortality.

Widdowson, H. (1980). Models and fictions. *Applied Linguistics*, 1, 165–170.

Widdowson, H. (1998). The theory and practice of critical discourse analysis. Review article. *Applied Linguistics*, 19, 136–151.

Widdowson, H. G. (2001). Coming to terms with reality: Applied linguistics in perspective. In D. Graddol, (Ed) *Applied Linguistics for the 21st Century, AILA Review*, 14, 2-17.

Widdowson, H. G. (2004). *Text, context, pretext. Critical issues in discourse analysis*. Oxford: Blackwell.

Wiggins, M. E. (1976). The cognitive deficit difference controversy: A Black sociopolitical perspective. In D. Harrison & T. Trabasso (Eds.), *Black English: A seminar* (pp. 241–254). Hillsdale, NJ: Lawrence Erlbaum Associates.

Wiley, T., & Lukes, M. (1996). English-only and standard English ideologies in the U.S. *TESOL Quarterly*, 30(3), 511–536.

Williams, G. (1992). *Sociolinguistics: A sociological critique*. London: Routledge.

Williams, G. (1998). Children entering literate worlds: Perspectives from the study of textual practices. In F. Christie & R. Misson (Eds.), *Literacy and schooling* (pp. 18–46). London: Routledge.

Williams, Q. (2017). *Remix multilingualism: Hip Hop, ethnography and performing marginalized voices*. London: Bloomsbury.

Winn, M. T. (2013). Toward a restorative English education. *Research in the teaching of English*, 48(1), 126–135.

Winn, M. T. (2018). *Justice on both sides: Toward a restorative justice discourse in schools.* Cambridge, MA: Harvard Education Press.

Winn, M. T., & Jackson, C. J. (2011). Toward a performance of possibilities: Resisting gendered (in)justice. *International Journal of Qualitative Studies in Education*, 24, 615–620.

Wodak, R. (1996). *Disorders of discourse*. London: Longman.

Wodak, Ruth (2015). *The politics of fear: What right-wing populist discourses mean.* London: Sage.

Wodak, R., de Cillia, R., Reisigl, M., & Leibhart, K. (1999). *The discursive construction of national identity.* Translated by A. Hirsch & R. Mitten. Edinburgh: Edinburgh University Press.

Yasukawa, K., & Black, S. (Eds). (2016). *Beyond economic interests critical perspectives on adult literacy and numeracy in a globalised world*, Rotterdam: Sense Publishers.

Young, R. (1990). *White mythologies: Writing history and the West*. London: Routledge.

Young, R. (1995). *Colonial desire: Hybridity in theory, culture and race*. London: Routledge.

Yunkaporta, T. (2019). *Sand talk: How Indigenous thinking can save the world*. Melbourne: Text Publishing.

Zita, J. (1992). Male lesbians and the postmodernist body. *Hypatia*, 7(4), 106–127.

Zuckermann, G. (2020). *Revivalistics: From the genesis of Israeli to language reclamation in Australia and beyond.* New York: Oxford University Press.

Index

Thrift, N., 116
Thurlow, C., 17, 98, 102, 109, 127
Tochon, F., 123
Todd, Z., 18
Toohey, K., 155
Tollefson, J., 31, 69, 131
Transformation, 32, 151 (see also
    preferred futures); cultural and linguis-
    tic practices, 32, 77, 81–2, 88–9, 145;
    of society, social relations, 12, 24–6,
    29–32, 37, 41–2, 77, 101–2, 146–7, 163;
    transformative pedagogy, 123, 138,
    146–7; transformative research, 156,
    159; and translanguaging, 18, 81
Translation, xiii, 33, 36, 158; and ethics
    of difference, 36; critical approaches,
    33, 36; interpreting, 36–7, 97, 153
Troemel-Ploetz, S., 92
Tsuda, Y., 67, 71
Tupas, R., 68
Tupas, R., & Rubdy, R., 73
Tupas, R., & Salonga, A., 73

Umbarila-Gómez, S. P., 144
UNDP, 4
UNHCR, 6
United Kingdom (Britain) xv, 76
United States of America (US), xvi,
    47, 87, 101 (see also North America);
    Americanization, 81; California,
    xv, 118; Chinese immigrants, 87;
    Colorado, 122
Universalism, xiii–xiv, 4, 28, 49, 53, 77,
    80, 85, 109, 143, 164; and difference,
    diversity, 35, 67; and gender, 97; and
    language rights, 71–2; and locus of
    enunciation, 80; and relativism, 60–1;
    universal grammar, 47–9; universal
    pragmatics, 106
Usher, R., & Edwards, R., 58, 60, 143

Validity, 106, 156, 159
van Dijk, T., 104, 106
Van Leeuwen, T., 52, 107, 127
van Splunder, F., 13, 44, 65
Vaughan, J., 83
Venuti, L., 33, 36

Voice, 100, 103, 117, 123–6, 140, 142–3,
    147, 151, 153, 158 (see also critical
    pedagogy); vs. genre, 119–26; silenc-
    ing, 32, 90–1, 123, 140, 153, 158; and
    symbolic power, 123–5

Walkerdine, V., 118
Wallace, C., 120
Walsh, C., 32, 24, 123
Waters, D., 87
Wee, L., 72
Weedon, C., 42, 60
Weiler, K., 123
White, Whiteness xiv, 7–8, 16, 28, 35,
    54–5, 146–7; applied linguistics, 7–8,
    10, 75, 143, 146, 163; epistemologies,
    27, 54–5, 60, 163; ignorance, 54; lan-
    guage norms, 16, 32, 119–20, 127–8,
    132, 136, 145–7; methodological, xiv;
    normativity, 16, 54–5, 75, 97, 119–20,
    127, 132, 143, 145–7, 157; public
    spaces, 32, 120, 146–7; supremacy, 8,
    16, 132, 136, 163; time, 54–55
WHO, 3
Widdowson, H., 11, 22–3, 49, 52, 108,
    126–7, 128n3, 160
Wiley, T., & Lukes, M., 120
Williams, Geoff, 135
Williams, Glyn, 14, 25, 34, 52, 57, 81,
    136, 151
Williams, Q., 82, 158
Winn, M. T., 145
Winn, M. T., & Jackson, C. J., 140
Wodak, R., 36, 57, 104–7, 109
Wodak, R. et al., 104
World Englishes, 51, 66–8, 74, 79, 81,
    90, 150
Essential World English, 67
Unequal Englishes, 66, 73
Worldliness of English, 82

Yasukawa, K., & Black, S., 118
Young, R., 59, 77
Yunkaporta, T., 18, 90

Zita, J., 98
Zuckermann, G., 83